The Biology of

Belief

The Biology of Belief

How our biology biases our beliefs and perceptions

Joseph Giovannoli

Rosetta Press, Inc.
Rosettapress.com

Library of Congress Cataloging-in-Publication Data
Giovannoli, Joseph
The Biology of Belief: How our biology biases our beliefs and perceptions / Joseph Giovannoli.—1st ed.

Includes biographical references and index.

ISBN 0-9708137-0-8 (cloth)
ISBN 0-9708137-1-6 (paper)

This book is printed on acid-free paper.

In loving memory of
my brother, Dr. Ralph T. Giovannoli,
whose humanity and gentle disposition
endeared him to all who knew him.

Contents

Notes to the reader   xiii

Preface   xv

Outline   xxi

Chapter 1

The Mind of God and the Mind of Man   1

> *The Human Paradox*
> *Our Earliest Beliefs*

Chapter 2

Problems Our Minds Have With Perception   11

> *Believing is Seeing*
> *Self-perpetuating Misperceptions*
> *The Planning Assumption*
> *Forced Beliefs, Belief Linkage, and Transitory Beliefs*

Chapter 3

The Biology of Belief Manipulation   37

> *Our Brains Have Design Problems*
> *One Way to Manipulate Someone's Beliefs*
> *Zealots and Alpha-State Trances*

Chapter 4

The Genesis of Mind, Self-organizing Knowledge, and Psychogenes   59

> *Self-organizing Knowledge and Darwin's Discovery*
> *Self-organizing Psychogenetic Knowledge*

Chapter 5

Our Ancestors' Beliefs and the Origin of Creation Myths   79

Ancestral Attempts to Make Sense of the World
Dreams and Hallucinations
Creating Beliefs to Satisfy Our Emotional Needs

Chapter 6

Creation According to Science—How the Earth Formed   99

The Early Universe
Our Star
Our Planet

Chapter 7

Brain Evolution at the DNA Level   113

Section 1
DNA Self-organizes
DNA Enables Cells to Cooperate
A Small Mutation Makes a Big Difference

Section 2
DNA and Brain Evolution
Feeling vs. Thinking – How DNA Evolved Our Paradox

Chapter 8

The Overt Process of Brain Evolution   133

Section 1
Evolution before Darwin
Early Life
Venturing onto Land
The First Mammals

Section 2
Large-scale Social Evolution Begins

Chapter 9

Where Darwinian Evolution Ends and Psychogenetic
Evolution Begins   153

The Gene-Psychogene Boundary
The Nature of Psychogenes
Psychogenes and Organized Ignorance

Chapter 10

Psychogenes and Cultural Evolution   181

Early Roman Psychogenes
The Assimilation of Early Greek Psychogenes
The Assimilation of Early Christian Psychogenes
The Christian Rejection of Greco-Roman Psychogenes
The Rebirth (Renaissance) of Greco-Roman Psychogenes

Chapter 11

The Noble Experiments and Aristotle's Resurrection   205

The Noble Early Greek Attempt to Replace Myth with Reason
The Noble Early Christian Attempt to Merge Faith and Reason
The Arabs Reintroduce Aristotle to Europe
Aristotelian Logic Ends Claims that Faith is Supported by Reason
Key Participants in the Noble Experiments
> *Plato*
> *Aristotle*
> *Augustine*
> *The Arab Philosophers*
> *The Reformers*
> *Giordano Bruno*

Chapter 12

The Battle for our Psychogenes   231

To Convince is to Conquer
The Rise of Secular Mythology
Whose Psychogenes Are Being Passed to Our Young?

Chapter 13

Reason, Myth, Psychogenetic Inertia and the Future   253

We See the Universe through Our Ancestors' Eyes
Old Psychogenes in a New World
Can Our Mythologies Adapt?
Blurring the Line between Myth and Science
Philosophers and Shamans

Appendix A: DNA Sequence Guessing Computer Program   281

Appendix B: "In God We Trust" Guessing Computer Program   283

Appendix C: Brain Wave Charts   285

Appendix D: Limbic Brain   287

Appendix E: Limbic Brain Components   289

Appendix F: Inferred Black Sea Flood Migrations   291

Notes   293

Bibliography   315

Acknowledgments   323

Permissions Acknowledgments   325

Index   327

Notes to the reader

Given the nature of this work, it does not use "BC" (before Christ) and "AD" (anno Domini or year of our Lord). Instead, "BCE" (Before the Common Era) and "CE" (Common Era) are used. Years without notation are CE. Dates of birth and death, or periods spent in office, are noted to provide a time context for the reader. Electronic documents, by their nature, might not have page numbers in their references. In addition to describing the objectives of this work, the Preface provides information on chapter arrangement that should be helpful to the reader.

Preface

During the past ten or so years, scientific journals have reported extraordinary research into how our brains function. Those research reports have included subjects such as how neurotransmitters influence brain activity, the effect of brain states on perception, how various brain regions coordinate their functions, the relationship between our limbic and neocortex brain structures, and the like. As I pieced together this evolving wealth of information, much of what was puzzling about human culture and our individual belief systems became understandable.

In examining the biological processes that enable us to believe, this book examines how our brain structures and the workings of our minds influence how our beliefs are created and transmitted, change, define our realities, determine our actions, alter our perceptions, and perpetuate our cultures. It explains why our thought-processes are imprecise and subject to manipulation by others without our conscious awareness. In addition to providing an insight into the processes that create our cultures and shape our personal beliefs, the book examines, for example, how our brain biology is at the core of the conflict between science and religion.

Much of what we believe today has been inherited from our ancestors in the form of religious and philosophical belief systems. Together, these systems have shaped our institutions and our cultures. The influence exerted by these very different ways of seeing the world is so finely integrated into the way we perceive reality that it has become transparent. By examining the biology of belief we should come to better understand why we believe what we believe, and perhaps understand why our inherited beliefs might cause problems for us in the near future.

Rather than beginning this work by researching the thinking of others, I chose to address each key question by examining the problem, developing original concepts to deal with it, and then studying the thinking of others to evaluate my concepts. I chose this approach to preserve the possibility of seeing old problems in new ways, which can be stifled by exposure to the thinking of others before we have taken time to think about the problem for ourselves, using our own experience and knowledge. By analogy, it is like being the first person to ski down a mountain. The temptation to follow existing tracks is high for everyone except the first skier, who is free to choose where to direct her or his skis. Original thought, unbiased by the thoughts of others, has a higher likelihood of venturing into new areas of inquiry and of discovering things previously unseen. The German philosopher Arthur Schopenhauer (1788-1860) cautioned that "It is dangerous to read about a subject before we have thought about it ourselves. ... When we read, another person thinks for us; we merely repeat his mental process."[1] Unfortunately, this approach runs the risk of frustration if you find that your insights are not new. Such was the case with aspects of my concepts of what might be the law of self-organizing knowledge, and of what I call "psychogenes" (sI'kOH-jEEns). I define *psychogenes* as *beliefs with perceived inheritance value* that are replicated between or within generations; i.e., beliefs with perceived inheritance value that behave like mental genes.

Investigating both self-organizing knowledge and psychogenetics was fundamental to understanding the biology of belief. As to self-organizing knowledge, the British philosopher Karl Popper (1902-94) characterized the biological process of natural selection as the acquisition and evolution of knowledge. In his view DNA, the genetic code made up of deoxyribonucleic acid, represents knowledge shaped by an organism's history of successful adaptation.[2] It is not clear whether he saw the knowledge aspect of biological evolution as a specific manifestation of a more generic concept that, under certain general conditions, knowledge is capable of self-organizing in various media—of which hydrocarbons represent but one. Although a number of theories analogizing social evolution to genetic evolution have been presented since Darwin's time, *memes* (e.g., self-reproducing ideas), as defined by Richard Dawkins in *The Selfish Gene,* describe the essential character of psychogenes. Dawkins describes memes as ideas that collect people. Given my requirement that a belief must be perceived by a potential recipient to have inheritance value, psychogenes appear to be a class of memes. Allowing for the effects of inculcation, belief-altered perceptions and other aspects of the biology of belief, psychogenes are beliefs that people find acceptable.

With all of history as a resource, and given the pervasive influence of beliefs, knowing at the outset where such research would lead was, for me, impossible. Belief system formation, cultural evolution, and the human mind, although apparently connected, involved too many categories of knowledge for me to have had a clear initial understanding of how to research the subject. It was also apparent how easily personal bias could influence one's perception of which areas of research to pursue and, perhaps, which not to pursue. Given the subject matter, the approach of "knowing" from the outset which areas to research is not necessarily a benefit. I found it necessary to inquire into a number of knowledge disciplines to ferret out a clear understanding of the biology of belief. The American biologist and philosopher Edward O. Wilson uses the word *consilience* to describe the process of combining objective information from different disciplines to create a common groundwork of explanation.[3] The word *consilience* was first used by William Whewell in his 1840 synthesis *The Philosophy of the Inductive Sciences*. While books that deal with less broad subjects enable the reader to settle into a comfortable feeling of knowing in advance how successive paragraphs are likely to fit into an overall picture, seeking consilience regarding the biology of belief might be unsettling to some readers, as it crosses traditional knowledge boundaries. This means that an evolving concept might not lend itself to a predictable pattern. In fact, combining ostensibly unrelated information might be the best way to clarify an overarching concept. In other words, although some chapters here might seem to deal with subjects that are unrelated to a common theme, the coming together occurs in later chapters.

My initial motivation for writing this book was to determine why rational minds are capable of believing in myth, and how this question relates, if at all, to the processes that shape our belief systems and drive cultural evolution. A subsequent motivation was to address recent attempts by religious fundamentalists, postmodernists, and others to discredit Darwinism. Also, it appears that some religious scientists are attempting to link science with religion by a strained analogy involving the Big Bang theory of the origin of the universe. Notwithstanding the mountain of fossil evidence in support of the theory of evolution, some of Darwin's detractors believe that his theory is unsupported because there are gaps in the fossil record. Deduction, interpolation, and extrapolation consistent with a solid theoretical model using real fossil evidence are apparently insufficient to dislodge this kind of thinking. Such denials of what most consider obvious by those of us whose perceptions are formed by mythology are the logical consequence of the biology of belief and its capacity to alter our view of reality.

To understand the biology of belief it is essential to understand how our brains evolved and how that evolutionary process has defined how they function. In this regard, the average American understands less about biological evolution than the average person in some third world countries. For these reasons, a detailed description is presented to show, in gradual, logical, and probable increments, how humans, and specifically the human brain, evolved from the first self-organizing molecules. Chapter 7 does this at the DNA level, and Chapter 8 at the organism level. To present aspects of the origins of our inherited mythological beliefs and to explain to those who find it difficult to believe how our universe formed according to cosmological science, a similar process is used in Chapter 6 to describe our current knowledge of the formation of the universe.

In attempting to unravel the puzzle of the biology of belief, writing this book has been a voyage of discovery through our collective past, although the voyage was occasionally more like experiencing a fanciful Baron Munchhausen illusion. It became apparent very quickly that, without a sense of history, many of us tend to think that our discoveries about things fundamental to humanity are novel. After thousands of years of the best minds pondering the same questions, it is very unlikely that our discoveries, insights, and many of our theories have never been considered at some time in our past. That being said, the body of knowledge created by insights of the best minds over thousands of years, when considered in its entirety, itself provides an opportunity for novel insights into how the individual pieces of the human puzzle relate to each other. And, when properly arranged, those combined pieces might reveal an enlightening view of ourselves. To this end, I have attempted to assemble and interrelate what I perceive to be the essential pieces of such a puzzle, namely, the biology of belief. In so doing I have quoted, where possible, those present and past who are or were among the first to reduce to writing fundamental and timeless truths about our basic nature. My contribution, such as it might be, is in seeing how their individual truths fit into a continuum of coherent knowledge.

In some cases, quotations from works that might be difficult to find are presented at length. As a general Western history reference I have relied on Will and Ariel Durant's *The Story of Civilization*. Without the electronic version of their eleven-volume encyclopedic work, it is unlikely that this book would have been completed. Although the details of Eastern culture are unique, I believe—and hopefully will show—that the fundamental human factors that created Eastern culture are essentially the same as those that created Western culture, which is the focus of this book.

JOSEPH GIOVANNOLI
October 1, 1999
Saddle River, NJ

Outline

Given the variety of knowledge disciplines encompassed in the following chapters, a description of how these chapters are structured is provided at this point for readers who might find this prior knowledge beneficial.

Chapter 1: The Mind of God and the Mind of Man. The first chapter opens quoting the last sentence in Stephen Hawking's *A Brief History of Time*: "If we find the answer to [why we and the universe exist], it would be the ultimate triumph of human reason—for then we would know the mind of God." This chapter suggests that Hawking and other scientists such as Newton and Kepler represent a paradox. Specifically, how do our best rational minds reconcile the rigorous demands of objective, logical thinking with mythological beliefs based on faith, to which objective logic is anathema? Stephen Hawking's reference to the mind of God brought into question the mind of man. To account for why otherwise objective scientists would consider a subjective, unprovable supernatural premise to explain a scientific unknown, this chapter posits that the Big Bang theory, relativity, quantum physics, and chaos theory have added a dimension to modern scientific thinking that is more flexible than previous thinking based on a more materialistic view of Nature. In addition, realizing that they cannot know what—if anything— existed before the Big Bang, some scientists might be tempted to deal with this frustrating limit by analogizing the Big Bang to any one of a number of creation myths. It is noted that Hawking's reference to the mind of God appears to be Neoplatonistic rather than theological.

Inasmuch as beliefs learned in youth influence our subsequent perceptions and the believability of new information, the next section considers the possibility that scientists are discussing religious beliefs because their earliest beliefs were learned before they had sufficient intellect to inquire into their truth. Events surrounding Charles Darwin's presentation of *On the Origin of Species by Way of Natural Selection* are reviewed in this light. Darwin's theory conflicted with two dominant beliefs held by many of his colleagues. The first was the biblical story of creation found in Genesis, which was clearly incompatible with Darwin's natural selection model. The second was an erroneous intuitive belief that all complex things require intelligence to create them. The chapter ends by asking whether seemingly disparate life experiences are diverse manifestations of a few fundamental truths, and suggests that the biology of belief may be one such truth.

Chapter 2: Problems Our Minds Have With Perception. This chapter presents a few mechanisms that demonstrate how our perceptions and beliefs can be adversely influenced by the biology of belief. The first section suggests that believing something to be true causes a perceptual bias that in turn supports that belief; i.e., belief alters perception and perception reinforces belief. The roles of intuition (neural network pattern recognition), brain hemisphere dominance, and problem-solving heuristics are examined. Extra-experiential intuitions receive special focus because our minds are limited by what we have experienced, ergo our intuitions are equally limited. It follows that if things supernatural are extra-experiential, the spirit world of our ancestors, at least in part, derives from the nature of intuition and related neural processes. The section suggests that faulty interpretations of intuitions create incorrect beliefs, which in turn corrupt our future perceptions. Generation after generation of belief-formation by this process creates defective belief systems and corrupted perceptions of reality.

The second section suggests that mistakes in perception can be self-perpetuating, i.e., incorrectly believing a thing to be true can cause "behavior" that reinforces the incorrect belief. An example is posited in which poor nutrition, inadequate stimulation in infancy, and other factors that lead to intelligence levels below one's genetic potential may have been misperceived by Thomas Jefferson, resulting in actions or inactions that perpetuated the conditions that caused below-genetic-potential performance among his slave population.

The third section posits that planning is exceptional in Nature, but that because we can plan, we assume that planning is common in Nature. This section cites research that shows that young children possess an inborn trait to attribute intent to apparently self-propelled things, an excellent foundation for adult assumptions about the intent and planning of unseen spirits. A most famous example of the planning assumption is presented in the form of the watchmaker argument. How can it be that a watch (a relatively complex device) requires a watchmaker, while the watchmaker (a very complex planner) happened without planning? The planning assumption suggests that if we didn't plan it, someone or something else must have planned it. Ergo, spirits of animist cultures are bodiless analogs of ourselves with the ability to make supernatural things happen intentionally—by planning. This section describes how Darwin confronted this aspect of our nature in *On the Origin of Species by Way of Natural Selection*. Research into what has been dubbed the "God module" suggests an additional motivation in support of belief in unseen spirits. Additional arguments are provided to show how the planning assumption and the human ego might have combined to give rise to anthropomorphism, and our evolution away from worshiping spirits in animal form to worshiping spirits in human form.

The fourth section addresses a series of mechanisms that contribute to our problems with perceiving reality as it is. *Forced beliefs* are described as beliefs we manufacture to protect other beliefs that are not supported by fact. Alternatively stated, they are beliefs that support defensive perceptions we require to avoid acknowledging that other strongly held beliefs are wrong or inconsistent. *Belief linkage* is described as the tendency to believe that someone or something possesses traits of similar people or things with which we are familiar. *Transitory beliefs* are described as beliefs derived from perceptions that are biased by a prior event. An example given is that a picture of a smiling face is perceived differently depending on whether it is shown to a subject following a picture of a happy scene or an upsetting scene.

The chapter summarizes the foregoing as sources of baseless linkages of cause and effect that are driven by our inborn need to ascribe meaning to events (a trait of the left brain hemisphere). It concurs with the Kantian view that our way of perceiving will forever be inextricably mingled with the thing perceived, and concludes that our beliefs about reality may be preventing us from perceiving it correctly.

Chapter 3: The Biology of Belief Manipulation. The third chapter begins with the observation that writings that deal with beliefs typically fail to consider how the nature of the brain and mind influence how and what we think. Three characteristics of the brain and mind are considered.

In addressing design problems our brains have evolved, we examine the relationship between reason and emotion; the nature of dreaming; causes of hallucinations; the effects of hormones, neurotransmitters and psychoactive chemicals; the nature of trances, hypnotism, brainwashing and meditation; why some of us become zealots and fanatics; and the nature of faith healing.

The next section addresses the Jekyll and Hyde nature of both barbarians and ecclesiastics. Brain characteristics related to memory, emotion, neurotransmitters, trance states and basic limbic system functions are reviewed and related to our behavior. For example, it analyzes how we misinterpret trance states and hallucinations as heightened states of spiritual awareness, and oxygen deprivation as near-death spiritual experiences.

The next section deals with how our beliefs can be manipulated without our conscious awareness. In short, the section describes how our reasoning and context-sensitive left brain hemisphere can be circumvented to access our gullible and context-insensitive right brain hemisphere for the purpose of altering our beliefs. It traces the process from Pavlov to hypnosis, alpha brain states, and eyes-open alpha-trance induction.

The final section describes the relationship between zealots, true believers, revival-meeting conversions, and alpha-state trances. It explains the four brainwashing steps of alertness-reduction, confusion, thought-stopping, and maintenance. The brainwashing process is related to religious fundamentalism and other zealotry. It describes how voodoo combines animism,

Roman Catholicism and alpha-trance states. Additionally outlined is a medical modality called "neurolinguistic programming," which is used to promote healing through manipulation of immune-system-suppressing beliefs. The section finishes with an analysis of the trance-state process underlying revival meetings.

Chapter 4: The Genesis of Mind, Self-organizing Knowledge, and Psychogenes. The first section questions whether the evolution of human intelligence is extraordinary or merely one step toward ever-increasing complexity, driven by the very nature of knowledge. The section quotes British philosopher Karl Popper's observation that the Darwinian theory of evolution by natural selection can be considered a theory of the evolution of adaptive "knowledge" of an organism by trial and error. The section goes on to describe the mechanism by which DNA (deoxyribonucleic acid) records knowledge, replicates itself, and adapts over time to changing conditions. The same process of recording, replicating, and adapting is described for genetic algorithms (digital DNA) in computer environments. This technology is used in self-learning robotic devices. The section finishes with examples of subtle interpretations of genetic adaptation in biological systems, such as evolving adaptations to evolving circumstances, co-evolution, and evolved behaviors. Also described is a likely cause of punctuated equilibrium based on genetic algorithm research.

The next section addresses the concept of self-organizing psychogenetic knowledge and begins with a number of queries. What kind of knowledge would result if beliefs were substituted for DNA nucleotide sequences? Is it possible that beliefs possess many of the properties of genes? Are inheritable beliefs the genes of social evolution that cause cultures and other social organisms to evolve or to become extinct? The section goes on to state that, in the Darwinian sense, beliefs can have survival value. It then queries why, after a million years of psychogenetic evolution, so little happened until about 100,000 years ago, and why human social evolution accelerated in the past five millennia. The answer presented is that complex language began to develop about 100,000 years ago and writing about 5,000 years ago. This section further suggests that the ability to reduce language to writing created an immensely enhanced ability to record and reproduce our heritable beliefs. We had achieved with writing and our ability to reason what DNA had achieved with nucleic acids and trial-and-error adaptation. Our libraries and other repositories of information contain the psychogenetic equivalent of our DNA. Moreover, this section suggests that inasmuch as psychogenes have the benefit of inductive and deductive reasoning in addition to trial-and-error adaptation to perfect their evolution, psychogenetic evolution is explosive when compared with biological evolution. It is the difference between a lightning bug and lightning. In addition to observing that psychogenetic evolution in the form of genetic engineering is beginning to free Darwinian evolution from its more than four billion year old dependence on random chance, this section observes that psychogenetic knowledge differs from DNA and genetic algorithm knowledge in that psychogenes self-assemble in the environment of our collective minds.

Chapter 5: Our Ancestors' Beliefs and the Origin of Creation Myths. This chapter begins by acknowledging that it is not possible to know with certainty what took place in the minds of our ancient ancestors. That being understood, the chapter proposes to glimpse the thoughts and beliefs of our ancient ancestors by considering archaeological findings and studies of contemporary primitive cultures.

The first section posits that our ancestors had no understanding of the nature of death and fertility; that dreams were likely thought to be windows into a spirit world; that drug-induced hallucinations were waking dreams; that plants, trees, animals, and natural events had human-like consciousness; that they could relate to their ancestor's spirits; and so on. A key factor in these beliefs is that our ancestors lacked the capacity to distinguish between the real and spirit worlds. The section suggests that their extra-experiential intuitions and the planning assumption made the existence of intelligent spirits intuitively obvious. This section further suggests that these primitive concepts evolved such that intelligent mythological spirits became omnipotent, immortal gods with animal forms, and these gods possessed supernatural powers that enabled them to relieve suffering, ensure fertility, and steel believers against the forces of Nature. Central to these beliefs was the animist belief that a bodiless force animated the universe and that shamans could unite the real and spirit worlds. This section ends with the observation that while their early religion helped our ancestors cope with their difficulties, it came with a price: the damage that results from misunderstanding reality and the damage that results from the sacrifice, ostracism, and hostility that necessarily flow from a need to deny the validity of competing beliefs.

The section on dreams and hallucinations suggests that a primitive mind would think that dreams are real, given that they experience the same emotional responses to dreams as to their waking world. The section explains that hallucinations are dream-like states that can be achieved through meditation, rhythmic rituals, drugs, sensory deprivation, fasting, and fatigue. The neurochemistry of hallucinations is examined. Joseph Campbell's connection between myth and dreams in *The Hero with a Thousand Faces* is cited: "Dream is the personalized myth, myth the depersonalized dream; both myth and dream are symbolic in the same general way of the dynamics of the psyche. But in the dream the forms are quirked by the peculiar troubles of the dreamer, whereas in myth the problems and solutions shown are directly valid for all mankind."

The next section links our emotional needs with the process of myth creation. It suggests that even if our myths disappoint us, it is easier to believe a comforting myth than to accept an unpleasant reality. When we most need reassurance, it would be unthinkable to let our disappointment force us to reject the very thing we depend on for reassurance. In considering the relationship between fear and myth, this section observes that fear easily overpowers reason, and that reason—at best—moderates fear. The brain biology responsible for this arrangement is considered. In examining the role of mystery in mythology, the ignorant and the educated are considered. For the ignorant, the writings of a 17th century Roman Catholic priest are presented: "If religion were clear, it would have fewer attractions for the ignorant. They need obscurity, mysteries, fables, miracles, incredible things." For the educated, the denigration of reason by myth is shown in East Indian teachings: "The first lesson that the sages of the Upanishads teach their selected pupils is the inadequacy of the intellect. How can this feeble brain, that aches at a little calculus, ever hope to understand the complex immensity of which it is so transitory a fragment?"

More recent writers are shown to argue against reason, relying on references to "direct perception," "immediate insight," and intuition. The Christian Bible's approach is shown in Eccles. 1:18: "For in much wisdom is much grief, and he that increaseth knowledge increaseth sorrow."

The end of this chapter describes the evolution of religions from earlier forms showing the persistence of aspects of older religions in modern ones. It also presents the neurobiological mechanism underlying this continuing process as viewed by modern psychology. According to *The Encyclopedia of Psychology*, "Although modern society places great emphasis on the importance of rational thinking, research suggests that human beings today are as prone to magical thought as were their primitive ancestors. There seems to be a universal inclination to infer symbolic and meaningful relationships among objects and events, and an inability or a disinclination to properly evaluate the experiences upon which these inferences are based."

Chapter 6: Creation According to Science—How the Earth formed. This chapter deals with the multiplicity of creation myths that attempt to explain how the universe came to be. These myths reflect the beliefs and limited knowledge of their creators and may represent the only information many of us have about the nature of the universe. One unfortunate effect of such myths is that scientific discoveries are routinely denied because they conflict with mythological teachings. Creation myths that derive from extra-experiential intuitions and the planning assumption are contrasted in this chapter with the present understanding of cosmological science regarding the formation of the universe from the Big Bang to the emergence of the primordial earth. This chapter sets the stage for the discussion of the evolution of life on earth.

To aid the reader, the final section of this chapter provides a summary of our progress toward consilience. It reminds the reader that we have considered the processes by which we acquire beliefs without having considered their merit, and described how our beliefs, assumptions, misperceptions, and evolved brain traits distort our perceptions of reality. We have considered how our biological nature makes it easier for some of us to believe in miracles, and for some of us to have our beliefs manipulated. We have argued that both genetic and psychogenetic knowledge is self-organizing, and shown how beliefs function individually and in belief systems. We have endeavored to explain the origin of beliefs we inherited from our ancestors by attempting to reconstruct our ancestors' world. And we have examined how dreams and hallucinations influenced our ancestors' perceptions, and considered their predisposition to animism and to emotionally satisfying belief systems. The final aspect of the summary reminds the reader how scientists believe the universe evolved to its present state from its apparent beginning—a story of creation inconceivable to our primitive ancestors.

Added to this summary is an indication of how later chapters will combine consiliently to provide a clearer understanding of the biology of belief. The following chapters examine how DNA self-organized to create the conflicted thinking organs in our heads, and how psychogenes in those thinking organs influence our perceptions, behavior and social evolution. Using successive periods of Western history as an example, the process by which psychogenes evolve over time is demonstrated. Attempts of philosophers and shamans to deal with the consequences of the evolved, conflicted nature of our brains is considered, and their successes and failures are reviewed. Both primitive and modern methods used to control our beliefs are considered, and, in the final chapter, a consilient merging of the foregoing elements is presented, together with an example of the effect the biology of belief may have on our global future.

Chapter 7: Brain Evolution at the DNA level. This chapter begins by explaining how DNA could have self-organized and thereafter progressed through a continuous sequence of increasing complexity, resulting in genetic code that defines the structure and functions of our brains. The two evolved brain structures of particular interest are the amygdala and the prefrontal lobes of the neocortex. The amygdala was inherited from our reptilian ancestors and screens incoming sensory information for any threat. The more recently evolved neocortex provides us with our reasoning ability, among other things. The chapter gives a detailed explanation of how our brains self-assemble during gestation and thereafter. It describes how the older emotional amygdala can dominate the more recent rational neocortex. And it explains that we have both an emotional and a rational mind, semi-independent faculties that see the world in different ways.

The chapter concludes with a description of how philosophers have tried to use reason to convince us that emotion must be controlled by reason; however, emulation and blind acceptance, not reason, are the primary processes by which our neocortex circuitry is shaped during our formative years. Moreover, it goes on to explain that theologians use emotion-influencing myths, methods and dogma in our formative years to inculcate in us their beliefs, to protect us from life's anxieties, and to help us avoid reptilian (sinful) behavior. Finally, the chapter suggests that our history shows that the uneasy balance between our amygdalae and prefrontal lobes has been responsible for the struggle between our myths and our philosophies, religion and science, and is the probable source of the paradox represented by Newton's fascination with the Apocalypse, Kepler's belief in witchcraft, and Hawking's reference to "the mind of God."

Chapter 8: The Overt Process of Brain Evolution. The "overt process" of brain evolution is the visible result of DNA evolution. This chapter describes the probable continuous evolution of organisms from single-celled creatures to mammals. Specifically noted are pivotal organism-level increases in complexity resulting from events in DNA evolution described in the previous chapter. Particular attention is paid to life forms that are in the human evolutionary chain and to circumstances that influenced the evolution of our brain structures.

Section 2 notes the first coming together of scattered human settlements, the appearance of Sumerian culture, and the evolution of writing, technology, and social organization. It examines how psychogenetic evolution logically follows from our evolved high intelligence, our capacity for language, and our increasing social complexity. The chapter concludes that after billions of years of evolving by accumulating molecular knowledge in the form of DNA, self-organizing knowledge had crossed a threshold with the Sumerian culture. After evolving organic life by refining DNA (using Nature's test of survival value), self-organizing knowledge began to evolve human culture and wisdom by refining human beliefs—not by selecting beliefs for their survival value as such, but by selecting them based on their perceived value to those who would inherit them.

Chapter 9: Where Darwinian Evolution Ends and Psychogenetic Evolution Begins. This chapter examines the evolutionary mechanism that limits genetic influence on cultural evolution, and further examines how that same self-organizing knowledge mechanism in a psychogenetic environment is able to influence cultural evolution in ways that genes cannot. Richard Dawkins' description of *memes* is explained and distinguished from *psychogenes*. Regarding the effect of Darwinian evolution on social behavior, the chapter posits that inasmuch as basic human urges are a matter of biological predisposition, one can understand how genes can affect individual behavior at the rudimentary levels of survival and reproduction. However, the jump from genes controlling individual behaviors to genes adapting to determine group behavior has a few problems. The influence of a reflexive DNA response becomes uncertain to the extent that it can be overridden by thinking. This section suggests that if Darwinian feedback is overridden by a belief, in a life and death decision based on one's response, it is conceivable that twins with identical physical genes could have opposite psychogene-based responses. The twin that responded correctly and survived would pass on the same genes as the one that made the wrong survival decision and Darwinian evolution would not have been relevant. However, it is likely that the surviving twin would pass on the successful psychogene to his or her offspring. This section concludes that complex human cultural evolution, unlike Darwinian evolution, appears to be driven by the mechanism of self-organizing knowledge in the form of psychogenes.

The remainder of the chapter considers the nature of psychogenes. It examines why societies maladapt as beliefs that were successful in their time cause problems when circumstances change. The allegory in Nietzsche's *The Three Metamorphoses* demonstrates that the education of children is the most malleable link in the transmission of beliefs. Spinoza is quoted to show that literal interpretation of inherited religious beliefs is a misapplication of the allegorical nature of biblical psychogenes. Efforts of social engineers to supplant traditional beliefs with their own through controlling education curricula and through the establishment of political correctness is viewed as an attempt to solve current social problems emanating from antiquated psychogenes. Incorrect economic short-term mass beliefs (the tulip bubble and South Sea Company bubble) are described and compared with metaphysical belief bubbles, which are less likely to burst given the absence of objective criteria to determine their truth.

The chapter concludes with the idea that, although knowledge can self-organize, there is no natural mechanism impelling psychogenetic knowledge to organize in ways consistent with reality. Evolution's fiat is that knowledge be suited to its environment, not that it be correct; i.e., the least stupid wins. For this reason, assemblages of ignorance can survive indefinitely if they are not challenged to adapt. And, inasmuch as our beliefs can be based on reality or illusion, our belief-altered perceptions necessarily reflect those underlying beliefs. The question this raises is whether those of us whose psychogenetic inheritance includes believing that myth is reality are better off than those of us who perceive reality more clearly. Setting aside the damage that illusory belief systems have done throughout history, is it possible that living the illusion and rejecting, perhaps by forced beliefs, the unpleasant realities of life may be more satisfying for most of humanity? How philosophers and theologians have dealt with this question is considered in a subsequent chapter.

Chapter 10: Psychogenes and Cultural Evolution. This chapter presents an example of cultural psychogenetic evolution. Although psychogenetic evolution is faster than biological evolution, it often takes a number of generations to produce fundamental psychogenetic change. From about 750 BCE to 1600 CE, Italian beliefs experienced many fundamental changes as Italy evolved from a republic to an empire; from the Roman state under Julius Caesar, to Christian domination through the Dark and Middle ages, and then to the Renaissance and the beginning of modern philosophy and science. This chapter considers the psychogenetic influences that gave rise to the Roman state, the consequences of conquering Greece and assimilating its culture, the psychogenetic influence of the rise of Christianity, and the influence of Greco-Roman beliefs on Italian psychogenes during the Renaissance.

The chapter concludes with the observation that although there are considerable differences in the ways cultures around the world have evolved, what is not different is the psychogenetic process by which they evolved. It is an evolutionary process that is fundamental to the biology of belief. However, unlike the fossils Nature has preserved, which fix for all time what our ancestors were, the nature of belief provides us with multiple histories, some based on the best objective evidence available and others based on what we would like our ancestors to have been.

Chapter 11: The Noble Experiments and Aristotle's Resurrection. This chapter compares the different methods by which shamans and philosophers have attempted to establish ethical cultures. Philosophers, in general, have appealed to our reasoning prefrontal cortex, while shamans have used intuition, interpretation of dream spirit-worlds, and emotional control of what we now know to be our amygdala's reptilian propensities.

The noble attempt of early Greek philosophers to replace mythical with non-mythical ethical systems is described. Thereafter, the noble early Christian attempt to merge faith and reason is examined. The undoing of the Christian merger of faith and reason, with the reintroduction of Aristotelian logic to Europe by Averroes, is described, together with brief considerations of the possible motivations of key players in both experiments.

The chapter ends by noting that the secular and ecclesiastical philosophers who most influenced the noble experiments fall into roughly two groups—poets and scientists. The poets' perceptions were emotional and intuitional, compared with the perceptions of the more reason-based scientists. The question considered is whether all their choices were more influenced by the biology of belief than by their free will. They were all intelligent. They all had detailed knowledge of both the good and evil of human nature and of the arguments for and against believing that something like a God could exist. Why did they choose as they did? How significant were their psychogenetic inheritances and planning assumptions? Were these philosophers accomplished thinkers with varying degrees of amygdala and prefrontal lobe dominance or of left- and right-brain hemisphere dominance? Does much of the difference simply reflect historically different myth-driven assemblages of organized ignorance? Are the volumes of well-reasoned philosophical arguments merely empty logic attempting to justify their inherited beliefs or emotional needs? The chapter concludes that whatever the answers, by myth and reason the participants in the noble experiments attempted to find the truth and to convince our ancestors to control their inborn reptilian instincts. Although the experimenters chose different methods to compensate for aspects of the biology that shapes our beliefs and actions, their common goal was clearly noble.

Chapter 12: The Battle for Our Psychogenes. The chapter begins by positing that our psychogenetic inheritance and other beliefs are beset constantly by organizations, governments, causes, mythologies, and individuals who need our cooperation to achieve their goals. If belief alters perception, then how we perceive something depends on what we believe about the thing perceived. And, if our beliefs can be biased through propaganda, then propaganda or public relations will influence our perceptions of events.

This chapter describes the efforts of Edward Bernays and myriad public relations pioneers who perfected the art of belief manipulation. Until perhaps the past million or so years, our ancestors interacted with their surroundings, not with the aid of reason, but with subconscious, intuitive, impulsive emotions. Primitive, unreasoning responses combined with cultural stereotypes, an inborn need to be part of a group, and fear, envy, and hate are some of the subconscious mechanisms propagandists use to control our beliefs and behaviors. What this means in a world filled with propaganda is that forming public opinion is more analogous to herding sheep than it is to well-reasoned debate. The section describes how and why Edward Bernays and Walter Lippmann used these subconscious mechanisms for public relations and propaganda purposes. The concentrating ownership of various types of information media in the hands of a limited number of large companies is considered regarding the increasing ease with which beliefs can be manipulated on a grand scale. This section considers what the combination of public relations belief-management and concentrating control of the media might mean for the future.

Also examined is the question of whose psychogenes are being passed to our young. Exposure of our young for a substantial part of their formative years to public relations and information about other beliefs and values interrupts the traditional process of enculturation. Commercially disseminated beliefs and values have numerous motivations, few if any of them concerned with the long-term welfare of their consumers. This section considers the influence of factors that favor nuclear families and disfavor more traditional extended families. Educated parents of nuclear families rely more on books offering child psychology theory to guide them through child rearing. They rely less on the psychogenes of family members who are no longer present to advise or participate in child rearing. Although psychological research has taught us much about ourselves, such research can be difficult because of the complexity of the brain, difficulty in determining which factors cause which results, and the length of time required to establish the credibility of some theories. Good-sounding reasons can be given to explain behavior, but are they true? Are theories being implemented for their quality or for their compatibility with political and social movements? The recent unfortunate experience with "facilitated communications" is cited as one example. An authority in psychological research is quoted as saying that "Much of psychology now consists of vague theories that don't spell out precise predictions.... Productive theories about the mind will have to risk being precise and opening themselves up to being disproved." Whether these theories will prove correct and will benefit us in the long run is not yet known. Neither is the effect of politically and commercially driven changes in our cultural psychogenes. What we do know is that they are altering our culture.

Chapter 13: Reason, Myth, Psychogenetic Inertia, and the Future. The initial section of this final chapter restates a number of points made in the book. Our evolved amygdalae and prefrontal lobes are the biological source of our reason and emotion and our Jekyll and Hyde nature. Myths are necessary to restrain the primal passions of much of society. And, excepting influences of our scientific discoveries, our fundamental nature is not much different from that of our ancient ancestors. Restated is Averroes' view that philosophers should not openly criticize mythologies for their transgressions against reason because myths are the source of morality and piety for a substantial part of society. The absence of a theological counterpart view protective of philosophers is noted.

In considering our future, the next section describes a biologically and psychogenetically driven population-increase scenario. Our success as a species in controlling our environment is cited as a driving force for environmental embrittlement. The cultural imperatives of primitive animistic societies acknowledge that their survival depends on Nature, while they are unaware of Nature's underlying laws. We, on the other hand, understand much about and utilize the laws of Nature, but have lost cultural imperatives that acknowledge our dependence on it. By pushing our life-sustaining systems to the limit, we embrittle ourselves. We lose the ability to accommodate Nature's surprises. Another suggested cause of embrittlement is the population-increasing effect of cultural and myth-based psychogenes that encourage mindless population growth. In this scenario, our future is influenced less by our capacity to reason and more by the inertia of religious, ethnic and other anachronistic psychogenes that view boundless procreation as beneficial.

The next section suggests that we must adapt psychogenetically to our changing world. Blindly following the dictates of our psychogenetic inheritance may be a formula for disaster. We may be facing circumstances that are capable of bursting mythological bubbles. Historical circumstances that created some contemporary mythological beliefs are examined, and this section suggests that it may be time to overcome our fundamentalist zealotry and to rethink our anachronistic mythological beliefs. While new social engineers are in a position to assist in this effort, this section suggests that cultural relativism, popular pseudopsychological theories and other such factors might be creating an ineffectual secular mythology. Added to this mix is the lack of interest in our problems on the part of belief-managing commercial interests that are using public relations with no discernable public benefit in mind. This section also suggests that social engineers may be willing to overturn beneficial, ethics-controlling religious psychogenes, with no idea of what will replace them.

The next section addresses apparent attempts by some mythologists to marry science (rational analysis) with religion once again, this time using the Big Bang instead of Neoplatonism. Claims that the Big Bang is the mythological moment of Creation would not only be impossible to prove or disprove, they would support, in the minds of many, claims that myth has a way of knowing that science does not. If this line of reasoning were to become widely accepted, it follows that mythologists could use the Big Bang-Creation argument to impugn Darwinism, fetal tissue research and other pursuits repugnant to their mythologies. This section also points out the inappropriateness of prominent scientists invoking mythological references in otherwise scientific presentations to the public, giving the impression that science is worshipping at the altar of myth. As personally satisfying as such mythological references might be, those views are personal, unscientific, and are as unprovable as creation myths. For a scientist to endorse mythology with the imprimatur of a body of knowledge created in part by scientists who suffered or died at the hands of mythologists is not good science, nor is it good *for* science. The section concludes that any accord between religion and science would be an illusion. They are systems with different beliefs, purposes, and perceptions of reality. Moreover, their conflicting beliefs reflect the biology of the conflicted minds Nature has given us.

The final section concludes with a few observations. Given the nature of the biology of belief, it seems certain that myth will shape much of our future. The history of the Enlightenment shows that a non-mythological understanding of reality leads society to disillusionment and to subsequent reliance on comforting myths. Realizing that their power derives from this biological propensity of our species, perhaps the keepers of our mythologies will make future decisions reflective of a better understanding of the flaws inherent in the biology that influences our beliefs.

Chapter 1
The Mind of God and the Mind of Man

In examining the nature of belief, this work deals with mythological belief systems—including religion, superstition, and occultism, among other things. And, given the nature of belief, some readers will find unsettling any attempt to analyze belief objectively, particularly those beliefs that rely on mystery. "For in much wisdom is much grief, and he that increaseth knowledge increaseth sorrow." (Eccles. 1:18) Inasmuch as my purpose is to analyze, not proselytize, perhaps I should caution readers with deep religious or mystical beliefs that they should read something more comforting.

One more thing before we start: Understanding the biology of belief involves understanding aspects of knowledge ranging from astronomy to zoology. As with weaving cloth, weaving these knowledge disciplines into a coherent fabric of understanding requires time to put the various threads of knowledge into place. The discussion of *consilience* in the Preface explains what the reader can expect as the early chapters begin to assemble these necessary—but at times seemingly unrelated—threads of knowledge into a fabric of understanding.

The Human Paradox

What began as a simple question raised by the last sentence of Stephen Hawking's book *A Brief History of Time* has led me to examine the fundamental nature of belief. That sentence said:

> If we find the answer to that [why it is that we and the universe exist], it would be the ultimate triumph of human reason—for then we would know the mind of God.

His statement reflected what I thought to be the human paradox. How does one of the best rational minds of our time reconcile the rigorous demands of objective, logical thinking with a mythological belief based on faith, to which objective logic is anathema? Hawking is certainly not the first scientist or natural philosopher[1] to invoke supernatural references. According to Will and Ariel Durant in *The Story of Civilization,* "Even Kepler and Newton mingled their science with mythology: Kepler believed in witchcraft, and Newton wrote less on science than on the Apocalypse ..."[2] More recently, another scientist claimed to prove the existence of God and universal resurrection using global general relativity theory. It appears, however, that his idea of God involves technology rather than a supernatural being.[3] Another contemporary scientist contends that modern physics reveals the basic oneness of the universe that "parallels" the tradition of Eastern mysticism. Here again, the imprimatur of science is linked to a mystical or metaphysical worldview.[4] I did not include Albert Einstein in this list. Notwithstanding his statement to Danish physicist Niels Bohr that "God does not play dice with the Universe," repetition of this quote in a mythological context was a source of irritation for Einstein. In responding to a letter that questioned the accuracy of an article about Einstein's religious beliefs, he wrote:

> It was, of course, a lie what you read about my religious convictions, a lie which is being systematically repeated. I do not believe in a personal God and I have never denied this but have expressed it clearly. If something is in me which can be called religious then it is the unbounded admiration for the structure of the world so far as our science can reveal it.[5]

In response to a similar evolution-related letter Einstein wrote:

> The misunderstanding here is due to a faulty translation of a German text, in particular the use of the word

"mystical." I have never imputed to Nature a purpose or a goal, or anything that could be understood to be anthropomorphic.

What I see in Nature is a magnificent structure that we can comprehend only very imperfectly, and that must fill a thinking person with a feeling of "humility." This is a genuinely religious feeling that has nothing to do with mysticism.[6]

Since the Renaissance, and especially during the Enlightenment, scientists have used secular reason to examine things also dealt with by theology. Although many scientists have found theology lacking, many others have not. Although this work could have referred to Kepler or Newton instead of Hawking, I read Hawking's *A Brief History of Time* when I was attempting to see more clearly the common thread that ran through human history. I was seeking something that would explain, in a fundamental way, the primary forces that shape collective human activity and social evolution. Stephen Hawking's reference to the mind of God caused me to focus my thinking on the mind of man. Without having read his book it is unlikely that I would have collected my thoughts and considered in detail what I see as the human paradox.

In general, scientists do not openly challenge theological beliefs. At most they fend off criticism from theists when a scientific finding conflicts with theological dogma. Whether or not they are theists themselves, they generally avoid openly discussing theology. Why, then, are we seeing mystical contentions by some scientists, and why at this time? Why would a scientist, a professional skeptic, a person who insists on objective proof before something is to be believed, be willing to consider a subjective, unprovable supernatural premise as a means of explaining a scientific unknown?

In recent time, the Big Bang theory has been receiving considerable attention. The theory, first proposed in 1927 by Belgian astrophysicist Georges Henri Lemaître (1894-1966), proposes that the universe originated many billions of years ago from the violent explosion of a very small concentration of immense energy of extremely high density and temperature. Although the theory does not explain what appears to be a very rapid expansion at the very beginning of the bang or the observation that the galaxies are presently *accelerating* away from each other, it does account for much of what we have observed. If we study the galaxies in view of Lemaître's theory, it appears that they began separating about 12 to15 billion years ago. It is as if the galaxies were like raisins in a rising loaf of raisin bread, and space were the dough. As the dough expands the raisins move further apart. So too, the galaxies are not traveling out into existing space. Expanding space and separating galaxies are part of the same process.

If this is what happened, scientists have no way of knowing what, if anything, existed before the Big Bang. No physical evidence prior to the Big Bang would survive. This "fact," and the obvious realization that we cannot create an experiment to reproduce the Big Bang, places a new and frustrating limit on scientists. It is a frustration that some might be tempted to resolve by analogizing the Big Bang to any one of a number of creation myths. In addition, relativity, quantum physics, and chaos theory have added a new dimension to modern scientific thinking, which is more flexible than previous thinking based on a more materialistic view of Nature.[7]

Hawking proposed a number of theories about the beginning point of the Big Bang. Very briefly, in his "singularity theory," at the time of the Big Bang the laws of physics would break down because the density of the universe and the curvature of space-time would be infinite. In another theory, the "no boundary proposal," the laws of physics would hold at the beginning of the universe. However, if either of these theories proved to be correct, we would be left with the same question. As Hawking stated in his 1988 work *Origin of the Universe*:

> Although science may solve the problem of how the universe began, it cannot answer the question: why does

the universe bother to exist? Maybe only God can answer that.

As with some other scientists, it is likely that Hawking does not believe in a personal God and that he refers to God as a metaphor for a creative force. In this context his "mind of God" reference in *A Brief History of Time* is characteristic of the Neoplatonists' view that the creation and orderliness of the universe derives from an ideal concept of divine wisdom, i.e., the mind of God. This seems to be supported by the fact that Hawking refers to God in connection with creation and not with the subsequent evolution of the cosmos.

Our Earliest Beliefs

It occurred to me that the reason scientists are discussing religious beliefs has to do with the nature of belief itself. We learn many of our basic or core beliefs before we are able to evaluate such things. The beliefs we hold today, which we learned in youth, are uninformed, nonvolitional beliefs. We had no capacity to evaluate what we were taught or to decide whether to accept or reject those teachings. They reflect the beliefs of our culture, and the beliefs of our parents and others who have influenced us in early youth. We may have reconsidered some of our early beliefs and chosen to keep or change them, but, to the extent that they have altered our perception, we are limited in our capacity to view them objectively. Learning to believe before learning to think is our conundrum. An empty mind cannot judge what it should believe. We need a critical mass of knowledge and belief to evaluate what to believe, a mass critical both for its size and its content. For beliefs once learned influence our perceptions and thereby limit the believability of things we experience later in life. The conundrum is epitomized in the following observation of the French scientist and philosopher René Descartes (1596-1650):

> The chief cause of our errors is to be found in the prejudices of our childhood ...[8] principles of which I allowed myself in youth to be persuaded without having inquired into their truth.[9]

Plato (427?-347?BCE) concluded that indoctrination was necessary to teach ethical behavior.

> [I]ntelligence is needed to discriminate between good and harmful pleasures; and for fear that intelligence may come too late we must inculcate in the young a habit of temperance, a sense of the golden mean.[10]

What to inculcate appears to be at the root of this problem. If each generation learns its core beliefs before it is able to evaluate them, then as a culture, ancestors who would be considered primitive by current standards created our oldest beliefs. Our ancestors' beliefs notwithstanding, reality is what it is irrespective of our collective imagination. Our minds contain beliefs that combine to form a useful model or representation of reality, but this is not reality. It is this fact that makes us look in bewilderment at the actions of others whose beliefs form a model of reality foreign to our own. Although we are inclined to think that our personal view of reality is objective because it is generally consistent with that of our immediate community, what our minds actually contain is a consensus reality model that reflects the perception biases of our culture as well as our own perception biases. In considering our "knowledge" of reality the English philosopher William of Ockham (1285?-1349?) observed that

> Our knowledge is molded and limited by our means and ways of perceiving things; it is locked up in the prison of our minds, and it must not pretend to be the objective or ultimate truth about anything.[11]

More than four hundred years later German philosopher Immanuel Kant (1724-1804) would come to the same conclusion in his *Critique of Pure Reason*. Kant's view has been restated as follows:

> Apparently, all our knowledge comes from the senses, and reveals not the external reality itself, but our sensory adaptation—perhaps transformation—of that reality. By sense, then, we can never quite know the "real"; we can know it only in that garb of space, time and cause which may be a web created by our organs of sense and understanding, designed or evolved to catch and hold that fluent and elusive reality whose existence we can surmise, but whose character we can never objectively describe; our way of perceiving will forever be inextricably mingled with the thing perceived.[12]

The reference to knowledge coming from the senses relates to sensing something by sight, sound, smell, taste, or touch. This is to be distinguished from belief by some that knowledge can be acquired from a soul or spirit, such as is associated with reincarnation. For example, Plato believed that an immortal soul has innate knowledge from past lives that teaching merely reawakens. The belief that innate knowledge is possible has been debated for millennia. In 1690, not long before Kant wrote his *Critique of Pure Reason*, British philosopher John Locke (1632-1704) published *An Essay Concerning Human Understanding*. In it he said:

> It is an established opinion amongst some men, that there are in the understanding certain innate principles; some primary notions, *koinai ennoiai*, characters, as it were stamped upon the mind of man; which the soul receives in its very first being, and brings into the world with it. It would be sufficient to convince unprejudiced readers of the falseness of this supposition, if I should only show ... how men, barely by the use of their

natural faculties, may attain to all the knowledge they have, without the help of any innate impressions; and may arrive at certainty, without any such original notions or principles. ... it seeming to me near a contradiction to say, that there are truths imprinted on the soul, which it perceives or understands not: imprinting, if it signify anything, being nothing else but the making certain truths to be perceived. For to imprint anything on the mind without the mind's perceiving it, seems to me hardly intelligible.[13]

Inasmuch as quality science requires the most accurate reality model possible, scientific beliefs must be verified using methods intended to eliminate bias and arbitrary beliefs. However, scientists, as do the rest of society, arrive at adulthood with myriad beliefs, rational and otherwise, which make up and influence their perceptions of reality. They are products of their socialization and education, and they too have their problems with accepting observations that conflict with their beliefs.

When Charles Darwin published *On the Origin of Species by Way of Natural Selection* in 1859 it met with a firestorm of controversy in the scientific community. Darwin's belief that the accumulation of slight variations in some offspring better adapted them to survive provided a scientific explanation for the theory of natural selection. His work lent credibility to a theory that conflicted with two dominant beliefs held by many of his colleagues. The first was the biblical story of creation found in Genesis, which was clearly incompatible with Darwin's natural selection model. The second was an erroneous intuitive belief that all complex things require intelligence to create them. Thomas Aquinas listed as a proof of the existence of God that the order and purpose we see in the universe cannot be the result of chance. If this belief were true, how then could the mindless process of natural selection be said to be purposeful?

For thousands of years philosophers have dealt with questions of individual and collective human thought and conduct, each attempting to identify the essential elements of the thing considered and the truths linking those elements. Is it possible that our seemingly disparate life experiences are, in fact, diverse manifestations of a few fundamental truths? Is there an insight that would enable us to perceive superstition, science, art, lawlessness and spirituality as different hues of the primary colors of our nature? Could such an insight explain why cultures that evolve independently are so similar?

This work examines how beliefs are created, how the structure of our brain influences them, how they are transmitted, by what means they change, how they define our realities, determine our actions, alter our perceptions, perpetuate our cultures, allow others to manipulate our thoughts and actions, and how our future might depend on how rapidly our beliefs can adapt.

Chapter 2

Problems Our Minds Have With Perception

We do not arrive at this time in our lives as blank slates. What has been written in our minds is now so habitual that we find it difficult to believe that things could be otherwise. Believing is Seeing; Self-perpetuating Misperceptions; Planning vs. Happening; and Forced Beliefs, Belief Linkage and Transitory Beliefs are presented to demonstrate a few problems we have with how we see the world.

Believing is Seeing

Much of our information about the world is confusing and imprecise. Although we use reason to deal with much of it, we rely on intuition to deal with questions for which answers are otherwise unavailable. Consequently, it would be valuable to know what intuition is and how it works.

Among other things, our brains are neural networks that can find patterns in large volumes of imprecise information. Pattern recognition takes place without our conscious awareness. When our minds find what might be a pattern, we perceive it as sensing something—an intuition, idea, feeling, impression, suspicion, hunch, insight, and so on. It is a pattern recognition process, not a reasoning process. Unlike reasoning, intuition does not allow us to trace back to determine why our mind made a particular linkage. Intuitions are subconscious conclusions without conscious reasons. Research on humans and other mammals suggests that intuition employs the neural networks of our brains in the following (simplified) process. Our brains comprise left and right hemispheres, and typically one hemisphere dominates as a result of events determined before birth. The right hemisphere perceives experiences in the moment. It has no sense of how an experience fits into a context of prior experiences. By comparison, the left hemisphere attempts to place experiences into a context of its existing knowledge. As it attempts to do this, the left hemisphere is endeavoring to ascribe meaning to experiences. As we will see, this process gives rise to many of our erroneous beliefs. The left hemisphere includes a left prefontal lobe that is capable of probability analysis and judgment. If you are left hemisphere dominant, cause and effect links "obvious" to your right hemisphere would be moderated by what seems probable to your left hemisphere. If you are right brain dominant, left hemisphere probability analysis is less influential and you are more likely to believe cause and effect linkages that do not, in fact, exist. Given this arrangement, when those of us who are right hemisphere dominant see a miracle, the left hemisphere dominant see a coincidence, because they are unlikely to accept supernatural or improbable intuitions as true. However, improbability is a judgment based on what we believe, and if left hemisphere dominant persons have been taught to believe that perceived supernatural phenomena are real, their conclusions about intuitions would be difficult to distinguish from those with right hemisphere dominance. It follows that our existing beliefs and hemisphere dominance combine to influence the believability of our intuitions about everything, including intuitions about things beyond our actual experience (our extra-experiential intuitions). The British philosopher and historian David Hume (1711-76) was apparently left hemisphere dominant. Note in his following quote his reliance on probability to reject supernatural explanations.

> The maxim by which we commonly conduct ourselves in our reasonings is that the objects of which we have no experience resemble those of which we have; that what we have found to be most usual is always most probable; and that where there is an opposition of arguments, we ought to give the preference to such as are founded on the greatest number of past

observations.… It forms a strong presumption against all supernatural and miraculous relations, …[1]

In addition to intuition, we use rules of thumb (heuristics) to make quick decisions about things. These are cause and effect beliefs (rules) we accumulate as problem-solving shortcuts. Research has shown that we tend to focus on a first factor to the exclusion of others in applying rules of thumb.

In one example, researchers ask volunteers to calculate the probability that a 40-year-old woman who has a positive mammography test actually has breast cancer. The correct answer involves not only the accuracy of the test, which gives a positive result in 80 percent of women with breast cancer, but also the base rate of the disease (1 percent among 40-year-old women) and the rate at which a mammography falsely reports breast cancer in healthy women.

Usually, volunteers asked to make this type of estimate focus on the first factor to the exclusion of the others and produce unduly high estimates, around 80 percent. Bayes' theorem, in which the base rate factors into a relatively complex calculation of the one-time probability of having breast cancer given a positive mammography, yields a prediction of 7.77 percent.

To explain such base-rate neglect, many researchers have invoked a judgment shortcut, or heuristic, known as representativeness, the tendency to assume that like goes with like. In the mammography problem, they propose, representativeness leads the volunteer to conclude that a positive test result and the presence of disease naturally go together. The ease of making that link fosters neglect of more complicated factors, such as base rate of the disease and the probability of false positives.

Gigerenzer, by contrast, views representativeness and other heuristics as fuzzy concepts that mask a fundamental point: The human mind did not evolve to perform statistical calculations that include percentages and other mathematical notions invented within the past 2 centuries. Humans and other animals instead rely on simple thinking mechanisms that operate on available information from their surroundings. At the core, these cognitive tools solve problems that have long proved crucial to survival and reproduction, such as distinguishing safe from poisonous foods, choosing a mate, and detecting cheaters in social exchanges (SN: 4/8/95, p. 220).[2]

When we focus on a first factor only, we can expect our rules of thumb to give us incorrect answers. This is in addition to other influences such as needing to answer quickly, needing to be consistent with our other decisions and beliefs, and being aware that we might have to answer to others for the decision we make. We find that our likelihood of perceiving a situation correctly is hampered not only by intuitions of questionable value, but by our method of solving problems and related beliefs and influences as well. Imperfect as they are, it is likely that our beliefs and how we employ them had survival value during our evolution. This is not a vindication of imperfection, however. The evolutionary process selects based on which is better suited to survive, not on which is correct. In other words, in matters of intelligence evolution selects the least stupid.

If intuition is a product of our minds, and our minds are limited by what we have experienced, then intuition is a product of our experience. For this reason, reliance on intuition is of questionable value when dealing with matters beyond our actual experience. It is of little help in dealing with things that change imperceptibly during a human lifetime, or that we cannot see or otherwise sense. In dealing with such things the mind will resolve uncertainty by selecting the most plausible perception consistent with what it believes to be true. If intuition is limited by our beliefs, experience and brain hemisphere dominance, then why would we place any trust in it to deal with things beyond our actual experience? Why would we expect our intuition to reveal insights inconsistent with our existing beliefs? If our ancestors saw the universe as unchanging it was because little observable change took place during their collective memory. That incorrect belief would support creation myth intuitions depicting static life forms in a static universe, both of which are inconsistent with our understanding of biological evolution and the history of the universe. Nonetheless, contemporary cultures are rooted in such inherited intuition-based beliefs.

Can it be that the spirit world was intuitively apparent to our ancestors? It has been suggested that certain spirits are equivalent to supernatural parents, that the child-parent relationship learned in youth is recreated in an adult-god relationship later in life. An alternative intuitive explanation of spirits might be the belief that if we can influence human-scale events, then something more powerful than ourselves must influence superhuman events. Are our gods simply constructs based on inappropriately interpreted intuitions and on emotions rooted in fear of death and the uncertainties of life? Faith in a supernatural power capable of relieving our suffering is therapeutic for those of us who feel helpless before Nature, not knowing why we are here, what our purpose is, what happens to us after death, and so on. Are our minds motivated to select certain intuitions because we find it difficult to consider the possibility that we may be insignificant in what may be a mindless universe, or that we are purposeless creatures with aspirations that are irrelevant to Nature? Perhaps an inspiring purpose gives our life meaning and is simply a source of great emotional satisfaction.

It should be apparent that the process by which we determine what is believable can be extremely imprecise. The problem does not end there. What we believe about something before we perceive it will alter our perception of it (belief alters perception, or believing is seeing). The process is self-corrupting. Faulty interpretations of intuitions create incorrect beliefs, which, in turn, corrupt our future perceptions, and so on. Generation after generation of belief formation by this process now influences our perceptions of our world. No one's belief system is immune from corruption by this process.

When two very different cultures meet for the first time, there is a brief opportunity to examine a common experience as seen through the belief-altered perceptions of differently evolved belief systems. One such event occurred when Captain James Cook first sailed his ship into Hawaiian waters in 1778. The Hawaiians, never having seen such a ship, saw trees moving on the water. The billowing sails were perceived to be the image of a Hawaiian deity. As a result, Captain Cook was greeted, at least initially, as a God. Their perceptions as well as their intuitions were influenced by their beliefs, as are ours, and those perceptions were handed down to subsequent generations of Hawaiians. What kinds of beliefs have we inherited thanks to the incorrect perceptions of our ancestors?

If our beliefs shape our perceptions, then what we are taught to believe about something before we encounter it will prejudice our subsequent perceptions of it. When Rogers and Hammerstein wrote the play *South Pacific,* they included a song entitled *You've Got to be Carefully Taught.* While the play was being fine tuned in performances outside of New York, before opening on Broadway, the authors were requested to remove this song because it was deemed offensive by a number of those who saw the play. The song was not removed. Oscar Hammerstein's lyrics were

> You've got to be taught to hate and fear.
> You've got to be taught from year to year.
> It's got to be drummed in your dear little ear.
> You've got to be carefully taught.
>
> You've got to be taught to be afraid
> Of people whose eyes are oddly made,
> And people whose skin is a different shade,
> You've got to be carefully taught.
>
> You've got to be taught before it's too late,
> Before you are six or seven or eight,

> To hate all the people your relatives hate,
> You've got to be carefully taught!
> You've got to be carefully taught!

Jean Meslier (1678-1733), a French priest who rejected the teachings of the Catholic Church, wrote:

> Our nurses are our first theologians; they talk to children about God as they talk to them of werewolves.... Very few people would have a god if care had not been taken to give them one.[3]

Notwithstanding the repetition of commonly held beliefs, our understanding of something does not necessarily improve by repetition or familiarity. Unfortunately, inasmuch as belief alters perception, prolonged belief-biased perception of something tends to reinforce our existing beliefs and may add nothing to our understanding of the thing perceived; i.e., belief alters perception and perception reinforces belief. This is the reason experience does not necessarily lead to wisdom. Greek-born Roman playwright Terence (190?-159? BCE) wrote, "You believe easily that which you hope for earnestly." Similarly, English philosopher, jurist, and statesman Francis Bacon (1561-1626) said, "For what a man had rather were true he more readily believes." Seeing is believing might be true for an unbiased observer, but for most of us, believing is seeing.

Belief bias also influences the degree of proof we require to perceive something as true or false, and, as we are more likely to believe something consistent with what we already believe, we may never believe something inconsistent with our present beliefs. Belief bias can result from transitory, linked, or deep-rooted beliefs. Your fundamental belief about the future will determine whether you see a glass as half full or half empty. The Rorschach test, which uses inkblots to provide a window into a viewer's beliefs, demonstrates the effect of deep-rooted beliefs on perception. A once-popular joke described a patient who saw perverted sexual acts on every page of every book of inkblots he was shown. His psychiatrist told him that he was a hopeless sexual deviant. Whereupon the patient retorted: "You have some nerve. You're the one with all the pornographic books."

If belief alters perception, what effect does the absence of belief have on perception? When Belgium withdrew from the Congo (Zaire), its former African colony, there were very few Congolese who had learned the beliefs necessary for a transition from colonial government to democratic self-government. Instead, the relevant Congolese beliefs were pre-colonial, tribal beliefs. As a result the Congo was vulnerable to charismatic totalitarianism during the power vacuum that followed Belgium's withdrawal. Even with the opportunity for freedom and self-government, absent the necessary beliefs to perceive their opportunity for democratic self-government, they followed the dictates of their belief legacy. To a limited degree, the same might be true of Russia after Communism. By comparison, the British colonies in North America functioned with a certain degree of autonomy prior to the Stamp Act. The effect such autonomy had on their belief evolution contributed in great part to their perception of themselves, on average, as Americans first and British subjects second. Combined with their experience was a knowledge of various forms of government beginning with the Greco-Romans.

More recently, when an attempt to stabilize Somalia was begun in the name of feeding the hungry, many expected that neutralizing the intimidation power of warlords in some way would promote the formation of a fledgling democratic state. How this could happen without introducing, through education or example, necessary democratic self-government beliefs into the Somali belief system is incomprehensible. To make democratic self-government beliefs part of the Somali belief system in one generation, much less one year, is a formidable task indeed. Existing democracies have the good fortune of inheriting their democratic beliefs from generations of countless ancestors who, at great personal sacrifice, created and preserved them.

Self-perpetuating Misperceptions

Much has been said recently about Thomas Jefferson's opinions regarding African-Americans. Was the author of the Declaration of Independence a bigot? Was some other mechanism at work that caused Jefferson to perceive his world as he did?

I define *self-perpetuating misperception* as incorrectly believing a thing to be true, and thereby causing behavior that reinforces the incorrect belief. In our infancy, our brains grew in response to sensory stimulation and nutrition. Exposure to toys and sounds of all sorts, such as music and speech, caused parts of our brains that processed that information to grow larger. This is evolution's way of adapting our brains to our environments. The opportunity for our brains to grow in this way is available to us only once and for a very short time. Those of us who lost that opportunity through the misfortunes of life, or whose mental processes were impaired by fetal exposure to PCBs (polychlorinated biphenyls) or exposure to lead or dioxin,[4] for example, are less mentally capable than our genetic inheritance would have permitted. Therefore, if we are unfortunate enough to be malnourished and under-stimulated from conception through the first few years of life we may grow to be less "intelligent" than someone with less genetic potential but better nutrition and stimulation. Does this mean that low intelligence scores necessarily follow poverty? We know this is not true. If resources, such as they are, are made available to nourish and stimulate the young, intelligence is maximized. It is a matter of parental beliefs as well as opportunity. If we disregard the importance of attitude and motivation, which are largely based on beliefs, and focus solely on physiological capacity, the effects of malnutrition and under-stimulation in early youth could result in below-normal intellectual performance. This in turn could reinforce the incorrect belief others may hold that our ethnic or other group is genetically mentally inferior. It could also reinforce such incorrect beliefs in the minds of those incorrectly believed to be genetically deficient. Such beliefs create assumptions of incompetence. Based on such assumptions, opportunities that would disprove the assumption are "logically" provided to others assumed more competent. The misperception is thereby reinforced and becomes self-perpetuating. Such self-perpetuating misperceptions might have led Thomas Jefferson to believe that slaves were mentally inferior—a belief otherwise difficult to explain in a person who risked his life for *his* belief in equality and who died unable to free his slaves only because he lacked the funds to satisfy a Virginia statute intended to prevent them from becoming public charges.

Lately there has been a great deal of discussion about differences in intelligence among various groups of humans. Whether current self-perpetuating misperceptions or the legacy of equivalent past misperceptions are a factor in such studies is difficult to determine. What is clear from numerous studies is that success in life does not correlate with test scores; it correlates with attitude. And attitude is largely psychogenetic. "Believe you are defeated, believe it long enough, and it is likely to become a fact," wrote Norman Vincent Peale. Every day, people interested in achieving take courses that stress the importance of correcting self-limiting beliefs. Such beliefs create a negative attitude by diminishing self-confidence; incorrectly linking cause and effect; failing to control anger, guilt and blame; lowering expectations; marginalizing the importance of goals; and the like. The best inheritance we can receive is good health, good nurturing, positive beliefs and an absence of self-perpetuating misperceptions.

The Planning Assumption

In the normal course of events evolution and natural forces determine the fate of virtually all life on Earth. We, however, (to the extent possible) use our intelligence to control our fate. We observe the world, learn cause and effect relationships, and satisfy our needs by creating causes that result in effects we want. We are the Earth's ultimate planning animal, and although we take planning for granted, it is extraordinary. We do it in everything from farming to space flight. We do it to control the things we fear. We do it without a second thought, but it is exceptional and rare in Nature. It requires intelligence, knowledge and conscious control. It is so ingrained in our nature that we attribute planning and planning-related motives to other life forms, and even to Nature. By the time we are a year old we attribute positive or negative intentions to self-propelled objects that pursue simple goals, suggesting that infants have an inherent capacity for discerning intentions in goal-directed actions of their parents and others.[5] Recently, when the family dog accidentally pushed down a one-year-old, the child responded as if the dog had acted intentionally. Do weather, volcanoes and lower order animals really demonstrate vengefulness, malice, or deceit? These are acts that typically require intent and planning. A respected publication described the evolution of dolphin sonar as follows: "Animals such as dolphins, which have been using sonar for millions of years, have somehow refined it to an extraordinary art."[6] I believe that natural selection, which provided dolphins with sonar, explains the continued evolution or refinement of dolphin sonar quite well, dolphin artistic talent notwithstanding.

Given our planning assumption, we find it difficult to imagine what life would be like without it, or that things we cannot make happen can come to be without planning. How can it be that a watch (an inorganic device) requires a watchmaker, while the watchmaker (an organism containing adaptive, self-replicating molecules) happened without planning? The process by which organisms and their components come to be necessarily follows the requirements of DNA-based biological evolution. Those rules are different from any rules required to explain planning-based entities that are primarily inorganic. The fusion of these different means of creating something may be at hand as genetic engineers learn to manipulate DNA-based biological processes. This is not to say that the many fundamental principles used for our inorganic inventions were not employed by evolved organic life forms. Actually, our attempts to duplicate physical principles employed by naturally evolved life forms have been the source of many of our "discoveries." Richard Dawkins, the British zoologist and expert on biological evolution, in his various writings on the subject has described evolution's mastery of echo-ranging as used in sonar and radar (dolphins and bats), infrared heat-detectors (snakes), electricity (eels), jet propulsion (squid), megaphones (mole crickets), optical sensors and lenses (sighted animals), dam building (beavers), antibiotics (fungi), garden tending (ants), milking of other life forms (ants), hypodermic needles (wasps), valved pumps (hearts), harpoons (snail mating dart), fishing rods (angler fish), and water pistols (archer fish). Although the list is far from complete, one could add explosive chemical reactions (bombardier beetle), saws (serrated sharks' teeth), flight (birds, bats and insects), and neural network computers (brains).

The planning assumption suggests that if we did not plan it, someone or something else must have planned it. One reason that animism is common to diverse cultures around the world is that all humans make the planning assumption. The spirits of animist cultures are bodiless analogs of ourselves with the ability to make things happen intentionally; i.e., to plan. Georgii Gurdjieff (1873?-1949), a Greek-Armenian spiritual leader, clearly manifested the planning assumption when he wrote:

> The evolution of man is the evolution of his consciousness, and 'consciousness' cannot evolve unconsciously. The evolution of man is the evolution of his will, and 'will' cannot evolve involuntarily. The evolution of man is the evolution of his power of doing, and 'doing' cannot be the result of things which 'happen.'

Charles Darwin had to confront what I call the planning assumption if *On the Origin of Species by Way of Natural Selection* was to be understood and accepted. In it he wrote:

Nothing at first can appear more difficult to believe than that the more complex organs and instincts should have been perfected not by means superior to, though analogous with, human reason, but by the accumulation of innumerable slight variations, each good for the individual possessor. Nevertheless, this difficulty, though appearing to our imagination insuperably great, cannot be considered real if we admit the following propositions, namely, – that gradations in the perfection of any organ or instinct, which we may consider, either do now exist or could have existed, each good of its kind, – that all organs and instincts are, in ever so slight a degree, variable, – and, lastly, that there is a struggle for existence leading to the preservation of each profitable deviation of structure or instinct. The truth of these propositions cannot, I think, be disputed.

While our gods are planners, Darwin was telling us that the process by which we came to be has no plan, no understanding, no intelligence, no judgment and no purpose. When George Bernard Shaw realized this, he wrote:

[T]he Darwinian process may be described as a chapter of accidents. As such, it seems simple, because you do not at first realize all that it involves. But when its whole significance dawns on you, your heart sinks into a heap of sand within you. There is a hideous fatalism about it, a ghastly and damnable reduction of beauty and intelligence, of strength and purpose, of honor and aspiration, to such casually picturesque changes as an avalanche may make in landscape, or a railway accident in a human figure. To call this natural selection is a blasphemy, possible to many for whom Nature is nothing but a casual aggregation of inert and dead matter, but eternally impossible to the spirits and souls of the righteous.[7]

23

Honor, beauty, purpose, aspiration and strength are emotion-packed concepts relating to virtue and self-worth. Shaw's heart sinks to think that their greatness does not derive from an equally great spiritual source. Otherwise stated, Shaw was saying that there can be no honor or purpose without spirituality. This might come as a surprise to a few billion of our fellow humans. Perhaps Shaw's concern was that any purpose that comes from within would reflect baser human values, and not a loftier view of what we should strive to be.

Although George Bernard Shaw was an atheist, his reaction to Darwin's theory of natural selection might suggest that the religious would have even more reason to find biological evolution and religious faith incompatible. Perhaps evolution and faith are paradoxically related. If the fear that weakens us thereby threatens our survival, then the faith that overcomes our fear will have survival value. And, if faith has survival value, it will selectively evolve. The resulting irony would be that the multitudes of faithful, whose beliefs reject biological evolution, might have faith because of biological evolution. Recent research suggests that evolution has provided some of us with neural circuitry specifically capable of giving us strong emotional feelings when we think about spiritual beliefs. A researcher at the University of California at San Diego has found that a cluster of neurons in the brain's temporal lobes becomes electrically active when some people contemplate spiritual matters.[8] The researcher discovered that a particular region of neurons in the temporal lobes of epileptics in some way became involved in subjects who reported profoundly spiritual experiences. When that region became electrically stimulated, some described their experience as becoming obsessed with religious spirituality. The researcher said, "There may be dedicated neural machinery [circuitry] in the temporal lobes concerned with religion." The circuitry was dubbed the "God module." In a very limited experiment, Epileptic patients were compared with people who described themselves as intensely religious, as well as with a randomly selected control group. It was determined that, unlike the control group, there seemed to be elevated God module activity in the epileptic group and the intensely religious group when they were shown words invoking spiritual belief as compared with words that invoked sexuality. Although a correlation might have been found, it should be noted that the research was based on a study involving a very small group of subjects. It is possible that the God module is a nexus of activity that is more generally taking place in the temporal lobes. It is also possible that the God module has a function not yet understood with a side effect resulting in profound spiritual or other feelings. Alternatively, neurons in the God module might develop in response to experiences in early youth. Medical research has shown that some people who have experienced neuron disturbance from stroke, tumor or trauma in the right frontal region of the brain develop an inordinate preoccupation or "heightened sensitivity" to and appreciation for particular stimuli such as food.[9] If we do have a God module, perhaps biological evolution has preferentially selected our God module-possessing ancestors over time because the God module improved their likelihood of survival. It might have given them the advantage of strength in the face of adversity.

If a God module evolved, that development may be similar to the way in which the brains of dyslexics appear to have evolved. As the brains of dyslexics mature their neural networks take longer to develop, and this enables them to visualize information in ways in which non-dyslexics cannot. For example, among the more famous dyslexics in history, Nikola Tesla (1856-1943), a pioneer in the development of commercial electrical power technology, was capable of designing devices in his mind, testing them in his mind, and revising the designs in his mind, and when he was satisfied that a design functioned properly, he would have the device built.[10] He received 111 U.S. Patents in the fields of electrical generating and metering, electric motor design, and radio and lightning technology. In another example, Michael Faraday (1791-1867), the British physicist and chemist who discovered electromagnetic induction, had the capacity to invent in his mind visualizations of electromagnetic fields. His visualizations were the basis of British physicist James Maxwell's (1831-79) now famous Maxwell's equations of electromagnetism. Einstein, who was also dyslexic, expanded on Faraday's field theory and brought to us concepts of space-time that have changed the way we see the universe.[11] Before writing became important to knowledge processing, dyslexia, which today is generally considered a disadvantage, might have been an evolutionary advantage. In a three-dimensional world of predators and prey, the ability to think visually might have had survival value. Indeed, the present trend toward having computers present large volumes of complex data in two and three-dimensional graphics may represent an adaptation of non-dyslexics to the world of visual data manipulation. Perhaps a picture *is* worth a thousand words. Einstein, Faraday, Edison, General George Patton, Winston Churchill, Lewis Carroll, William ButlerYeats, and Leonardo DaVinci, among others, all demonstrated characteristics we associate today with dyslexia. The extent to which they may have been less able in other information processing areas appears to be a small price to have paid for the ability to see with the mind's eye. In the same way Nature provided some of us with slight variations in neural circuitry capable of superior visualization, it might have provided some of us with a God-module-based religious fervor.

Not long after the introduction of Darwin's *On the Origin of Species by Way of Natural Selection,* many thought that the matter was settled in Darwin's favor by the Thomas Huxley and Bishop Wilberforce debate. Perhaps, for the most part, it was settled in the scientific community. However, over half a century after Darwin explained how natural selection and biological evolution are related, an American high school teacher named John Scopes was prosecuted for violating a Tennessee law against teaching the theory of evolution. Although there were many motivations, including commercial interests, which created the show trial nature of the proceedings, the trial did serve to spotlight the Tennessee law. Clarence Darrow defended Scopes, and William Jennings Bryan prosecuted. Scopes was found guilty and fined a nominal sum, but the conviction was reversed on technical grounds. Bryan's predisposition to the planning assumption is evident in his criticism of the theory of evolution. "There is no more reason to believe that man descended from some inferior animal than there is to believe that a stately mansion has descended from a small cottage."

The planning assumption may be responsible, at least in part, for our anthropomorphistic view of the world as well. Anthropomorphism appears to be the child of our planning assumption, an inborn attribution of intent to apparently self-propelled things and our ego. It attributes human motivation to inanimate and imaginary objects, plants, animals and natural phenomena. The Greek Sophist Protagoras (c. 485-410 BCE) declared that "Man is the measure of all things." Perhaps as our ancestors learned to control things in Nature they saw themselves as superior to that which they controlled. And the more they controlled, the more their egos became inflated. This may account for their evolution from reverence and fear of simple spirits to their respect and fear of spirits in the form of animals on which their survival depended or whose abilities they admired, and then to their respect and fear of spirits in our own form. It logically follows that today's lack of respect for Nature derives from our long evolution away from being awed by Nature to being awed by our accomplishments in science, which is, ironically, Nature without the mystery.

Forced Beliefs, Belief Linkage and Transitory Beliefs

By one definition *intellect* is the measure of our capacity to change our beliefs when they are unsupported by observation or reason. If we do not believe the thing perceived or to be perceived is possible, our perception will be distorted in ways consistent with our then existing beliefs. This is the source of assumptions or anticipated perceptions, other perception-related biases, and *forced beliefs*, which I define as defensive perceptions, i.e., a form of denial or rationalization. When a person you believe to be honest does something dishonest, your belief that he or she would not be deceptive may blind you to inconsistencies or duplicities that would be obvious to others. Your forced belief that the person you endorsed is not duplicitous distorts your perception of the situation, your lack of inquiry into his or her possible duplicity notwithstanding.

Unlike beliefs distorted by perception, forced beliefs are beliefs manufactured to protect other beliefs that are not supported by fact; i.e., other opinions. Forced beliefs manifest themselves as defensive perceptions that are presented as factual to avoid acknowledging that other strongly held beliefs are wrong or inconsistent. We rationalize and otherwise defend our forced beliefs even when we know we are manufacturing them. A contemporary forced belief is the denial that men and women are different in certain essential areas unrelated to reproduction. To protect the belief that women should have equal opportunity and equal treatment, some force the belief that women and men have equal capability, notwithstanding objective research that shows that evolution has given men and women a number of different and complementary mental and physical capabilities that have better adapted them together to survive and reproduce.

Knowing that a person is male, female, young, or old will presuppose knowledge about that person based on your linked beliefs about similar people. The evolutionary survival value of belief linkage may be that it enabled us to avoid hazardous situations given minimal information. However, some social disadvantages of belief linkage include presumed knowledge of something of which we are ignorant, failure to recognize when further inquiry is appropriate, and prejudicial stereotyping.

Transitory beliefs are more situational. When you see an upsetting picture followed by a picture of someone smiling, you perceive the smile as callous. That same smiling face following a happy picture will cause you to see it as festive. It is the transitory belief that something good or unpleasant has taken place that influences how you interpret the next event you perceive. The bias is independent of which of your senses is involved. When

28

expecting to taste orange juice, your first sip tastes like orange juice even if it is grapefruit juice. Does not a critic's review of a play tend to fulfill its own conclusion by implanting a belief that alters how the audience perceives the play? Is not an early lie more effective than the belated truth? When writing to persuade, is it not best to make your case early to get the reader "on your side"? Does our need to rush to judgment arise from emotional discomfort we feel when we do not know what to believe?

Baseless linkages of cause and effect, which we create from our own experiences, derive from our need to ascribe meaning to events we observe. Such baseless linkages and meanings are often wrong. Children of divorced parents, for example, often believe that they are the cause of the divorce. Beliefs derived from erroneous linkages of cause and effect are at the root of many of our psychological problems. One function of psychoanalysis is to seek out the events in early life that created erroneous beliefs, and, once found, to change the troublesome beliefs by convincing us that they derive from baseless linkages of cause and effect motivated by our need to ascribe meaning to events.

Proper science requires that scientists guard against misreading data to fit what they believe they will find. To eliminate the effect of possible perceptual biases, results must be reproduced by other scientists to confirm the absence of bias. In medicine, double-blind studies are done for this reason.

Delusion is defined as a false belief strongly held in spite of invalidating evidence. Inasmuch as our perceptions are belief dependent, and beliefs need not be based in reality, the difference between delusion and "right thinking" is the degree to which our underlying beliefs are not supported by reality. However, delusion is not measured against reality, but against a belief-biased consensus or community view of reality. How can we recognize those who have the gift to see reality clearly through the haze of our widely held arbitrary beliefs? How many DaVincis, Einsteins and Edisons have lived their lives in frustration and ridicule, waiting in vain for permission to become geniuses?

Mythologies have established extra-experiential beliefs that encompass virtually all human activities as well as the known universe. Often, facts that threaten such beliefs are countered with forced beliefs (manufactured beliefs or denied realities) presented to avoid acknowledging that another strongly held belief is wrong. While we willingly accept scientific discoveries not in conflict with our myths, forced beliefs explain denials of the validity of biological evolution by intelligent people who are actually protecting their literal belief in the biblical description of creation. Forced beliefs appear to be rooted in belief-distorted perception, and are not necessarily disingenuous.

Although creation myths have claimed knowledge of everything from the formation of the universe to the origin of life, I know of no creation myth that correctly and unequivocally contradicted beliefs extant at the time and place of its formation. For example, heliocentricity (the Earth revolves around the sun), the prior existence of dinosaurs, and biological evolution were discovered by scientists and not predicted by any creation myth of which I am aware. Although no rational argument has been presented that contradicts these discoveries, believers have denied—and, in defense of their myths, some still deny by forced belief—the truth of such discoveries. In defending their myths some believers in mythology have killed philosophers and scientists for their heretical discoveries. The need of mythologists to defend their beliefs is extraordinarily strong. How else could killing those who do not believe what you believe be explained? I know of no instance where philosophers have killed mythologists for their beliefs. To give credit where it is due, Charles Darwin was laid to rest in Westminster Abby. Also, a Papal commission of the Roman Catholic Church acknowledged in 1992 that the Church had made an error in 1633 when it sentenced Galileo to life imprisonment (commuted to house arrest) for his belief in the theory of heliocentricity. More recently, in December of 1999 the International Theological Commission of the Roman Catholic Church completed a document entitled *Memory and Reconciliation: The Church and the Faults of the Past.*

Through a general reference in this document and a Universal Prayer, subtitled *Confession of Sins and Asking for Forgiveness,* delivered in a subsequent Papal mass, it appears that the Church acknowledged, among other things, its error in 1600 when it burned Giordano Bruno alive for his belief in heliocentricity. The relevant portion of the mass was

II. CONFESSION OF SINS COMMITTED IN THE SERVICE OF TRUTH

A representative of the Roman Curia:

Let us pray that each one of us,
looking to the Lord Jesus, meek and humble of heart,
will recognize that even men of the Church,
in the name of faith and morals,
have sometimes used methods not in keeping with the
    Gospel
in the solemn duty of defending the truth.

Silent prayer.

The Holy Father:

Lord, God of all men and women,
in certain periods of history
Christians have at times given in to intolerance
and have not been faithful to the great commandment
    of love,
sullying in this way the face of the Church, your
    Spouse.
Have mercy on your sinful children
and accept our resolve
to seek and promote truth in the gentleness of charity,
in the firm knowledge that truth
can prevail only in virtue of truth itself.

We ask this through Christ our Lord.

R. Amen.[12]

The phrase "defending the truth" appears to refer to section 5.3 "The Use of Force in the Service of Truth" set forth in *Memory and Reconciliation: The Church and the Faults of the Past.*

5.3. The Use of Force in the Service of Truth

To the counter-witness of the division between Christians should be added that of the various occasions in the past millennium when doubtful means were employed in the pursuit of good ends, such as the proclamation of the Gospel or the defense of the unity of the faith. "Another sad chapter of history to which the sons and daughters of the Church must return with a spirit of repentance is that of the acquiescence given, especially in certain centuries, to intolerance and even the use of force in the service of truth."[13]
This refers to forms of evangelization that employed improper means to announce the revealed truth or did not include an evangelical discernment suited to the cultural values of peoples or did not respect the consciences of the persons to whom the faith was presented, as well as all forms of force used in the repression and correction of errors. Analogous attention should be paid to all the failures, for which the sons and daughters of the Church may have been responsible, to denounce injustice and violence in the great variety of historical situations: "Then there is the lack of discernment by many Christians in situations where basic human rights were violated. The request for forgiveness applies to whatever should have been done or was passed over in silence because of weakness or bad judgment, to what was done or said

hesitantly or inappropriately."[14] As always, establishing the historical truth by means of historical-critical research is decisive. Once the facts have been established, it will be necessary to evaluate their spiritual and moral value, as well as their objective significance. Only thus will it be possible to avoid every form of mythical memory and reach a fair critical memory capable—in the light of faith—of producing fruits of conversion and renewal. "From these painful moments of the past a lesson can be drawn for the future, leading all Christians to adhere fully to the sublime principle stated by the Council: 'The truth cannot impose itself except by virtue of its own truth, as it wins over the mind with both gentleness and power.'"[15]

Fundamental to the scientific method is an acknowledgment that reality is supreme and what we believe about it merely represents our attempt to understand it. Independently verifiable beliefs about reality that explain what has happened or predict what will happen are thought most likely to be correct; an example of the former being Darwin's explanation of biological evolution and of the latter being Halley's predicted return of the comet that now bears his name. But even the remotest possibility that a belief may be wrong causes scientists to treat it as a theory and not as a law. There are virtually no absolutes in science, and, to separate fact from illusion, every accepted belief is subject to challenge by anyone at any time.

Science has concerned itself with how Nature works, unconcerned, for the most part, with myths or superstitious matters. Even so, since Galileo's time, when heavenly bodies were found to be imperfect, and idealized medieval mythological concepts of the universe were found wanting, one by one, mythological concepts of the physical world have been replaced by scientific models. It seems that what is yet unknown to science is the only safe haven for myths, superstitions and the occult. However, this process of science displacing myth may have reached a limit with creation. If the Big Bang theory is correct, science is unlikely to discover anything that happened prior to about 15 billion years ago, if indeed there was anything prior to the Big Bang. Any prior assemblage of matter would have been disassembled in the Big Bang. So far, Georges Lemaître's Big Bang theory is supported by observation. It explains cosmic background radiation found in the early 1970s by Arno Penzias and Robert Wilson, the ratios of light to heavy elements we find in the universe, and Edwin Hubble's 1929 observation that the more distant a galaxy the more rapidly it is moving away (Hubble did not know that the galaxies were actually accelerating). If the Big Bang was the event that formed the present universe, we may be dealing with an old problem once again. Our beliefs about reality may be preventing us from perceiving it correctly. Perhaps Hawking's no boundary proposal will show us that the universe has no boundary, no edge, no beginning, and no end. Another theory, which correctly predicted that we would find specific irregularities in the background radiation of the universe, may answer the question. It is called *The Wave Function of the Universe*. It was developed by Stephen Hawking, Andre Vilenkin, Alex Linde, and others, and posits that the universe came into existence because of its "natural properties." By comparison, the Big Bang theory makes no reference to natural properties of the universe bringing about the Big Bang, and leaves much room for speculation by some that the Big Bang came about because of "supernatural forces," i.e., the moment of Creation or Genesis.

The way our brains evolved has left us with biological processes that now profoundly influence how and what we believe. In the few examples of this chapter we have seen how our existing beliefs strongly influence how we perceive reality. Perception is not an objective process of seeing and believing. If anything, the reverse is true. As Kant would say, our way of perceiving will forever be inextricably mingled with the thing perceived. Self-perpetuating misperceptions are examples of how corrupt perceptions of reality can be self-reinforcing. While belief linkage and transitory beliefs might have become part of our genetic behaviors because they have survival value, forced beliefs may be with us more for their value to our egos than as a result of the perception-altering nature of our beliefs. A major underpinning of animism and mythology is the planning assumption. It is embodied in the argument that if watches need watchmakers then people need makers (gods) as well. Is this logic the result of an inherited survival behavior? If by our first year of life our brains have the inherent capacity to attribute "intent" to the actions of people and of self-propelled objects that are incapable of intent, then should we be surprised that as adults we assume intent behind the ultimate self-propelled object, the universe? These and other aspects of the biology of belief will be examined in detail in later chapters.

Chapter 3
The Biology of Belief Manipulation

It is curious that so many writings that deal with belief fail to consider how the nature of the brain and mind influence how and what we think. Inasmuch as understanding brain traits is fundamental to understanding the biology of belief, we will consider how our brains function and how their functions shape and alter our perceptions and beliefs.

Our Brains have Design Problems

What we call "mind" is the brain at work. In general, the mind manifests itself as thought, perception, emotion, volition, memory, imagination and the like. It is our conscious and subconscious, our spirit, knowledge, intelligence, and our ability to reason. All of these capabilities, and more, derive from the structure and neurochemistry of the thinking organ in our heads, which, along with its capabilities, has its limitations. To understand the human mind we will examine the relationship between reason and emotion, the nature of dreaming, what causes hallucinations, the function of hormones and neurotransmitters, why some chemicals are psychoactive, what trances are and why they happen, why some of us can be hypnotized or brainwashed, what happens when we meditate, how zealots and fanatics come to be, the nature of faith healing, and what all this has to do with what the human mind believes.

The key difference between ourselves and the rest of life on Earth resides in the way our brains are structured. All but a small percentage of our genetic code is identical to that of our closest living primate relative. And included in that small percentage of genetic code is the molecular blueprint for our neocortex, which provides us with our reasoning ability. Without it we would be less than human. In fact, we would be what we were millions of years ago, when our brain capacity was equivalent to that of contemporary chimpanzees.

We happened to be born when the present model of Homo sapiens is being produced, and it should be apparent that we have a few design problems. Biological evolution selected Homo sapiens based on our fitness for survival, not for our intellectual or emotional perfection. In fact, if living in emotional and intellectual conflict had survival value there is no reason to think we would not have evolved that way. Then again, perhaps we did. One of our problems is that the limbic part of our brain is essentially an emotional autopilot we humans inherited from our ancient ancestors. The benefit is that, before we were able to reason, the limbic brain provided us with the emotion-based actions we needed to survive and reproduce. Unfortunately, now that we can reason, both reasoning and emotion control our actions. Therein lies the conflict. Our arrangement of neural circuitry subordinates reason to the deep-seated reptilian emotions and behaviors emanating from the primitive reptilian part of our brains. Although emotions are part of what is most admirable in human thought and conduct, when our brain evolution was at the reptilian stage, we had no humanizing neocortex to provide an alternative to reptilian behavior. Reptilian behavior is variously defined as despicable, mean, nasty, obnoxious, disgusting, repugnant, vile, foul, shocking, detestable, reprehensible, abhorrent, perfidious and, in general, the product of low moral standards. Imagine what your behavior would be like if you saw the world through the eyes of an alligator. Keeping our neocortex-based reason subordinated to our older reptilian brain enables us to respond to threats in milliseconds. If our neocortex evolved to dominate our reptilian brain we could easily reason away our feelings, and that would likely threaten our survival. Imagine that the pilot of your airplane waited a few seconds longer while his neocortex decided to maneuver to avoid an imminent midair collision. Instead he or she responds virtually instantly. In fact, it often takes considerable effort for our reasoning neocortex to overcome the reflexive, emotional decisions of the reptilian part of our brain. And the more circumstances evoke emotional responses, the less rational thought prevails. For this reason, crimes of passion (committed in "hot blood") are punished less harshly than premeditated or rational crimes (committed in "cold blood"). The law recognizes that we cannot always control our emotions.

Federal Statute 10 USC Sec. 919 Art. 119 provides:

> (a) Any person subject to this chapter who, with an intent to kill or inflict great bodily harm, unlawfully kills a human being in the heat of sudden passion caused by adequate provocation is guilty of voluntary manslaughter and shall be punished as a court-martial may direct.

Manslaughter is defined in Federal Statute 18 USC Sec. 1112 as follows:

> (a) Manslaughter is the unlawful killing of a human being without malice....
> Voluntary [as used in *manslaughter* is defined as]
> —Upon a sudden quarrel or heat of passion.

If premeditated, the same act of unlawful killing would be considered murder and would be subject to more severe penalties.

For better or worse, our emotions are automatic. And, while providing us with the things spoken of by poets, our emotions ensure our survival through passion, fear, aggression, and the like. The story of Jekyll and Hyde is an example of instinctual emotions versus reasoned intellect where the author separated the two into clearly defined persons. Hyde acted without the civilizing influence of intellect and Jekyll, unable to control Hyde, was forced by his intellect to kill himself to stop Hyde. The British writer Leonard Woolf (1880-1969), considering the history resulting from our nature, wrote "The sordid and savage story of history has been written by man's irrationality, and the thin precarious crust of civilization which has from time to time been built over the bloody mess has always been built on reason."[1] For those of us who think he was talking about our barbarian ancestors, think again. Mark Twain described the contribution religion made to the bloody mess.

> During many ages there were witches. The Bible said so. The Bible commanded that they should not be allowed to live. Therefore the Church, after doing its duty in but a lazy and indolent way for eight hundred years, gathered up its halters, thumbscrews, and firebrands, and set about its holy work in earnest. She worked hard at it night and day during nine centuries, and imprisoned, tortured, hanged, and burned whole hordes and armies of witches, and washed the Christian world clean with their foul blood.
>
> Then it was discovered that there was no such thing as witches, and never had been. One does not know whether to laugh or to cry. Who discovered that there was no such thing as a witch—the priest, the parson? No, these never discover anything. At Salem, the parson clung pathetically to his witch text after the laity had abandoned it in remorse and tears for the crimes and cruelties it had persuaded them to do. The parson wanted more blood, more shame, more brutalities; it was the consecrated laity that stayed his hand.[2]

If the priest and the barbarian arrive at the same horrible result while professing beliefs at opposite ends of the moral spectrum, then may we conclude that, in the end, their behaviors were influenced more by their common emotional nature than by their morals or their capacity for rational thought?

Some believe that our reasoning ability came into its own with the development of language. When we began to create and use language we began to reduce concepts to word symbols. This, in turn, enabled us to increase the complexity and precision of our thinking. With our newfound capacity for logical, analytical thought, we were able to transcend our predominantly emotional view of the world. Reasoning, however, is a process that needs good information if it is to arrive at good conclusions. Inasmuch as our ancestors were just beginning to discover how the world works, their limited understanding necessarily limited their conclusions. This, together with other problems the brain has with how it perceives the world, led to simplistic ancestral belief systems we have observed in equivalent, contemporary primitive cultures. In other words, there is much more to reasoning than acquiring the ability to reason.

Memory is essential to our reasoning process. By studying people with brain damage we have begun to understand what makes memory happen. Brain damage can occur in many ways, including intentionally. A last resort treatment for epilepsy in the 1950s was a surgical procedure that damaged the brain's temporal lobes. One side effect of the surgery was loss of the ability to form new permanent memories. Memories before the surgery were unaffected, but post procedure memory lasted for no more than minutes. It was determined that these patients all suffered damage to the hippocampus, a structure within the temporal lobes. Research has determined that the hippocampus is centrally involved in moving memories about objects and events from temporary to permanent storage. Once the information is stored permanently, the hippocampus is no longer part of the process. However, if the hippocampus is damaged the information does not move to permanent storage and is forgotten.[3]

The memory you are experiencing right now is taking place in your prefrontal cortex. It will remain in your consciousness as long as neurons *containing* the information remain active. If the information is passed to your hippocampus before the prefrontal cortex neurons go inactive or displace the thought, that memory will not have been lost, at least for now. In the presence of glutamate (a neurotransmitter) a complex chemical process called "long-term potentiation" takes place that should result in the hippocampus storing the information for from hours to days.

Permanent storage of information is another matter. This requires physical changes in brain neurons and in the connections among neurons. It is these physical changes that make long-term memory possible and that make beliefs, once learned, so difficult to change. What we call memory is a neural network learning process that is believed to take place during sleep. Recent research done by Matthew Wilson, at the Massachusetts Institute of Technology, and Bruce McNauqhton, at the University of Arizona, has revealed much about the process.[4]

When mice are placed into a new environment, the experience causes nerve cells in the hippocampus to fire off coordinated electrical signals in ways that depend on where the mouse is in the environment. It is thought that the mouse is constructing a neural-map equivalent of its surroundings and the different groups of firing neurons represent recordings of different things in the environment. Thereafter, during slow-wave sleep (not REM sleep, when dreaming takes place), the same groups of hippocampal neurons reproduce the earlier firing pattern. It is as if the events of the day are being replayed and perhaps recorded in permanent memory. An interesting aspect of this process, according to Dr. Wilson, is that, while neurons in the hippocampus are reproducing the earlier firing patterns, neurons in the neocortex parallel the firing pattern of the hippocampal cells.

Although the process of firing-pattern reproduction takes place during slow-wave sleep, it has been shown in other research that interrupting REM sleep disrupts the process of moving object and event information from the hippocampus into permanent memory. We dream during REM sleep, and if dreaming and permanent memory formation are connected through REM sleep, we do not know what the connection might be. It has been suggested that dreams may occur when the prefrontal lobes of the neocortex attempt to make sense of impulses that result from the process that creates permanent memories. Also, research has shown that the nearby amygdalae (almond shaped parts of the limbic system at the back of the temporal lobes, shown in Appendix E) are able to add fear to permanent memories. In Arthur C. Clarke's *2001: A Space Odyssey,* Hal, the thinking computer, asked if it would ever dream. Given what we know about dreaming it seems unlikely.

While our cerebral cortex processes sensory input and memories to create reasoning, the more primitive limbic system busily orchestrates our emotions into actions, as shown in Appendix D. In addition to using nerve impulses to control our body's activities, the limbic system releases messenger molecules into the blood. The molecules circulate to receptor sites on various organ cells throughout the body and activate or deactivate their functions. Using messenger molecules is not unique to the limbic system. For example, our kidneys are blood pressure sensitive. Adrenal glands located on the kidneys release adrenaline into the blood to increase blood pressure by increasing the heart's pumping rate, among other things. Molecular messengers, although not as fast acting as nerve impulses, have a lasting effect and can orchestrate multiple organs simultaneously. Neurotransmitters are messenger molecules that affect the brain and neurological system. They bind to receptor sites on neurons to alter neurological activity. Noradrenalin, dopamine, endorphins, and dozens of other molecules are neurotransmitters. They influence human behavior, attitude, perception, temperament, love, and aggression, among other things. Serotonin, a major inhibitory neurotransmitter, affects mood, appetite, memory, and learning. It can both inhibit and enhance these functions. Stress during childhood can result in permanently low levels of serotonin and high levels of noradrenalin. If severe enough, the combination can account for a quick temper and violent behavior. The drug Prozac, which is prescribed for a variety of mood disorders including aggression, increases the availability of serotonin in the brain by decreasing its rate of elimination.

Dopamine is another inhibitory neurotransmitter. Among other things, it affects the basal ganglia, which control muscle movement. Insufficient dopamine causes the muscle tremors of Parkinson's disease. Dopamine also regulates the flow of information from other parts of the brain to the prefrontal lobes. It is thought that insufficient dopamine can cause incoherent and delusional thoughts. Too much dopamine in the limbic system and not enough in the neocortex might create paranoia or reduced social interaction. Insufficient dopamine in the prefrontal lobes might reduce our ability to remember telephone numbers long enough to transcribe them. Dopamine is also thought to create pleasure feelings. It is believed that endorphins may make more dopamine available to the prefrontal lobes. "Runner's high" is thought to occur when exercise creates very high levels of endorphins (to control pain), which in turn causes more dopamine to reach the prefrontal lobes, causing a sense of pleasure or "high" to the runner.

It appears that we can be influenced by molecules from other people as well. Everyone emits varying amounts of pheromones from their skin. When they become airborne and we inhale them, research suggests that vomero nasal organs (VNO) located inside our nasal opening, respond to the pheromones. Once activated, it is thought that VNO nerve impulses sent to the brain cause us to respond in some way, such as feeling good.

Along with the other things we inherit are the levels of emotion-altering molecules our bodies naturally produce. On average, gender-specific molecules are probably the most influential, given the pervasive effects of testosterone and estrogen. Although low levels of norepinephrine or noradrenalin are related to depression, gender-specific hormones influence how men and women deal with depression. Women tend to focus on what they are experiencing while men tend to focus on how to resolve it. Men are less inclined than women to talk about what is troubling them and are less receptive to emotional bonding. While women tend to feel more connected by sharing their experience, men might interpret the sharing experience as trivializing their difficulty or as a threat to their self-sufficiency. In depression, as with the other things in life, our gender-specific hormones cause men to find satisfaction in problem solving and self-sufficiency while they cause women to find satisfaction in shared experiences and emotional kinship.[5] Given the survival imperative of evolution, gender-specific hormones have given men and women different bodies and abilities to perform complementary functions necessary to their survival and procreation. It is clear that hormones, like beliefs and trance states, can alter our perceptions.

Cilicin, a molecule found in certain mushrooms, is similar to serotonin and can bind to serotonin receptors. Eating cilicin-containing mushrooms will cause cilicin to bind to serotonin sites in the thalamus. The thalamus, like a switching station, determines which sensory information reaches various parts of the brain. The prefrontal lobes are the part we use to reason and make decisions. Anything that disrupts the thalamus can disrupt the flow of sensory information to the prefrontal lobes. This in turn can cause abnormal thoughts to occur in our minds. If enough cilicin binds to serotonin sites in the thalamus the excessive sensory impulses flowing to the prefrontal lobes cause them to manufacture thoughts. In other words, if you eat enough cilicin-containing mushrooms, you will hallucinate. During dream sleep, blood flow to the thalamus increases while flow decreases to the complex thinking areas in the frontal brain. This combination, it is theorized, reduces our sense of time and self-awareness during dreaming, and contributes to our forgetting dreams on awakening.[6]

When mushrooms or other plants containing serotonin equivalents are used in a religious context, the hallucinations make imagined images more vivid and therefore more believable than those of a vague dream. The hallucination becomes a transcendent experience, but thought in this mental state is illusion. Instead of using cilicin, the same result can be achieved through sensory deprivation. Sensory deprivation is thought to increase the number of serotonin receptor sites in the thalamus, causing an otherwise normal level of serotonin to disrupt the thalamus and allow excessive sensory impulses to reach the prefrontal lobes. The following passage from the ancient philosophical writings of India, the Upanishads (800-500 BCE), describes what we know today as a fasting- and sensory-deprivation-induced hallucination:

> For a fortnight one must fast, drinking only water;[7] then the mind, so to speak, is starved into tranquillity and silence, the senses are cleansed and stilled, the spirit is left at peace to feel itself and that great ocean of soul of which it is a part; at last the individual ceases to be, and Unity and Reality appear. For it is not the individual self which the seer sees in this pure inward seeing; that individual self is but a series of brain or mental states, it is merely the body seen from within. What the seeker seeks is Atman,[8] the Self of all selves, the Soul of all souls, the immaterial, formless Absolute in which we bathe ourselves when we forget ourselves.

An alternative explanation would be that the subject's interpretation of events in ways consistent with his or her beliefs has combined with a fasting-induced hallucination or dream state to create a dream or illusion consistent with the hallucinator's beliefs. Hallucinations are typically achieved by meditating, rhythmic rituals, ritual fasting, fatigue, or drugs. Hallucinations resulting from smoking opium introduced the phrase *pipe dreams* into our vocabulary.

Another example of how brain chemistry can manufacture "reality" is found in near-death experiences. Unlike prefrontal lobe hallucinations, near-death experiences occur when your brain is deprived of oxygen—as can occur during surgery. When oxygen levels begin to decrease across your vision-processing neurons at the back of the brain, the neurons activate, and their output is the same as if you were seeing a white light. It is like an incandescent light bulb flashing as it burns out, except that the light lasts longer. You first "see" a white dot that gets larger as more and more of your vision neurons are deprived of oxygen. The tunnel perception is created because the neurons that are not yet deprived of oxygen do not activate, and you perceive their output as black. Seeing a small white spot on a black background reminds you of being in a black tunnel and seeing the small bright tunnel opening. As more neurons are deprived of oxygen you see the white spot grow larger. It reminds you of getting closer to a tunnel opening. Ultimately, when all your vision neurons are deprived of oxygen, you "see" only white. You have reached the tunnel opening. Further evidence of the biological origin of near-death experiences is that they also occur in people who have been physically incapable of sight from birth. One case occurred when a congenitally blind person was deprived of oxygen for minutes in a near drowning accident. People who have had near-death experiences also report having an overwhelming feeling of well being. This occurs because oxygen deprivation also causes your brain to release a flood of endorphins, which bind with your opiate receptors, producing what is typically described as a runner's high.

One Way to Manipulate Someone's Beliefs

One of the problems with the way our brains function has to do with the ease with which others can influence it. I am not referring to someone convincing us of something using reason; quite the contrary. This problem exists because the way our brains function makes it possible for us to be influenced by circumventing our ability to reason. In its simplest form we can be persuaded to accept someone's suggestion about what is true. In its most severe form we can be brainwashed. In essence, the different ways in which our left and right brain hemispheres deal with context, the nature of our different brain activity states, the ways in which our brains can be caused to malfunction, and other factors have made it possible for people to develop methods to manipulate what we believe without our realizing that it is happening. The degree to which this is possible varies from person to person, but, that fact notwithstanding, our control over our beliefs is not as secure as you might think. Most of us have seen demonstrations of hypnosis. Understanding what it is and how it works is essential to

understanding   neurolinguistic   programming,   persuasion
techniques, and brainwashing.

The Russian physiologist Ivan Pavlov (1849-1936) found
that dogs can be retrained easily after they have been stressed,
physically exhausted, or deprived of sleep. One theory suggests that
shared stressful activity has been a unifying force for our ancestors.
For example, group activities like rhythmic chanting and clapping,
drumming and music making, dancing, and rituals, such as those
used in Voodoo ceremonies, when practiced to the point of
exhaustion may have established common group beliefs using
Pavlov's conversion process.[9]

Although it is likely that we humans have experienced
hypnotic trances throughout our history, it is relatively recently that
hypnotic trances have been used by medical professionals for
treating mental conditions, controlling pain and nausea, relaxing
anxious   patients,   relieving   postsurgical   depression,   and
counteracting some sexual dysfunctions. Hypnotizeability is
thought to peak between the ages of 10 and 12 years. People who
achieve high scores on hypnotic susceptibility tests, such as the
Stamford Scales of Hypnotic Susceptibility, tend to have a history
of imaginative involvement. Hypnotic trances begin with an
"induction" and are "deepened" to increase the likelihood that
hypnotic "suggestions" will be acted upon. Induction can involve
relaxation, monotonous stimulation, involvement in fantasy,
activation of unconscious motives, and initiation of aggressive
behavior. Once a trance is induced, a rhythm at the approximate
rate of the human heart-beat will increase its depth. Thereafter,
suggestions can be "planted" with a command from an authority
figure.[10]

What is happening in the brain to make hypnosis possible?
Sensors sensitive to weak electric fields, when placed on the scalp,
register overall electrical activity resulting from neuronal activity in
the brain. Charts of brain electrical activity are shown in Appendix
C. As neuronal activity changes with our mental state, electrodes
on the scalp surface can detect electromagnetic wave patterns of
different frequencies. The patterns range from 1/2 to well over 13

cycles per second (Hertz or Hz), and have been grouped and labeled with Greek letters. Brains oscillating at frequencies of 3 Hz and lower are in a delta state, at 4 to 7 Hz are in theta, at 8 to 12 Hz are in alpha, at 13 to 19 Hz are in beta, and at 20 to 100 Hz are in gamma. When we are in the waking state we usually have a high degree of beta activity. Passing from being awake to being asleep involves passing through a series of brain states. Although the states overlap and involve some complexities, the process begins with alpha immediately preceding sleep and ends with delta in the deepest sleep state. Rapid eye movement (REM) sleep, associated with dreaming, demonstrates a wave pattern similar to the post-alpha or beginning sleep state.[11] Gamma wave activity at about 40 Hz has been associated with perception and learning arising from synchronized activity of clusters of neurons. Experiments suggest that the electrical peaks of large numbers of neurons may synchronize to unify recorded neural information into a coherent perception or recollection. According to Wolf Singer of the Max Planck Institute for Brain Research in Frankfurt, Germany, gamma activity "could well be the mechanism that binds neurons into functionally coherent assemblies."[12]

Of the various brain states, one in particular is significant regarding our beliefs. A *trance* is an altered state of consciousness, like sleepwalking, which involves the alpha state. Typical signs of being in an alpha trance are body relaxation, dilated pupils, and a high degree of suggestibility. A relaxed feeling results from an alpha-related release of opiate-like molecules such as enkephalins and beta-endorphins, introducing an addictive element to the alpha trance. We are much more likely to accept suggestions from an authority figure while we are in a deep alpha trance than in a fully conscious beta state. To varying degrees, when in this condition, our beliefs can be altered through commands or suggestions given by the person controlling the trance. And experiences during a deep trance might not be remembered unless you are instructed to remember.

How is an eyes-open alpha trance induced? Recall that hypnotizeability varies from person to person, but a substantial part of the population is susceptible to an eyes-open alpha trance. Electrical measurements have shown that during a trance state the right brain hemisphere is much more active than the left brain hemisphere. In a simplified view the right hemisphere deals with emotions and imagination, and functions without the capacity to relate present experiences to the past or the future. This is quite unlike the left hemisphere, which is analytical and rational, and constantly strives to find meaning in experiences and to place them into an overall context. The evolutionary advantage of seeking explanations for why events occur may be that our ancestors were better able to respond to recurring events and not merely treat them as if they were happening for the first time. It appears that an unfortunate aspect of this survival trait is that the left hemisphere, in attempting to ascribe meaning to events, often incorrectly links cause and effect, thereby creating a false memory of events and their meanings.[13] Imperfect as it is, given the left hemisphere's context evaluation of information, it is better able to detect charlatans and thereby protect the context-deficient, gullible right hemisphere. That electrical activity in the left hemisphere is low during alpha trances while the right hemisphere is active suggests that during alpha trances our connection with reality and the source of our skepticism is diminished and that we are much more likely to believe what we are told.

Regular meditation for at least an hour every day, for at least a few weeks, is very likely to cause a prolonged state of alpha with little strong beta. Excessive and continual meditation is part of some spiritual rituals, and the resultant stifling of virtually all left hemisphere rational thought and the resulting feeling of detachment from reality is perceived by some as disinterested wisdom and freedom from desire—or a higher state of consciousness. It appears to fit the description of Buddhist Nirvana.

Meditation and self-hypnosis are voluntary activities. However, when alpha trances are induced involuntarily and a manipulator alters our beliefs, we call it brainwashing. Then again, if we agree with the manipulator, we may call it conversion, motivation inducement, or being born again. In other words, even though the induced alpha state subject is unaware that his or her beliefs are being manipulated, others may agree that it is a good thing—if they believe in the purpose. Ordinary citizens are converted into single-minded military units by experiencing boot camp training. Criminals are rehabilitated when they experience religious "rebirth." People are "healed" at revival meetings. Human-potential organizations use this kind of belief manipulation to help some to deal with their counterproductive and self-destructive beliefs.

Zealots and Alpha-State Trances

As you would expect, all kinds of people are using belief manipulation for all kinds of reasons. Cults and propagandists as well as evangelists use it. Examples range from politicians using manipulation techniques to win elections to cults and human-potential organizations using manipulation techniques for unscrupulous profit. In brainwashing, what the brainwasher describes as education, conversion, persuasion, or whatever, is actually manipulation of someone's beliefs for the benefit of the brainwasher, with little concern for the interests of the subject. A brainwasher's objective is to change what you believe to what he or she wants you to believe. It can be accomplished in four steps—alertness reduction, confusion, thought stopping, and maintenance.

Alertness reduction can be achieved by an exclusive diet low in protein and high in carbohydrates, such as drinks with high sugar content, cookies, or fruits and vegetables. It produces a light headed or "foggy" mental state. Diets high in sugar and low in protein, fat, and complex carbohydrates upset normal brain chemistry and impair your ability to reason. Fatigue associated with strenuous activity and sleep deprivation can impair your ability to reason as well. After your alertness has been reduced, programmed confusion can be achieved by overloading you with information, questions, guilt, self-doubt, or humiliation, perhaps in combination. By now your left prefrontal lobe, which examines new information by comparing it with what you already know, will have been impaired. The right hemisphere of your brain, which cannot evaluate the context of new information, is extremely likely to believe what it is told. With your reasoning capacity low and your level of confusion high, a suggestion is given to you in very clear terms. You are relieved to respond to a clear suggestion amid the confusion.

Thought stopping involves placing you in a trance-like alpha state. It is achieved in stages. Focusing on a simple mental task such as meditation, chanting, or rhythmic marching or dancing at first calms you; if that focusing is prolonged, you will hallucinate. You will focus solely on your brainwasher's agenda and will ignore everything else. And it will all be done within the context of the movement, cause, organization, or whatever wants to control your thinking. When you are under your brainwasher's control, you will be taught the cult's beliefs while any of your unacceptable pre-existing beliefs will be "washed" away. And while your belief system is being altered, pleasant words will be spoken to celebrate your conversion or being "born again." Control will be maintained through reinforcement at regular meetings or by your living with other converts, and you may be kept away from your family and others who are likely to interfere with the brainwasher's agenda. Maintenance is intended to reinforce your new beliefs and to create a sense of belonging.

Those of us most susceptible to brainwashing are what Eric Hoffer describes as "true believers." They believe that they are incapable of self-direction or self-actualization. They are the insecure joiners and followers who want to be told what to believe. They look to others for meaning, enlightenment, and dogmatic structure. Because they want to be told what to believe, true believers make perfect followers in politics, business, social causes, and organized religions. The danger they pose is that they can be manipulated by charismatic leaders to become zealots and fanatics. This is typically done in movements that focus on a common enemy to establish unity. Such groups want everyone to believe what they believe, and may use coercion to achieve their goals. The wisdom in the American Constitution in separating church and state is rooted in an understanding of the danger inherent in allowing "true believers" access to the ultimate means of coercion, the power of government to legislate, police, and make war. The danger of such zealots was noted in the following statement attributed to Louis D. Brandeis (1856-1941), associate justice of the U.S. Supreme Court: "The greatest dangers to liberty lurk in insidious encroachment by men of zeal, well-meaning but without understanding."

If we prohibit falsely shouting "Fire!" in a crowded theater, what position should we take on inflammatory words spoken to an audience of zealots? What of words that would not move an ordinary person to violence, but would be considered a moral directive to a zealot? Is a zealot with little free will an instrumentality of the speaker controlling him or her? Is that the lesson of the World Trade Center bombing? Should zealot leaders be held to a higher standard for incitement speech given the higher suggestibility of their audiences—a characteristic well known to and perhaps cultivated by zealot leaders? If zealot speech were held to a higher standard, then who among us will decide when speech is zealot speech and when it rises to the level of unlawful incitement? Imagine what would happen if a prosecutor indicted a Christian minister for inciting the bombing of an abortion clinic or the killing of clinic personnel. Appropriately, the word *assassin* derives from an 11th and 12th century Islamic fundamentalist sect that killed moderate Muslim political leaders, Crusaders, and others.

Our beliefs determine the value of information available to us. Information consistent with our beliefs is held in high regard, while information we prefer not to believe is variously ignored or disregarded. Depending on whose beliefs are offended, the information source may be defamed, belittled, attacked, criticized, mischaracterized, villainized, denigrated, coerced, or eliminated. This "shoot the messenger" approach is most pronounced among propagandists or zealots who may respond irrationally when their beliefs are challenged. If we see ourselves as defined by our beliefs, then our "beliefs" become "self," and to challenge belief is to challenge self. It appears that self and mythological beliefs merge most completely among the most narrowly educated, those educated with narrow beliefs and little or no exposure to other belief systems during their formative years. It follows that a narrowly educated monoculture is most likely to reject foreign ideas and is least likely to perceive foreign ideas in the same way the foreign believer perceives them. Polycultures, by virtue of their exposure to multiple belief systems, are less likely to have narrow beliefs. In addition, because in polycultures there is typically economic interdependence among people with different beliefs, polycultures have an incentive to tolerate foreign beliefs. Monocultures will become less narrow in time to the extent that their populations are exposed to other beliefs through mass communications and global commerce. In any culture, mutual respect and tolerance are the essence of morality, but that essence cannot be attained by people who are uneducated except for narrow religious beliefs that extol intolerance and mindless adherence to a distorted mythological view of the world. Rational information presented to a zealot will be perceived in a manner consistent with the zealot's beliefs, and the more irrational the beliefs the more irrational the perception. An astute observation attributed to Oliver Wendell Holmes, Jr. (1841-1935), associate justice of the U.S. Supreme Court, is that "The mind of the bigot is like the pupil of the eye: the more light you pour upon it, the more it will contract." As does everyone else, zealots believe their perceptions are correct, and people act in ways consistent with their beliefs.

Zealot fundamentalist killings are found throughout history. Pre-Christians engaged in human sacrifices and persecutions. Christians killed during the crusades, various Inquisitions, the Salem witch trials, and the like. More recent fundamentalist killings involved a machine gun attack on an Islamic mosque by an Israeli Jewish fundamentalist; bombing of the World Trade Center in New York city by Islamic fundamentalists; bombing of a Federal office building in Oklahoma City by militant, religious extremists; and anti-abortion Christian zealot killings of abortion clinic medical staff. What of parents who refuse medical treatment for religious reasons, thereby causing their children to die from curable causes such as ear infections? Non-believers perceive the death as unnecessary and possibly criminal while the parents perceive the death as God's will. What is incongruous is that, while these parents are acting in a manner consistent with their religious beliefs, others who claim to have the same beliefs criticize them for actually expecting their God to help them. Instead, they are encouraged to place the fate of their child in the hands of secular science.

Although brainwashing can be effective in certain situations with a limited segment of the population, it has little practical use for swaying the mass of society. Persuasion techniques are another matter. Although persuasion techniques do not employ all of the elements of brainwashing, they can change people's beliefs without their consent or their awareness. Neurolinguistic programming (NLP) is a recognized medical modality developed in the early 1970s to reprogram limiting beliefs that negatively influence patients' immune systems. It has been found that positive beliefs aid the healing process and that negative beliefs about our prospects for being healed can inhibit the immune system. Negative memories produced by long forgotten events that caused trauma or confusion are remembered as feelings or phobias we currently associate with things and events. By using *reframing* (altering beliefs to change liabilities into assets) and *anchoring* (creating a strong association between a thought or sensation and a desired event), NLP practitioners identify negative beliefs (memories) and replace them with pleasant, positive beliefs. It is done non-cognitively by inducing an alpha brain state in the subject and accessing and manipulating the context-deficient right hemisphere while the context-seeking left brain hemisphere is distracted. Although NLP is beneficial, our problem is that persuasion techniques can be used by almost anyone for reasons not so beneficial.

An advisor who helped shape the political career of President Bill Clinton was discovered having a liaison with a prostitute. In reporting what many considered an unfortunate but minor event, many news reports emphasized that the advisor had represented Republicans in the past. The repetition of the word Republican was so strong in the reporting that I came away with a mental image that the discredited advisor primarily advised Republicans and just happened to be advising the president. The whole matter seemed irrelevant. However, that the reporting created an impression opposite to the facts of the story was unsettling. Methods of influencing public opinion by means of spin or propaganda are considered in more detail in Chapter 12.

In the 17th century, Roman Catholicism syncretized with African Dahomean animism and ritual on the French slave plantations of the Caribbean. The resultant hybrid belief system is what we know as *voodoo* or *vodoun*, which means "god" or "spirit" in the Fon language of Nigeria. It worships the Christian God who is called "bon dieu" or "Bondye." Also worshipped are local deities, deified ancestors, saints, the dead, twins, and spirits called "Ioa" (from the Yoruba language). Shamans called priests ("houngan") and priestesses ("manbo") manage voodoo rituals. According to Voodoo beliefs, Ioa involve themselves with human affairs and can take possession of human souls during voodoo rituals. Voodoo temples have a central post from which Ioa descend to "mount" worshipers. This occurs during ceremonies that begin with rhythmic drumming, singing, and feasting. Sexual relations between humans and spirits are found in Greek mythology and in the example of the virgin birth in the Bible as well. In time, some worshipers build to emotionally frenzied dancing and enter a trance state. Ioa spirits specialize in things such as the dead, war, and fertility, and when an Ioa "mounts" an entranced believer, its stylized characteristics are demonstrated in the believer's behavior. In the trance state a possessed believer is believed to be able to communicate with ancestors, give advice, and perform cures. The voodoo ritual combines European theology, African animism, and alpha-inducing trances.

Religious revival meetings also predate neurolinguistic programming. It is believed that during a revival meeting in

Massachusetts in the 18th century, a revivalist preacher named Jonathan Edwards discovered that a revival meeting that employs guilt, apprehension, and tension in the proper way can "convert" sinners very effectively. Edwards apparently discovered the technique by accident. A present-day revival meeting that employs belief manipulation will set up an environment that aids in inducing trances. This will include music with an alpha-state-inducing beat, much like rhythmic methods used by hypnotists. The purpose of inducing an alpha state is to increase the likelihood that the audience will accept as true what it is told. Speakers will use speech rhythms to induce a trance. The words may sound monotonous and will be spoken at about one word per second. It is a method used by some trial attorneys. Once the audience is in an alpha trance, a preacher will speak to the audience using personal words such as *you* and *your* instead of unemotional, analytical words. Personal words communicate more on a subconscious level and are used to induce hypnotic trances.[14] A sense of fear may be created by preaching about religious retribution. For subjects who are emotionally stressed, a frightful experience can induce a trance state.[15] In time, the preacher will involve people from the audience and will perform dramatic "healing," which is a form of hypnotherapy.[16] If a subject's malady involves a repressed psychological condition (not unlike those dealt with by neurolinguistic programming), he or she might experience a catharsis that may cure the malady. Even if the subject has a biological disease that cannot be cured psychologically, the symptoms may be relieved temporarily by the preacher's hypnotic suggestion. This would be similar to a hypnotic suggestion that enables a subject to place his or her hand in hot water and believe that the water is cold. To believers at the meeting it would be perceived as a miraculous cure. Religious conversions or revivals can be accomplished using similar methods. For those who are "born again" by their alpha-state revival experience, their beliefs may be altered permanently. Once converted they will neither realize nor believe that their epiphany has been orchestrated and will likely perceive it as a miraculous transformation.

In addition to the problems presented by true believers wanting to be told what to believe, it seems evident that methods of circumventing our reasoning ability and methods of covertly inducing alpha brain states represent threats to the beliefs of the uninformed and the vulnerable. Given the way in which our brains are structured, these methods can expose our beliefs to manipulation without our awareness or consent. And, once manipulated, we cannot tell the difference between induced beliefs and our considered beliefs. They become part of our belief system and we defend them as if we knowingly chose to accept them, completely unaware that our beliefs have been altered. Unpleasant though it may be, this is part of the biology of belief. We cannot expect our perceptions to be perfect. The evolutionary process that created our brains was driven by a need to survive, not by a need to perceive reality with precision. It follows that our brains have inherent strengths and weaknesses, and, to the extent that our weaknesses can be exploited, our perceptions and beliefs can be manipulated by those who understand the workings of the biology of belief.

Chapter 4

The Genesis of Mind, Self-organizing Knowledge, and Psychogenes

Understanding the process by which our brains evolved can provide an insight into how our minds and beliefs came to be. Many of us believe that biological evolution is simply the result of competition between predators and prey, or of competition between or within species for the same resources, with the losers becoming extinct and the winners evolving. As it turns out, the primary influences on the process of natural selection are the properties of biochemically active matter, the solar system, and Earth's characteristics. The sun, the moon, other planets, comets, asteroids, the Earth's axis tilt, the climate, continental drift, volcanoes, Earth's natural resources, circumstances that cause or disrupt genetic isolation, glaciation, the tendency of species to produce more offspring than the environment can support, the possible gravitational effects of nearby stars, and ionizing radiation have all played important roles in shaping the evolution of life on Earth.

Self-organizing Knowledge and Darwin's discovery

Is the evolution of human intelligence extraordinary, or is it merely one step toward ever-increasing complexity, driven by the very nature of knowledge? Although as a process, evolution is constant, as a product, evolution reshuffles itself every minute of every day. Each life form thus evolved treats its environment, including other nearby life forms, as a resource. What we see as predation, competition, or microbial disease is simply other life forms using their genetic knowledge to survive and reproduce. What may not be intuitively obvious is that the very nature of matter and how it interacts provides natural selection with the power to perform incredibly complex feats we humans would accomplish, if possible, through planning and the intelligent use of information. It is as if Nature were taking a multiple-choice test with no limit on time or the number of times it could take the test. After repeatedly submitting tests it completed by guessing different choices for every question, eventually it would submit the correct combination of guessed answers. It might be easier to imagine a computer plodding through every possible combination until it selects all the right answers.

To understand the power of natural selection it will be helpful to consider how matter and information relate to the process. Of the countless ways in which atoms and molecules combine, some combinations are self-organizing. This is apparent in the organized and often symmetrical patterns found in snowflakes and other inorganic crystals. By comparison, organic molecules are capable of much more complex combinations. Once organized, molecules are like the letters on this page. If they are arranged randomly they mean nothing. However, once organized, they become information. The same is true of self-organizing molecular sequences. Another important property of matter is that, among the countless possible combinations, it can combine in ways that make it self-replicating. RNA (ribonucleic acid) and DNA (deoxyribonucleic acid) are forms of matter that are capable of self-replication in the presence of appropriate enzymes. By combining self-organization and self-replication, matter can acquire and reproduce information.

As we must learn to assemble letters into words and words into sentences to achieve some result, the same is true of molecules if they are to achieve some molecular result. We learn either by instruction or by trial and error (iteration). Although geneticists are able to "instruct" DNA by inserting nucleotide sequences into existing DNA, there were no means to instruct molecules four billion years ago. For molecules to assemble into meaningful arrangements they had to experience trial and error evolution. From such simple beginnings and after perhaps hundreds of millions if not billions of trial and error arrangements of molecules, "dead" matter "learned" to self-replicate into "living" matter. Or, if you prefer, random matter learned to become self-replicating organized matter as self-organizing molecular information evolved into self-replicating molecular knowledge as it adapted to its changing environment. The British philosopher Karl Popper (1902-94) saw biological evolution as a process of knowledge acquisition.

> [W]e can look upon the Darwinian theory of Evolution by natural selection as a theory of the evolution of adaptive knowledge of the organism by a process of trial (= mutations) and of error-elimination (= selection). The mutations themselves are always blind. They are accidental. But the changed organism, mutated organism, is far from blind. It possesses all the adaptive knowledge of its predecessors, or most of it; and so the changed organism, which incorporated the trial and faces the pressures of its error-eliminating environment, this changed organism is not blind....[1]

Deoxyribonucleic acid or DNA is the key to self-replication. It is the material of our chromosomes and genes. It determines our physical makeup and our inborn traits. The amount of DNA required to define animals as complex as ourselves is considerable. If the molecular threads of DNA in one of our cells were unraveled it would total about eight feet in length. However, in large part our DNA is made up of sequences that, at this time, have no apparent function.

DNA consists of two long chains of nucleotides (molecules) twisted into a double helix (twisted ladder) joined by hydrogen bonds and/or geometric compatibility[2] between the complementary bases adenine and thymine or cytosine and guanine. DNA mindlessly stores genetic knowledge as sequences of these nucleotides. Natural selection continually refines that knowledge to better adapt it to its environment. How does DNA replicate itself? When the double helix is unzipped along its length (by an enzyme), each half of the helix selectively attracts the correct nucleotides necessary to replace the missing unzipped half. The self-organizing nucleotides thereby produce two complete DNA strands from the original unzipped strand.

While binary computers store knowledge as sequences of zeros and ones, a two state or binary system, DNA stores knowledge in double binary form. Instead of using 0 and 1 sequences, DNA uses adenine, thymine, cytosine and guanine sequences (ATCG). Adenine combines with thymine and cytosine combines with guanine. DNA strands are made of sequences of these combinations; e.g., TCAGTGATTCGGA. DNA makes proteins by attracting A to T and C to G and vice versa. Using the DNA of our example we would produce a protein made of the following amino acid sequence: AGTCACTAAGCCT or adenine-guanine-thymine-cytocine, *et cetera*. Once a protein is formed, it separates from the section of DNA (or messenger RNA) that formed it and goes about its business. By this process DNA has become the molecular generator of proteins, the stuff of which much of life is made.

In Nature, only the DNA sequences of the fittest life forms are "remembered." The DNA sequences of life forms that die without replicating are "forgotten." Today, DNA accounts for as many as 30 million presently existing life forms. That represents an estimated 2 percent of all the life forms that have ever lived on Earth. This process, by which knowledge self-organizes into successively better-adapted DNA sequences, is what we see as biological evolution. And the engine that drives evolution, by making better adaptations possible, is the trial and error molecular refinement of DNA. At the nonmolecular level we see it as Nature permitting the best adapted of each generation of each life form to survive and reproduce. In other words, that appropriate natural molecular means have recorded, reproduced, and adapted by increasing in complexity is evidence that self-organizing molecular knowledge is a highly stable state of interacting matter.

Nature's trial and error refinement of DNA is time consuming. For the process to work, an efficacious change in the

DNA sequence must occur, and eventually that change alone or in combination with other DNA changes must provide a survival advantage to future offspring if the change is to become more or less permanent. The process can be simulated in a computer. For example, a hypothetical one thousand nucleotide DNA sequence represented as a string of letters in a simple computer program was reproduced by trial and error. The program, shown in Appendix A, guessed one letter of the sequence at a time. After each letter was guessed the process was repeated for the next letter, and so on. The possible letters for DNA are limited to A, T, C, and G, representing the four possible DNA nucleotides. Based on running the program more than 500 times to guess correctly the entire string, it took as many as 4,396 and as few as 3,238 guesses to match correctly the entire one thousand nucleotide sequence. The program, which ran on a common personal computer, took a few seconds to guess the entire correct sequence. In a rudimentary comparison, to achieve the equivalent mutations in a human population, assuming an average human generation of 20 years, one mutation per generation, and a sufficiently large beginning population as the sole variables, the worst case of 4,396 random nucleotide mutations (guesses) would take 87,920 years. The human genome (our entire DNA) comprises about 3 billion nucleotide base pairs that self-assembled (not one at a time) over about 4 billion years. By comparison, a similar program to guess the phrase "In God we trust" used fifty-three possible characters—twenty-six letters of the alphabet, each in upper and lower case as well as a space character. That program, shown in Appendix B, reproduced the phrase exactly by trial and error in less than one second. The program was run more than 500 times and required as few as 259 and as many as 810 guesses to match the "In God we trust" sequence.

Although DNA sequences can be changed by random replicative errors in the mechanics of replication or by viral or other outside interferences, there are two primary ways by which DNA sequences change: externally caused mutation and sexual reproduction. DNA mutates when something upsets its nucleotide sequence, such as defective replication or exposure to ionizing radiation, carcinogenic chemicals, damaging viruses, or free radicals (a form of oxygen that can damage DNA). In asexual or self-replicating reproduction, a life form, e.g., a bacterium, replicates its DNA exactly, producing offspring identical to the parent unless something causes its DNA to mutate. In sexual reproduction, however, pieces of DNA from each parent combine to form a new DNA sequence in the offspring. It is this capacity of sexual reproduction to create new DNA sequences with each new generation that enables natural selection to make large and rapid changes in the appearance and function of plants and animals. For example, light colored moths unfortunate enough to have lived in England during the early industrial revolution were genetically forgotten as soot-covered tree bark contrasted with their light color, making them easy prey for birds. Dark moths fared better, but their even darker offspring fared the best. However, the order we see in the cosmos is not the result of self-organizing knowledge. There is no known cosmological process for recording, reproducing, and adapting. The kind of order we see is merely *perceived* equilibrium. If knowledge is to be capable of self-organization, it must have a suitable means to record, reproduce, and adapt to changing conditions. DNA and RNA are examples of suitable hydrocarbon-based molecular means.

Are there other means suitable for knowledge to self-organize? By combining mathematics and electronics we have created computers capable of recording, reproducing, and manipulating information. But manipulation is not necessarily adaptation. To accomplish a task with a computer we write a series of instructions that are converted into executable mathematical code. In turn, this code is executed sequentially by the computer's central processor. This type of programming relies on human logic and planning, and, if some condition is not accounted for in the instructions, the program may malfunction or "crash" when the unexpected condition is encountered. This type of programming does not adapt. It cannot genuinely acquire knowledge from experience. Although we are impressed with the power of logic, it is not used by Nature in the non-intellect-driven self-organization of knowledge.

Can a computer program be written that can adapt to changes in its environment? In the early 1950s John Henry Holland was researching this problem at the University of Michigan.[3] On reading evolutionary biologist R. A. Fisher's book *The Genetic Theory of Natural Selection,* Holland realized that mathematical code, analogous in function to Nature's genetic code, could be developed to simulate biologically evolved knowledge in a computer. The mathematical analog of DNA or RNA would be a genetic algorithm. Such an algorithm would comprise a recipe of instructions (genetic information) which, when executed by a computer processor, would cause behaviors relevant to the informational organisms possessing the algorithm. Such organisms would have no physical being, but would live and reproduce as organized bits of data in a world of information. They would have no intelligence except in the way they would function to optimize themselves to survive in a constantly changing informational environment. Holland developed a genetic algorithm that was a DNA-like computer-resident entity capable of acquiring knowledge from experience. With the ability to adapt to its environment entirely on its own, the genetic algorithm provided the remaining element needed for computers to achieve self-organizing knowledge.

Creating simple genetic-algorithm-based organisms was a start. The question in Thomas Ray's mind was whether it was possible to create a genetic-algorithm-based ecosystem in a computer.[4] Thomas Ray was teaching at the University of Delaware in 1989 when he began a most ambitious project. He planned to create genetic-algorithm-based organisms that survived by competing for computer processor time and memory space in a computer memory environment he called "Tierra." Processor time was needed to execute and reproduce their "genetic" code, and memory was the space in which they recorded and reproduced themselves. The actual process Ray created was more complicated than the following description of Tierra.

Tierran organisms entered a circular queue and each in turn received a slice of processor time from the computer's central processor. The act of processing an organism's code copied it to another part of the memory environment and, on occasion, the replication resulted in a child organism in need of its own memory space and processing time. To enable Tierrans to evolve, alterations in their algorithm's genetic code were introduced in a number of ways. Some bits of their genetic code were changed at random, other bits were changed during replication, and still others during code execution. Death came to all Tierran organisms, but not at the same age. If their code adapted appropriately they lived longer. Death was essential to keep Tierra from becoming overpopulated and thereby exhausting its supply of memory.

So much for theory. On January 3, 1990, after two months of programming, Ray introduced the first Tierran into its carefully structured computer environment. The creature was eighty instructions long and was known as Ancestor. Contrary to the predictions of many, everything worked. Descendant clones were created and in time the oldest organisms began to die. Mutants appeared that were seventy-nine instructions long and soon outnumbered the original Ancestor population. Soon creatures with shorter instruction sets evolved a way to replicate as well. They had an evolutionary advantage because their reduced number of instructions enabled them to produce more offspring for a given number of central processor cycles. They were more efficient. Then something new appeared in Tierra. A creature with forty-five instructions began to compete for the position of most numerous creature. It would alternately outnumber the next most numerous creature and then its numbers would decline and soon rise again. What was happening? Creatures of fewer than about sixty instructions should not possess enough information to replicate. To replicate they had to be borrowing replication code from another creature. The new organisms had to be parasites.

With fewer instructions needed to reproduce, their numbers increased rapidly. However, as their host organism's numbers declined, so too did the parasites. This accounted for the alternate surging of parasite and host populations. Mutating hosts soon evolved immunity to the parasites and virtually destroyed the parasite population as the new host population became dominant. However, mutating parasites evolved a way to defeat the immunity and the battle continued. Without human intervention, Tierra was experiencing the same measure-countermeasure process so familiar in biological systems. Tierra was ten minutes old, and, already, knowledge was self-assembling.

Ray was able to do things with his artificial ecosystem that are virtually impossible with biological systems. He could analyze to the smallest genetic level what changed with each generation of Tierrans. In one experiment he turned off the mutation processes and found that mutations continued. His analysis suggested that parasitic tampering with host genetic code caused "sloppy replication." This suggests that parasites alone may account for some of the diversity we find in biological systems. In experiments that ran for a very long time, long stable periods were followed by bursts of diversity—what is called "punctuated equilibrium" in biological systems. In one example, a single Ancestor evolved descendants and parasites. In turn, hosts evolved immunity. This relationship remained stable for millions of computer processor cycles. Suddenly, hyper-parasites appeared. They had the same number of instructions as the Ancestor, but almost one-fourth of the genome was different. The now dominant hyper-parasites eliminated parasites. A long period of stability followed. In time hyper-parasites evolved a more efficient, symbiotic method of reproduction. They began sharing code needed for replication. The new hyper-parasites could not reproduce without another hyper-parasite that could provide the reproductive code they needed. It was a kind of sexual reproduction. Although it was a more efficient way to reproduce, this change provided new parasites an opportunity to flourish. The stable period ended as newly mutated hyper-hyper-parasites thrived on intercepted reproductive code as it passed between hyper-parasites. Tierra had evolved a venereal disease.

Similar work done by William Daniel Hillis at M.I.T.[5] with computer-based organisms indicated that, during long stable periods, mutations continue to accumulate at the genetic code level even though organisms show no outward appearance of change. When a threshold number of mutations is reached that result in an evolutionary advantage, those mutations spread rapidly through the population.

This kind of research raises a number of questions. Do the rules governing self-organizing knowledge apply equally to inorganic and organic systems? If so, what does this research imply about biological systems? Is it possible that the punctuated equilibrium we see in Earth's fossil record, such as during the early Cambrian period, results from the accumulation of unseen genetic mutations during periods of apparent stability? Do the similarities of evolutionary functions in physical and nonphysical knowledge systems confirm Darwin's theory? Is Darwinism only one example of the concept that knowledge will self-assemble given appropriate means for recording, reproducing, and adapting? Does the concept of self-assembling knowledge suggest that the difference between chaos and order merely depends on the nature of interacting environmental constituents and the amount of time random chance has operated?

Our experience with self-organizing knowledge has led to a number of innovations. Self-adaptive robotic devices and artificial limbs are becoming common. A new engineering discipline called "genetic programming" is solving design problems using self-adaptive computer programs. This system defines what needs to be done rather than how to do it.[6] For example, such programs can evolve the shape of a lens given only the focal requirements of light passing through it. The technology should keep science fiction writers busy for some time, and will likely change our world.

Even though we understand the process of genetic self-organization well enough to replicate organic evolution in inorganic environments, still, some of us find it difficult to understand how such a process can evolve complex structures and organs such as wings or eyes. Our incredulity would not be much different from that of our ancestors at their first sighting of a wheeled chariot or cart. It is thought that the wheel was first invented for making pottery, where it was arranged in a fixed position spinning parallel to the ground and driven by the potter's feet. The realization that such wheels could be used in a non-fixed vertical arrangement on a cart came much later. So too, wings can evolve by successive genetic mutations that create successively longer and more feather-like scales, from which proto-feathers might have begun to evolve because the warmth feather-like scales would have provided could have provided an evolutionary advantage by enabling activity in colder regions. Animals with such mutations might escape predators by gliding farther than their shorter-scaled siblings. Flying fish are a much simpler example of such an evolved adaptation. More complex organs such as eyes require much more involved evolutionary adaptations. By analogy, large-scale integrated circuits such as complex personal computer microprocessors containing millions of transistors were not envisioned when the transistor was invented. Other inventions and adequate time were needed to evolve something as complex as a microprocessor.

Another difficulty we have with regard to the mechanism of evolution is seeing things as evolved adaptations to evolving circumstances. Much has been written about the apparent incomprehensibility of giraffes' evolving long necks suitable for their eating from the tops of trees. These analyses generally assume that the trees were always there and that giraffes' necks had to grow to enable them to reach the tops. It is a scenario that is not credible because it does not reward an elongating neck until it has reached the treetops. This analysis combines dynamic evolution with a static view of circumstances; i.e., that the trees in question were always as high as they are now. If this scenario were viewed dynamically, the trees would have been increasing in size over time and the giraffes would have been growing longer necks in response. They would have coevolved. Evolution is replete with interdependent species adapting to each other's changes. It has occurred between predators and prey and between insects and the flowers they pollinate. Alternatively, if giraffes were competing with other species for food, there might have been two or more species evolving longer necks as they competed for food ever higher on the available trees.

A detailed analysis of this type of apparently incomprehensible evolved body part or organ is presented by Richard Dawkins in his books *Climbing Mount Improbable* and *River out of Eden*. The assumption we have made is that giraffes' necks are long to enable them to eat from the tops of trees. Is that true? We observe that they eat from all levels, not just the tops. If we do not assume that acquiring food is the evolutionary motivation for their elongated necks, what could the motivation be? Could they have evolved long necks for the same reason some birds evolved incredibly long tail feathers—as a mating advantage? When combined with their stubby horns, giraffes' swinging, massive necks are formidable weapons. We observe that male giraffes swing their necks in an attempt to horn-butt their rivals when competing for females. Are long-necked males better able to compete for mates than shorter-necked males? Is eating from the tops of trees an inadvertent consequence of a trait evolved for mating?[7]

Much like past arguments against biological evolution that cited the "inexplicability" of the giraffe's neck, a contemporary argument cites what is called "irreducible complexity." According to this argument, if you take away any part of a complex biological structure, such as that of a bacterial flagellum (a molecular motor with a rotating shaft that drives a kind of propeller), the design will fail. In other words, because evolution works on the whole organism, it would have to bring together all of the elements of a bacterial flagellum at the same time for evolution to have produced that particular molecular arrangement. This is not how evolution works. Planning, on the other hand, as the argument goes, would do just that, and planning requires intelligence; ergo, something equivalent to a god would explain the bacterial flagellum, while biological evolution cannot. However, while there are, in fact, a number of proposed scientific explanations for the coming together of the parts of the bacterial flagellum by means of biological evolution, supporters of the irreducible complexity argument have not explained how the god came together, and that explanation would inevitably be considerably more irreducibly complex than the explanation for the bacterial flagellum.

Genetic knowledge in the form of variations in attribute adaptations is what led Darwin to his discovery of the mechanism of natural selection. His voyage on the Beagle laid before him a pattern of physical variations, including fossil remains, which Darwin recognized to be the result of natural selection. The early Greeks were aware of natural selection, but could not explain why it happened. Darwin's insight was that every part of reproducing a life form is subject to variation from generation to generation. And that variations, which better adapted the life form to its changing environment, were what Nature was selecting. It would be another century before molecular biologists would discover how DNA and RNA store genetic knowledge and how their mutations cause the variations that Darwin observed.

Genetically learned behavioral attributes are subtler than physical attributes. It is what causes a frog to sit motionless as a snake passes within inches. In addition to smell (which is not highly directional) the snake's genetic knowledge resides in its sensitivity to motion. The frog's genetic knowledge resides in its inborn response to remain motionless. Along with our other biological inheritances, our genes program emotions into us. They are as automatic as blinking our eyes. They evolved before we had the brain capacity to know that we had them, and they came at the cost of many lives in countless events of natural selection over millions of years. They are part of us, refined by Nature to ensure our survival in the hostile world of our ancestors. We know them as sex drive, hunger, fear, rage, and the like. If you have not thought of emotions as genetic knowledge then consider this: In animals incapable of rational decision-making, what is the source of behaviors that enables them to survive? Urges, emotions, imprinting, and the like, which are genetic mechanisms evolved by natural selection, enable simpler animals to survive and reproduce. Although rational thought helps, only a small minority of life forms possess it, and the ones that do not, do quite well without it, as do many of our fellow humans.

In the following quote from *On the Origin of Species by Way of Natural Selection,* Darwin described the accumulation of genetic knowledge in terms of inheritance (remembering), profitable variations (new knowledge), and non-survival (forgetting):

> How do those groups of species, which constitute what are called distinct genera, and which differ from each other more than do the species of the same genus, arise? All these results, ... follow inevitably from the struggle for life. Owing to this struggle for life, any variation, however slight and from whatever cause proceeding, if it be in any degree profitable to an individual of any species, in its infinitely complex relations to other organic beings and to external Nature, will tend to the preservation of that individual, and will generally be inherited by its offspring. The offspring, also, will thus have a better chance of surviving, for, of the many individuals of any species which are periodically born, but a small number can survive. I have called this principle, by which each slight variation, if useful, is preserved, by the term of Natural Selection, in order to mark its relation to man's power of selection [selective breeding]. We have seen that man by selection can certainly produce great results, and can adapt organic beings to his own uses, through the accumulation of slight but useful variations, given to him by the hand of Nature. But Natural Selection, as we shall hereafter see, is a power incessantly ready for action, and is as

immeasurably superior to man's feeble efforts, as the
works of Nature are to those of Art.

The difference between selective breeding and natural selection is
that, in the former, we choose which offspring survive, and in the
latter, Nature chooses.

Although Darwin did not know of DNA or RNA, he could
see their effect, which he described as "any variation, however
slight and from whatever cause proceeding." Today, we have
mapped the DNA of simple organisms, and we have built machines
that can recreate DNA segments (nucleotide sequences) to an
impressive degree. Given the knowledge contained in DNA maps
of simple organisms, and machines to translate that knowledge into
complete DNA, it seems likely that we will be able to replicate the
DNA of simple organisms. Under the right conditions, that DNA
could produce a living organism. In other words, an organism's
genetic knowledge can be stored in a book or computer and, even if
the organism becomes extinct, at some later date, given an
appropriate means of gestation, that knowledge can be used to
reproduce the living organism.

Self-organizing Psychogenetic Knowledge

What kind of knowledge would result if beliefs were substituted for
nucleotide sequences? Is it possible that beliefs possess many of
the properties of genes? Are inheritable beliefs the genes of social
evolution that cause cultures and other social organisms to evolve
or to become extinct? On the basis that inheritable "beliefs"
influence cultural evolution as genes influence biological evolution,
I refer to them as "psychogenes" (sI'kOH-jEEns) or mind-genes.
With the understanding that beliefs learned in youth are often never
challenged or tested for their validity, for a belief to survive over a
succession of generations it must have perceived inheritance value.
For this reason psychogenes typically deal with matters having
general relevance. Belief that humans normally have two kidneys

would have inheritance value relevant to understanding physiology. Belief that a particular person has two kidneys would have value for a surgeon who is about to remove one, but, generally would have no inheritance value. By analogy to physical genes, it follows that psychogenes cease to exist or become unused when they become irrelevant, are superseded, or are no longer believed to be true. Simply stated, whereas Darwinian evolution is driven by survival value, psychogenetic evolution is driven by perceived inheritance value. It is necessary to use "perceived" as a condition because, for example, formative beliefs learned before we were able to reason may be perceived to have inheritance value even though we may not have given the matter any thought since learning them. Alternatively, changing social conditions, resentment, exposure to foreign psychogenes, peer pressure or simply misunderstanding the relevance or importance of a psychogene may result in its not being transmitted for lack of perceived inheritance value. Although, in the strictest Darwinian sense, beliefs can have survival value, not all beliefs relate to survival. As they evolve, self-replicating, heritable beliefs adapt to reflect the changing nature of the believers, their then-existing belief system, and their physical and social environments.

Beliefs taken as a whole can constitute a unique human organization, culture, or body of knowledge. A group's constitution, laws, or other rules are formal listings of its core psychogenes. Even if a group's core psychogenes are not formally stated, the degree to which all members of the group inherit or adopt such core psychogenes is a measure of the group's cohesiveness. We have a need to determine who is "us" and who is "not us." Discovering that a stranger is of the same religion, nationality, or ethnic origin, for example, can win her or him immediate acceptance because of assumed common beliefs. Alternatively, we can become upset if we discover that someone we thought believed what we believe actually believes the opposite.

Unlike biological organisms with each cell containing identical genes, each of us with our unique combination of heritable beliefs can be said to represent one cell of a social organism; the degree of our psychogenetic diversity being least in monocultures and greatest in diverse cultures. In the same way in which Nature selects physical organisms with genes best suited to survive in a given environment, it selects social organisms with psychogenes best suited for the group to survive. The link between belief and social survival is that people act in a manner consistent with their beliefs, and survival is determined by what we do—even if we do the right thing based on an incorrect belief.

The four DNA code letters A, T, C, G and the four RNA code letters A, U, C, G are used by Nature to create the words that embody the information of genetic evolution. In other words, the physical properties of hydrocarbons have determined Nature's alphabet, but it is not the only alphabet capable of storing information. With the evolution of intelligence, a crucial evolutionary change took place—the development of human language, and in particular recorded language. The letters of our alphabets, number systems, and other forms of recorded information are to psychogenetic evolution what the amino acid sequences of DNA and RNA are to genetic evolution. As is true for DNA, psychogenes comprise information we use to adapt and evolve. Given that DNA by its nature must function within a biological and hydrocarbon-based organic system, adaptations that require things beyond the capacity of DNA to learn or to produce cannot be accomplished by biological evolution as such. Psychogenes have no such limit. Setting aside the argument that all psychogenetic evolution is an accomplishment of biological evolution, psychogenes enable us to do things that biological evolution cannot. While DNA is limited to interacting with the world through the hydrocarbon-based organisms it can produce, psychogenes are limited only by what thinking organisms can produce.

Natural selection, by using trial and error to select the best adapted physical genes, has been painfully slow in bringing us to our present state of evolution. By comparison, psychogenetic evolution, which employs inductive and deductive reasoning as well as trial and error selection, has been astoundingly rapid. However, with almost 1 million years within which to evolve psychogenetically, why did so little happen before about 100,000 years ago and why did human social evolution accelerate in the past five millennia? What we learn from DNA is that organisms become more capable when their genetic information is assembled, verified, and reproduced reliably. For social organisms, except for the imprecise conduits of story-telling, apprenticeship, and oral history, our preliterate ancestors had no permanent means to record, accumulate, and pass on the volumes of information necessary to evolve socially. By comparison with the time required for genetic evolution, the time required for dramatic social evolution has been minuscule since language and writing emerged to support psychogenetic evolution..

The point of departure from purely genetic evolution appears to have begun with the formation of small human social groups. Although our ancestors had brains equal to ours in size about 1 million to 700,000 years ago, psychogenetic evolution did not become significant until they invented language. Language provided two key benefits for humans; the obvious benefit being communication with others and the advantages that provided. It was possible to collect, organize, discuss, and teach what had been learned. The less obvious benefit was that it enabled our ancestors to "talk to themselves." Thinking involves manipulating symbols in our minds. By naming everything, language provided those symbols and made creating rules for their use possible. The second invention, writing, made it possible to record those symbols for later examination and study. Without writing, our ancestors were not able to accumulate information effectively. Before writing, they recorded important events and other information orally in the form of stories and with cave and rock paintings. By inventing language and writing, our ancestors invented the first information age. Although such things are difficult to date accurately, it is estimated that rudimentary language began to develop approximately 100,000 years ago. Writing began as pictographic markings on clay tablets in Sumeria about 5,500 years ago and in Egypt about 500 years later. The oldest evidence of writing that represented the sound of speech (phonetic writing) is from Sumeria about 4,300 years ago.[8] With the ability to write, we began to preserve and publish our heritable beliefs. We had achieved with writing and our ability to reason what DNA had achieved with nucleic acids and iteration. Our libraries and other repositories of information contain the psychogenetic equivalent of our DNA.

It appears that all human social evolution prior to the development of writing, as important as it was, is infinitesimal compared with what has happened since. Compared with the rate of biological evolution, psychogenetic evolution is explosive. This is not surprising, since the process of biological evolution is dependent on random chance. Although guessing is an option, psychogenes have the benefit of inductive and deductive reasoning to perfect their evolution. To paraphrase Mark Twain, it is the difference between a lightning bug and lightning. We did not wait 20 million years to perfect our ability to travel and breathe under water (return to the sea). We use self-contained under water breathing equipment or submersible machines. Not only is it faster than waiting to evolve, we are saved the inconvenience of growing flippers. Astronauts practice their routines under water to simulate weightlessness in orbit. Shortly thereafter they perform the practiced routines in an environment with no water, no air, and virtually no gravity, all with the same body type we had 30,000 years ago. To accomplish this we did not adapt with genes, we adapted with psychogenes. And, in a somewhat ironic twist, psychogenetic evolution in the form of gene splicing and other genetic engineering techniques is beginning, in a limited way, to free Darwinian genetic evolution from its more than four-billion-year-old dependence on random chance.

By recording psychogenes in the neural networks of our minds, by replicating them through writing and other means of transmission, and by profitably adapting them through reason or reflex to changing circumstances, Nature has demonstrated yet another form of self-organizing knowledge. Unlike self-organizing knowledge driven by DNA or genetic algorithms, self-organizing psychogenetic knowledge differs in the means by which psychogenes are recorded, replicate, and adapt. Instead of relying on molecules or computer bits, psychogenes are recorded as connection patterns in the neural networks of our brains. Instead of replicating by a molecular process or by moving bits of information in an electronic environment, psychogenes can replicate by example or through symbolic communication between minds. And adaptation need not rely on time-consuming and mindless good fortune. To varying degrees, animals capable of psychogenetic evolution can adapt using reason and through the recognition of cause and effect relationships. Although inextricably linked with the physical world, psychogenetic knowledge differs from DNA- and genetic-algorithm-driven knowledge. Psychogenes self-assemble in the environment of our collective minds, and understanding them is essential to understanding the biology of belief.

Chapter 5

Our Ancestors' Beliefs and the Origin of Creation Myths

It is likely that ignorance and fear of Nature, belief that dreams are real, the perceived existence of a dream spirit world, the planning assumption, extra-experiential intuition, a need to ascribe meaning to events, and a need for control over their lives to achieve purpose and peace of mind caused our primitive ancestors to attribute conscious life to natural objects and to Nature itself. It is not possible to know with certainty what our ancient ancestors were thinking as they evolved from nomadic makers of stone tools to artisans with a rudimentary vocabulary, rock and cave paintings, agriculture, and domesticated animals. That being said, archaeological findings and studies of contemporary primitive cultures may provide a glimpse into our ancestors' thoughts and beliefs.

Ancestral Attempts to Make Sense of Their World

Imagine the year is 50,000 BCE and you are one of your ancestors. You find yourself in a world of which you are profoundly ignorant. Death and fertility are both mysterious. The world is a confusing and dangerous place. You think dreams are real windows into a spirit world. You may eat certain plants that cause you to hallucinate—which you believe is a waking dream. You believe that your tribal shaman, a medium between the visible world and an invisible spirit world, explains your dreams, predicts or controls natural events, and heals the sick. You observe flowers that move to face the sun as it crosses the sky. You believe that plants, trees, animals, and natural events have human-like consciousness and spirituality. You decorate your weapons with the images of the animals you hunt because you believe the images capture the animals' spirits and give you power over your prey. You treat the animals you kill and the trees you cut with respect because you believe the spirits of all things are interconnected. You worship the spirits of your dead ancestors. You may eat the bodies of slain enemies to obtain the power of their spirits. Your parents, who protected you in youth, are now dead, and in their place you believe in a spirit that will protect you. For your protection, you offer barter in the form of offerings and rituals. Prior to developing language you think in simple symbolic form, which contributes to your lack of distinction between the real and spirit worlds. As your speaking skills increase in precision and complexity you begin to separate the material and spirit worlds in more sophisticated mythologies. You observe that celestial cycles are related to weather and life cycles on earth, and conclude that celestial spirits control the stars, the weather, life on earth, and all things in the universe. As the winter cycle progresses, the sun crosses lower and lower in the sky and living things find it difficult to flourish. You are not sure that the sun will not continue to descend, and eventually drop below the horizon, never to return. You are elated at the winter solstice when the sun reverses course and its path begins to rise and warmth and life begin to return to your Earth. You interpret eclipses as celestial dragons attempting to devour the sun and moon, and you prevent those disasters with your dances and rituals. You record lunar, solar, and celestial cycles in stone circles and by cutting marks on bones. Your intuition and the planning assumption tell you that the things around you possess spirits that think and feel as humans do. Eventually, you conclude that the complexity of Nature must be the work of an intelligent spirit, and your inability to understand Nature translates into your inability to understand the intelligent spirit that created it. Your shaman discovered the trance-inducing effects of certain plants and thought it a gift from one of your animal spirits. Some of his wall paintings use pigments bound together with the marrow of animals depicted in the paintings. Some paintings show the trance-inducing plants. Others show geometric designs commonly seen during drug-induced hallucinations. Your creation myth contains things specific to your environment and your understanding of Nature. As time passes, your mythological spirits (bodiless animal analogs) evolve into various omnipotent, immortal gods with animal forms, possessing supernatural power that can relieve your suffering, ensure fertility, and steel you against the forces of Nature. All this you believe without question, and most fundamentally, you believe that a bodiless force animates the universe. You and your fellow humans have become animists in a belief system that uses shamans to unite the real and spirit worlds.

Before we look at these ancestral beliefs condescendingly, we should be mindful of a few things. Our ancestors managed their fears, they lived in balance with Nature, and they survived to make our generation possible. Could it be that the modern soul derives from their concept of a personal spirit, and that astrology and modern gods evolved from inherited beliefs about celestial forces and spirits? It is obvious that modern religions did not spontaneously generate. With their similar terminology, fundamental concepts, and traceable evolution, it is apparent that today's religions evolved from early animistic beliefs. Animism was the primitive religion of our ancient ancestors. And, by the time Greek civilization peaked, the primary focus shifted from creation myths that supported gods in animal form to creation myths that supported gods that looked like us. This evolution was so complete by the 16th century that European Christians debated whether the natives they encountered in North and South America were actually human. Michelangelo Buonarroti (1475-1564) cast his vote in favor of their being fellow humans when he painted them into the human family as part of his work in the Sistine Chapel. What European Christians found in the Americas were cousins whose mythology, unlike their own, had not evolved much beyond the animism of their European ancestors. In a way, Europeans stood face to face with their ancestors and did not recognize them. In Chief Seattle's speech before the Commissioner of Indian Affairs for the Washington Territories on January 10, 1854, he wrote (with some literary license taken by the reporter)

> Your God loves your people and hates mine; he folds
> his strong arms lovingly around the white man and leads
> him as a father leads his infant son, but he has forsaken
> his red children; he makes your people wax strong every
> day, and soon they will fill the land; while my people
> are ebbing away like a fast-receding tide, that will never
> flow again. The white man's God cannot love his red
> children or he would protect them. They seem to be
> orphans and can look nowhere for help. How can we
> become brothers? How can your father become our
> father and bring us prosperity and awaken in us dreams
> of returning greatness? [1]

Animism continues today in many cultures around the world.
Recent ecological concerns and a growing awareness of the
interconnectedness of the biosphere have renewed interest in
animism as a religious movement.

Animism, or any mythology, is useful to the extent that it
enables its believers to cope with the vicissitudes of life. The price
for this usefulness, however, is measured in the damage that results
from its conflict with reality and from the sacrifice, ostracism, and
hostility that necessarily flow from a need to deny the validity of
competing beliefs.

My attempt to reconstruct the beginnings of mythology
addresses certain timeless human and natural factors that influence
the creation of myth. It seems apparent that fertility, adversity,
community, death, ignorance, mystery, fear, dreams, intuition, and
the planning assumption are key factors that shape our myths. It is
also apparent that every culture has a need to explain how our
universe was created and that those myriad explanations are culture
specific and have evolved over thousands of years into the revered
and immutable beliefs we hold today.

Dreams and Hallucinations

What do dreams have to do with myths? If a dream experience can create the same emotional response as a real experience, then why would not a primitive mind think that dreams are real? If your dreams defined your reality, it would be as surreal as the spirit worlds of our ancestors. Dreams may be involved in a complex process that sorts out what the brain will remember from what it has experienced. Some researchers believe that dreams and permanent memory formation are unrelated. Other research suggests that the long-term storage of memories may take place during the period of sleep when we experience rapid eye movement (REM sleep). The process that converts temporary information into long-term memories may create false experiences fabricated from the emotions and other information the brain processes.

In a way, we may be dealing with inadvertent consequences. By analogy, we did not evolve a capacity for language, which began to develop about 100,000 years ago—much too short a time for evolution to produce significant neurological change. We evolved the capacity for some other purpose or purposes, such as predicting the trajectories of objects thrown during hunting. Whatever its evolutionary origin, that capacity just happens to be well suited to our creating language. In a similar way, given the complex neurochemistry of the brain, the evolved capacity to convert short-term memories into long-term memories may produce dreams as a side effect or inadvertent consequence. Anything that prevents the thalamus from controlling the flow of sensory information to the prefrontal lobes can cause abnormal thoughts to appear in our minds. Whether dreaming is the result of memory formation or some other cause is not important. That some direct or indirect brain function causes dreaming is what is important.

Hallucinations are dream-like states that can be achieved through a number of means, among them meditation, rhythmic rituals, drugs, sensory deprivation, fasting, and fatigue. The hallucination results from disrupting the normal flow of neural impulses in the brain. Eating cilicin-containing mushrooms can disrupt the thalamus (the part of the forebrain that relays sensory impulses to the prefrontal lobes where thought, reasoning, and memory are processed). Once disrupted, the thalamus excessively passes sensory impulses to the prefrontal lobes, causing us to perceive artificial experiences (hallucinations). When such mushrooms are used in a religious context, the hallucination becomes a transcendent experience. Sigmund Freud extended the concept to include other forms of cultural knowledge he believed are unconsciously created ideas:

> I recognized the presence of symbolism in dreams from the very beginning. But it was only by degrees and as my experience increased that I arrived at a full appreciation of its extent and significance, and I did so under the influence of ... Wilhelm Stekel. ... Stekel arrived at his interpretations of symbols by way of intuition, thanks to a peculiar gift for the direct understanding of them. ... Advances in psycho-analytic experience have brought to our notice patients who have shown a direct understanding of dream-symbolism of this kind to a surprising extent. ... This symbolism is not peculiar to dreams, but is characteristic of unconscious ideation, in particular among the people, and it is to be found in folklore, and in popular myths, legends, linguistic idioms, proverbial wisdom and current jokes, to a more complete extent than in dreams.[2]

The American mythologist Joseph Campbell observed:

> Dream is the personalized myth, myth the depersonalized dream; both myth and dream are symbolic in the same general way of the dynamics of the psyche. But in the dream the forms are quirked by the peculiar troubles of the dreamer, whereas in myth the

problems and solutions shown are directly valid for all mankind.[3]

Creating Beliefs to Satisfy Our Emotional Needs

Myth, whether from dreams or otherwise, provides us with a sense of control over the essentials of life, and peace of mind through "understanding" our world. It links us with immortality (non-death), and in some cases with a supernatural parent or guardian capable of protecting us. It frightens some of us into socially acceptable behavior, conforming our individual needs to those of the group. Even if our myths disappoint us, it is easier to believe a comforting myth than to accept an unpleasant reality. Throughout history both firmamental and terrestrial events have been interpreted by our ancestors using knowledge of their day. In Hawaii a volcanic eruption was proof that the Goddess Pele was unhappy about something. In Egypt the sun was pulled across the sky by Ra. Even contemporary personifications are more comforting and comprehensible to those of us who do not understand or accept what science has learned about Nature. Francis Bacon acknowledged, "I had rather believe all the fables in the [Golden] Legend, and the Talmud, and the Alcoran, than that this universal frame is without a mind."[4]

It is a fact of human behavior that disappointment can lead either to rejection or acceptance. Rejection of something that disappoints us is normal. If it fails, don't do it again. But the reverse is also true. If it fails, defend it. It is much like maxims about love and separation. If "absence makes the heart grow fonder," then why is "out of sight—out of mind" also true? It depends on the degree of love involved. If love is weak, then "out of sight—out of mind" is true. If love is strong, then "absence makes the heart grow fonder." This is true of religious belief as well. When belief (faith) is weak, disappointment with unfulfilled expectations will likely lead to disbelief. However, when belief is strong, unanswered prayers or a personal tragedy are met with feelings of inadequacy—of inability to understand the ways of God. Such things can increase the need to strengthen faith. At our time of greatest need for reassurance it would be unthinkable to let our disappointment cause us to reject the very thing we depend on for reassurance. This is the mechanism that makes discussions of faith-based beliefs with a devout believer quite pointless. It is one reason for my recommending in Chapter 1 that those with deep religious, or mystical beliefs should read something more comforting. The other reason is that some of us may have a specific portion of our brain (a God module) that predisposes us to seek comfort in and derive strength from mythology. What purpose would be served by disturbing those of us who are so predisposed, except, perhaps, to prevent their most zealous brethren from burning books, witches, philosophers, abortion clinics, other people's churches, or the U.S. Constitution.

What role does fear play in mythology? The emotion of fear is stronger than reason in determining our actions. At best, reason moderates emotion. That reason is no match for emotion is reflected in our recognition that crimes committed in the provoked heat of passion are treated less severely than those committed rationally and without passion; i.e., in "cold blood." If the unknown elicits fear and uncertainty, and mythology assuages fear and uncertainty, then emotion will choose comforting myth over inadequate reason. For this reason transcendence, prayer, ritual, mystery, and mind-altering experiences are to emotion what logical thought is to reason.

It appears that fear originates in the amygdalae (almond-shaped masses in the front portion of the brain's temporal lobes). Research shows that drugs that block learning when injected into the hippocampus block the learning of fear when injected into the amygdala. Rats treated with blocking drugs show no sign of fear.

Fear clearly has survival value. However, too much fear can paralyze, while too little fear can imperil. As to too much fear, William Shakespeare said, "To fear the foe, since fear oppresseth strength, gives in your weakness strength unto your foe." As to too little fear, Leonardo DaVinci observed, "Just as courage imperils life, fear protects it." Too little fear apparently is not the concern of myth. To the contrary, it is a purpose of myth to encourage one to persevere in the face of adversity. And to the extent that myth can remove fear, it empowers its believer to overcome adversity. Virgil (70-19 BCE) asserted that "They can conquer who believe they can.". In other words, fear begets myth that strengthens us against that which is feared. By promising eternal life, myth can transform into optimists those of us who would otherwise see life as an endless fear of dying. This is the real power of myth. On the other hand, if, as Livy (BCE 59-17 CE) claimed, "We fear things in proportion to our ignorance of them," and if fear begets faith, then the most faithful are likely to be the least informed.

What is the role of mystery in mythology? Jean Meslier, a 17th century Roman Catholic priest said, "If religion were clear, it would have fewer attractions for the ignorant. They need obscurity, mysteries, fables, miracles, incredible things."[5] Mythology defends its arbitrary beliefs by introducing mystery, denigrating rational disagreement, and requiring its believers to have faith; i.e., belief without proof. How a trinity can be one, how a being can be everywhere at once, and so on, are conundrums used by myth to add mystery and weaken its believers' reliance on practical experience and rational analysis. The trinity being one also avoids what some would consider polytheism. Not all experience is denigrated, however. "Knowledge" is revered if it is based on emotionally satisfying intuition about things beyond our experience. According to Charles de Gaulle, "Prestige cannot exist without mystery, for one reveres little what one knows well."

An ancient East Indian view of the relationship between intellect and mythology was this:

> The first lesson that the sages of the Upanishads teach their selected pupils is the inadequacy of the intellect. How can this feeble brain, that aches at a little calculus, ever hope to understand the complex immensity of which it is so transitory a fragment? Not that the intellect is useless; it has its modest place, and serves us

well when it deals with relations and things; but how it falters before the eternal, the infinite, or the elementally real! In the presence of that silent reality which supports all appearances, and wells up in all consciousness, we need some other organ of perception and understanding than these senses and this reason. "Not by learning is the Atman (or Soul of the World) attained, not by genius and much knowledge of books.... Let a Brahman renounce learning and become as a child.... Let him not seek after many words, for that is mere weariness of tongue."[6] The highest understanding, as Spinoza was to say, is direct perception, immediate insight; it is, as Bergson would say, intuition, the inward seeing of the mind that has deliberately closed, as far as it can, the portals of external sense. ...[7]

The Christian Bible is among the detractors of knowledge. Eccles. 1:18 "For in much wisdom is much grief; and he that increaseth knowledge increaseth sorrow." Jean Meslier concluded "If you must worship something, worship the sun, as many peoples do, for the sun is the real creator of our life and health and light and warmth and joy."[8] It is possible that Meslier was not fully aware of the influence pre-Christian mythology had on Christian beliefs. Even today, in Rouen, France, where Joan of Arc was burned alive in 1431, those familiar with the medieval Catholic cathedral seem unable to explain the significance of the sun symbol prominently displayed on the cathedral's roof. Manly P. Hall described the evolution of certain early Christian beliefs as follows:

Many early priests and prophets, both pagan and Christian, were versed in astronomy and astrology; their writings are best understood when read in the light of these ancient sciences. With the growth of man's knowledge of the constitution and periodicity of the heavenly bodies, astronomical principles and terminology were introduced into his religious systems.

The tutelary [protective] gods were given planetary thrones, the celestial bodies being named after the deities assigned to them. The fixed stars were divided into constellations, and through these constellations wandered the sun and its planets, the latter with their accompanying satellites....

The sun, as supreme among the celestial bodies visible to the astronomers of antiquity, was assigned to the highest of the gods and became symbolic of the supreme authority of the Creator Himself. From a deep philosophic consideration of the powers and principles of the sun has come the concept of the Trinity as it is understood in the world today. The tenet of a Triune Divinity is not peculiar to Christian or Mosaic theology, but forms a conspicuous part of the dogma of the greatest religions of both ancient and modern times. The Persians, Hindus, Babylonians, and Egyptians had their Trinities. In every instance these represented the threefold form of one Supreme Intelligence. In modern Masonry, the Deity is symbolized by an equilateral triangle, its three sides representing the primary manifestations of the Eternal One. ...

The origin of the Trinity is obvious to anyone who will observe the daily manifestations of the sun. This orb, being the symbol of all Light, has three distinct phases: rising, midday, and setting. The philosophers therefore divided the life of all things into three distinct parts: growth, maturity, and decay. Between the twilight of dawn and the twilight of evening is the high noon of resplendent glory. God the Father, the Creator of the world, is symbolized by the dawn. His color is blue, because the sun rising in the morning is veiled in blue mist. God the Son, the Illuminating One sent to bear witness of His Father before all worlds, is the celestial globe at noonday, radiant and magnificent, the maned Lion of Judah, the

Golden-haired Savior of the World. Yellow is His color and His power is without end. God the Holy Ghost is the sunset phase, when the orb of day, robed in flaming red, rests for a moment upon the horizon line and then vanishes into the darkness of the night to wander in the lower worlds and later rise again triumphant from the embrace of darkness. ...[9]

Many deities have been associated with the sun. The Greeks believed that Apollo, Bacchus, Dionysos, Sabazius, Hercules, Jason, Ulysses, Zeus, Uranus, and Vulcan partook of either the visible or invisible attributes of the sun.

The Norwegians regarded Balder the Beautiful as a solar deity, and Odin is often connected with the celestial orb, especially because of his one eye. Among the Egyptians, Osiris, Ra, Anubis, Hermes, and even the mysterious Ammon himself had points of resemblance with the solar disc. Isis was the mother of the sun, and even Typhon, the Destroyer, was supposed to be a form of solar energy. ...

One expression of the solar energy is Solomon, whose name SOL-OM-ON is the name for the Supreme Light in three different languages. ...

At the vernal equinox, the sun had grown to be a beautiful youth. His golden hair hung in ringlets on his shoulders and his light, as Schiller said, extended to all parts of infinity. At the summer solstice, the sun became a strong man, heavily bearded, who, in the prime of maturity, symbolized the fact that Nature at this period of the year is strongest and most fecund. At the autumnal equinox, the sun was pictured as an aged man, shuffling along with bended back and whitened locks into the oblivion of winter darkness. Thus, twelve months were assigned to the sun as the length of its life. During this period it circled the twelve signs of the zodiac in a magnificent triumphal march. When fall came, it entered, like Samson, into the house of Delilah (Virgo), where its rays were cut off and it lost its strength. ... The coming of the sun was hailed with joy; the time of its departure was viewed as a period to be set aside for sorrow and unhappiness. This glorious, radiant orb of day, the true light "which lighteth every man who cometh into the world," the supreme benefactor, who raised all things from the dead, who fed the hungry multitudes, who stilled the tempest, who after dying rose again and restored all things to life—this Supreme Spirit of humanitarianism and philanthropy is known to Christendom as Christ, the Redeemer of worlds, the Only Begotten of The Father, the Word made Flesh, and the Hope of Glory. ...

The pagans set aside the 25th of December as the birthday of the Solar Man. They rejoiced, feasted, gathered in processions, and made offerings in the temples. The darkness of winter was over and the glorious son of light was returning to the Northern Hemisphere. With his last effort the old Sun God had torn down the house of the Philistines (the Spirits of Darkness) and had cleared the way for the new sun who was born that day from the depths of the earth amidst the symbolic beasts of the lower world. ...

For reasons which they doubtless considered sufficient, those who chronicled the life and acts of Jesus found it advisable to metamorphose him into a solar deity. The historical Jesus was forgotten; nearly all the salient incidents recorded in the four Gospels have their correlations in the movements, phases, or functions of the heavenly bodies.

Among other allegories borrowed by Christianity from pagan antiquity is the story of the beautiful, blue-eyed Sun God, with His golden hair falling upon His shoulders, robed from head to foot in spotless white and carrying in His arms the Lamb of

God, symbolic of the vernal equinox. This handsome youth is a composite of Apollo, Osiris, Orpheus, Mithras, and Bacchus, for He has certain characteristics in common with each of these pagan deities. ...[10]

This Virgin mother, giving birth to the Sun God which Christianity has so faithfully preserved, is a reminder of the inscription concerning her Egyptian prototype, Isis, which appeared on the Temple of Sais: "The fruit which I have brought forth is the Sun."

While the Virgin is associated with the moon by the early pagans, there is no doubt that they also understood her position as a constellation in the heavens, for nearly all the peoples of antiquity credit her as being the mother of the sun, and they realized that although the moon could not occupy that position, the sign of Virgo could, and did, give birth to the sun out of her side on the 25th day of December. Albertus Magnus states, "We know that the sign of the Celestial Virgin rose over the Horizon at the moment at which we fix the birth of our Lord Jesus Christ. ..." Among certain of the Arabian and Persian astronomers the three stars forming the sword belt of Orion were called the Magi who came to pay homage to the young Sun God. The author of *Mankind—Their Origin and Destiny* contributes the following additional information: "In Cancer, which had risen to the meridian at midnight, is the constellation of the Stable and of the Ass. The ancients called it Prarsepe Jovis. In the north the stars of the Bear are seen, called by the Arabians Martha and Mary, and also the coffin of Lazarus." Thus the esotericism of pagandom was embodied in Christianity, although its keys are lost. The Christian Church blindly follows ancient customs, and when asked for a reason gives superficial and unsatisfactory explanations, either forgetting or ignoring the indisputable fact that each religion is based upon the secret doctrines of its predecessor.[11]

What pre-Christian sun gods have in common today is that they are relatively insignificant. These deities, so essential to the lives of long dead generations, are now mere vestiges. Joseph Campbell observed that

> In the later stages of many mythologies, the key images hide like needles in great haystacks of secondary anecdote and rationalization; for when a civilization has passed from a mythological to a secular point of view, the older images are no longer felt or quite approved. In Hellenistic Greece and in Imperial Rome, the ancient gods were reduced to mere civic patrons, household pets, and literary favorites. Uncomprehended inherited themes, such as that of the Minotaur—the dark and terrible night aspect of an old Egypto-Cretan representation of the incarnate sun god and divine king—were rationalized and reinterpreted to suit contemporary ends.[12]

Implicit in Campbell's observation is that those gods "reinterpreted to suit contemporary ends" were originated by ancestors who, at the time, were suiting their contemporary ends by creating them.

Why are gods vengeful? One answer may be found in perceptions of natural events either misunderstood or misperceived. Another answer may be incorrect interpretation of cause and effect. If we believe in imagined realities, then what happens when we are set upon by Nature despite doing what our mythologies demand to appease our gods? Is not the confrontation of reality and imagined reality perceived as divine displeasure? Is this the source of our vengeful gods? Religious belief systems free us from the fear of death and travail, but not from the fear of divine retribution. Perhaps the clash of myth and reality serves a few purposes. In addition to vengeful gods resolving discrepancies between reality and erroneous myth-based predictions, perhaps they serve to ensure compliance with codes of behavior in people more likely to respond to fear than reason. And perhaps they free shamans from responsibility for their inability to predict through myth the behavior of their gods or of Nature.

The Greeks had gods who were immortal versions of themselves. With the possible exception of some human frailties, the Christian view of God found in Genesis is similar. "And God said, Let us make man in our image, after our likeness." This static view of creation raises an interesting question. If humans are created in God's image, and if humans have evolved and perhaps continue to evolve, then does God's appearance also evolve? And if so, what was it before mammals or life first appeared on Earth? The answer for some is that God waited until humans evolved sufficiently and then gave them souls. The answer for many others is simply to reject the evidence of biological evolution in favor of an ancient worldview that defines their mythology. Doubters of such myths are equally ancient. The Kabbala (1200?-700? BCE) claims

> The gods are the creations of the created. They are not emanations of The Eternal. They are made by the adoration of their worshippers. It is not the gods that do the work of creation. This is done by the great natural forces working each according to its nature; the gods come into their procession after the egg of manifestation has been laid in the darkness of the cosmic night.[13]

Xenophanes (570-475 BCE) criticized certain Greeks for their anthropomorphic theology that ascribes human behavioral characteristics to the gods as well as creating gods in their own image. Perhaps our collective ego is at the root of this process. William of Ockham said:

> [A]ll that we perceive is will, the ego asserting itself in every action and thought. Reason itself and all the glory of intellect are tools of the will; the intellect is merely the will thinking, seeking its ends by thought.[14]

The need to anthropomorphize is still with us. In their quest for equality, some in the feminist movement have decided that God is female. The male will exerting itself has been followed by the female will exerting itself. Will certainly does not defer to reason. Without a mate, one wonders what use a god would have for genitalia.

If we had evolved as totally objective, rational beings with no need for emotion, it is likely that we would have no need for gods. This seems to be borne out by observations that the least likely to believe in supernatural things are among our most objective thinkers, while the least objective among us are most likely to believe in a spirit world. Since Galileo, the Western scientific community has generally separated itself from such subjective constructs because they are anathema to the objectivity required by quality science. In science, subjective imaginings must pass objective tests to be accepted. Mysticism has no such requirement. In fact, religious scholars either denigrate or dismiss rational objectivity in matters of faith. Instead, intuitive "knowledge" is revered. In myth systems, feeling that a belief is true supersedes knowing objectively that it is true. It is an emotion-based process, intended to assuage the emotional concerns of believers.

It is likely that there have been many thousands of creation—and other—myths since we attained the capacity to dream them. Clearly, our egos notwithstanding, being a member of a contemporary majority religion does not give any special importance to our myths. Wait a while. When Christianity began, the worshipers of Greek, Roman, and other deities, the then-religious-majority, viewed Christians as "pagans." Today the situation is reversed, and we have no idea what the dominant religions a thousand years from now will think of our myths. Will the mindless application of myth-based beliefs formed in response to conditions extant thousands of years ago create an unlivable future? Will future myths evolve that require reproductive and ecological self-control to deal with our legacy of overpopulation and indifference, if not contempt, for Nature?

By combining mysticism and useful beliefs in parables and symbolic forms, our ancestors' myths have conveyed the essence of the spiritual aspects of our cultures from generation to generation. Whether centered on trees, animals, or supernatural parents, they have given meaning to our lives and, to varying degrees, they have given us comforting, imagined control over the world in which we find ourselves. *The Encyclopedia of Psychology* describes the origins of magical thought as follows:

> Although modern society places great emphasis on the importance of rational thinking, research suggests that human beings today are as prone to magical thought as were their primitive ancestors. There seems to be a universal inclination to infer symbolic and meaningful relationships among objects and events, and an inability or a disinclination to properly evaluate the experiences upon which these inferences are based. ... While occultisms reflect an attempt, through magical thinking, to understand the workings of nature, they operate by and large outside conscious awareness, and often may serve the needs to increase personal power and to find solace in the face of existential anxiety. ... It is unlikely that human beings will ever be free of such needs or of the propensity for magical thought. Occultisms will in all likelihood always be with us in one guise or another, waxing when social organization is undergoing rapid change leading to widespread anxiety, and waning during periods of social stability.[15]

Whether from dreams or otherwise, creating beliefs to satisfy our emotional needs is the fundamental source of friction between our intellect and our emotions. Understanding this biological reality is fundamental to understanding the biology of belief. It explains why faith systems are disturbed by the relentless pursuit of objective knowledge by science, and why so many scientists ignore religion. Moreover, it explains why faith systems have been both destructive and helpful. Peace of mind has its price. By denying reason and requiring faith as payment for peace of mind, subjective belief systems are free to indulge any prejudice, imagine any enemy, and demand any retribution from which no one is safe.

Chapter 6

Creation According to Science—How the Earth Formed

Why are the history of the universe and biological evolution two primary focal points of the conflict between myth and science? If relieving our fears and uncertainties is a fundamental purpose of mythology, then explaining where the universe came from and how we came to be should be common to all mythologies. And so it appears to be. However, various claims to knowledge of the creation of the universe notwithstanding, creation myths reflect the beliefs and limited knowledge of their creators. For this reason, relatively new discoveries such as heliocentricity and biological evolution often conflict with the old myths and are routinely denied, at least initially. Since the development of experimental science, we have seen mythical concepts of the physical world steadily replaced by scientific models. It is, therefore, not surprising that myth-based opposition to science and to scientific discoveries continues, even though science concerns itself with how the universe works and usually does not address myths or superstitious concerns. Scientific reasoning is merely a process of rational testing of beliefs or postulates to separate fact from illusion.

Unlike creation myths that derive from extra-experiential intuition and the planning assumption, the following is my understanding of the rich and complex story of creation that science has thus far been able to unravel. It makes assumptions, extrapolations, and interpolations that are unavoidable, given the undertaking and the often unsettled and incomplete state of our knowledge. That we cannot account presently for more than ninety percent of the mass of the universe is of no small concern when attempting to understand its evolution. The belief that much of the universe is composed of presently invisible or so-called "dark matter" is based on calculations that cannot explain the motions of galaxies, for example, without adding the gravitational force of dark matter to their observable mass. Also, that galaxies are accelerating apart in an expanding universe is not explained by present theories. Although future research undoubtedly will change aspects of our present understanding of cosmology and other scientific findings mentioned in this book, it is not unreasonable to believe that much of what is presented will be confirmed.

One purpose of this chapter is to explain what science has discovered about the creation of our universe and the Earth to readers whose knowledge derives from mythological teachings. In the process, this chapter explains cosmological influences on the mechanism of biological evolution. Another purpose is to set the stage for an understanding of the process of biological evolution on Earth, which has resulted in the evolution of the human brain and the biology of belief. Readers familiar with this subject may prefer skip to the last two paragraphs of this chapter.

The Early Universe

Inasmuch as we have no way of knowing what happened before the Big Bang, if, indeed, anything happened, the story of creation begins about 12 or 15 billion years ago when all the mass and energy of the universe occupied an extraordinarily small volume. Its temperature exceeded one million billion degrees Celsius. When its mixture of matter, antimatter, and all kinds of high-energy particles exploded, the universe began expanding. When the universe had expanded to the size of our solar system, protons, neutrons, and electrons formed from more fundamental subatomic particles. By the time the universe was about 1,000 times the size of our solar system, neutrons and protons formed nuclei of hydrogen, helium, deuterium, and lithium. The universe was now about three seconds old. It was too hot to be transparent or to permit newly formed atomic nuclei to capture electrons to form atoms. That would take another 300,000 years. And when the universe had cooled enough to form atoms, the atoms combined under the influence of gravity to form stars.[1] By the time the universe was less than a billion years old, an entire generation of stars had lived and died, and some massive galaxies had formed.[2]

When a star first forms, gravity creates intense pressure and temperature at its core, causing hydrogen to fuse into helium. The process is the same as that of an exploding hydrogen bomb, but on an enormous scale. It is the continuous flow of energy given off by this nuclear fusion that prevents gravity from collapsing the sun's core even farther. When virtually all the core hydrogen is converted to helium, the core shrinks until there is sufficient temperature and pressure to fuse helium to create carbon. The process of creating successively heavier atoms continues until iron is formed. Unlike lighter atoms, iron does not give off energy when it fuses; it consumes energy. So nuclear burning stops with iron, and gravity collapses the core.

How long a star will last is directly dependent on its mass. More massive stars consume their nuclear fuel faster than less massive ones. In medium size stars such as our sun (of which we are aware of about 100 billion billion), the iron stage is reached in about 10 billion years. Stars smaller than our sun can burn for very much longer. In stars with a mass about 20 times that of our sun, fusion is more rapid and iron is formed in about 10 million years. Stars the size of our sun gradually brighten as they convert hydrogen into helium. In its infancy, our sun was about 70 percent its present brightness. Over the next billion years our sun will increase in brightness by about 10 percent, perhaps enough to vaporize our oceans. In the past decade our sun has increased the energy it delivers to Earth by about .5 watts/square meter to 1,367 watts/square meter.[3] By about 6.5 billion years from now, the sun's luminosity will about double. By that time, hydrogen at the sun's core will be depleted, but hydrogen in the shell of gas surrounding the core will continue to fuse into helium. This will cause the sun's outer layers to expand, cool, and appear redder. Our sun will have metamorphosed into what is called a "red giant." This phase will take over a billion years, during which the sun will expand to well beyond the orbit of mercury. As helium begins to fuse into carbon in the core the sun will begin to shrink. It will take about 100 million years to consume the remaining helium in its core. It is now 12.3 billion years since the sun first lit the solar system. When helium in the core has been consumed, helium in a gas shell surrounding the core will ignite. This consumed helium core surrounded by newly ignited helium gas will be enclosed in a shell of burning hydrogen. As the core contracts, it will draw in the two burning shells. The helium gas shell will experience a series of explosions, which will begin a final brightening and expansion of the sun that will last for about 20 million years. During this phase the sun will increase its diameter to beyond Earth's present orbit. Although the Earth will have long since lost its biosphere, the enormous loss of mass experienced by the sun during its later years will reduce its capacity to hold Earth in its present tight orbit. It is thought that the resultant increase in the size of Earth's orbit may keep it from being engulfed by the expanding sun. Over the following few million years, the sun's outer layers will dissipate and reveal its smoldering core. Unlike the dense cores of neutron stars formed when larger stars reach the end of their cycle, the sun's core will not collapse beyond the density permitted by electron repulsion of its core atoms. Its smoldering remnant will have become what is called a "white dwarf," perhaps to be orbited by Earth until the next cataclysm.[4]

Stars about 20 times more massive than our sun experience a very different end. When such stars reach the iron state, gravitation in the star's iron core is so intense that the core collapses. Unlike smaller stars, the mass of iron in the core of large stars is sufficient to compress the nuclei of iron atoms together. Electron repulsion is completely overcome. The collapse takes just a second. If enough material is present to create gravity so intense that light cannot escape, a black hole is formed. If less material is present, a neutron star is formed instead. The explosion following collapse blows the outer stellar material into space and releases the equivalent of all the energy released by our sun in its lifetime. It is as bright as a billion suns. Such an exploding star is called a "type II supernova," and appears as a bright spot in the night sky lasting a few weeks. In 1054 Chinese astronomers observed such a bright spot in the night sky. It was the supernova that produced what we now call the Crab nebula. The most recent supernova observation was made on February 24, 1987. The shock waves of supernovae create heavier elements such as uranium, lead, gold, and radioactive material—which accounts for the rarity of these heavy atoms. In this way, beginning with hydrogen, stars have manufactured most of the material from which planets are made.[5]

When the universe was first able to form stars, it must have looked like slow motion fireworks. The initial explosion or Big Bang left the universe a glowing, opaque fireball. As it cooled, stars were speeding away from each other in the expanding universe. Not long after that, large stars began exploding—sending debris in every direction.[6] Oxygen, nitrogen, and carbon, formed as the star burned, were thrown out at high speed and collided with slow-moving protons. The collisions formed lithium, beryllium, and boron.

In the gas clouds between stars, conditions were right for the formation of molecules such as hydrogen gas, water, carbon monoxide, ammonia, alkanes (methane series), polycyclic aromatic hydrocarbons (naphthalene), acetylene, and glycine (an amino acid).[7] In a 1993 experiment, hydrogen gas and naphthalene were exposed to 9,400 volts. An infrared spectrum analysis of the yellow-brown residue produced by the discharge revealed a close resemblance to a similar analysis of the Murchison meteorite that fell to Earth in Australia in 1969. It is thought that ionized hydrogen exposed to intense stellar outbursts would create conditions similar to those in the high-voltage experiment. More than 100 chemicals have been detected in interstellar clouds.[8] Exploding stars and interstellar synthesis are the primary processes by which hydrogen was converted into the heavier elements and compounds. It is thought that as solar systems formed within galaxies, stellar radiation modified interstellar chemicals to form ethane from acetylene, for example.[9, 10] Many of the hydrocarbon compounds created by these processes are common building blocks of life as we know it. If autogenesis required the presence of such compounds, lightning storms in Earth's early atmosphere (simulated in the 1993 experiment) may have produced the required compounds, perhaps making the interstellar contribution unnecessary.

The cloud of dust and debris left after a massive star explodes is called a "nebula." In time, matter in nebulae condenses into spinning disks of stars, gas, debris, ice, and dust. Each such spinning disk is a galaxy that can take the shape of a pinwheel or a flat disk with a bulge at its center. It is thought that at least some galaxies have black holes at their centers. A black hole is an object so massive that the velocity needed to escape it exceeds the speed of light, in which case we can not see it directly because light that might emanate from or reflect off it cannot escape its gravity. The disk shape is attributed to the spin plane of matter at the center of the disk. Each star in a galaxy is the center of its own spinning disk of matter, which may include planets and rings of debris such as our asteroid belt, all aligned roughly in the spin plane of the star. In turn, each planet could be the center of its own system of moons or rings. Moons, in turn, are capable of capturing and orbiting objects, a fact on which we relied in planning the 1969 moon landing. Even asteroids have been found to have tiny moons.[11]

The first galaxies formed about one billion years after the Big Bang, and incorporated stellar remnants and interstellar compounds. Recent observations of the cosmos indicate that there are in excess of 50 billion galaxies distributed along the boundaries of spherical voids, like the film on connected soap bubbles.[12] The voids measure in the hundreds of millions of light years across.[13]

Our galaxy began to form about 10 billion years after the Big Bang, and our star (the sun) is near the outer edge of our galaxy. When we look at the night sky we see an edge view of hundreds of millions of stars. Their number and density appear as a band of white we call the Milky Way. Calculations indicate that there is a black hole of about 2.7 million solar masses at the center of our galaxy. The radiation associated with matter being drawn into such a black hole is thought to be obscured by a vast dust cloud between Earth and the center of our galaxy.

Our Star

Our solar system, comprising our star, the Earth, other planets and orbiting material, formed about 5 billion years ago from a collapsing cloud of dust, gas, ice, and debris. A simplified description of the process is that as the cloud tumbled in on itself, it began to spin faster and faster, like a skater bringing her arms closer to her body to spin faster. The collapsing cloud was a chaotic affair driven primarily by gravity, electromagnetism, and inertia.[14] German astronomer and mathematician Johannes Kepler (1571-1630) determined that objects travel around the sun in elliptical orbits. Some objects orbited in nearly circular paths while the orbits of others were acutely elliptical and not necessarily coplanar—a combination that generated collisions of all kinds. In time, random agglomerations of matter attracted and held more and more gas, dust, and debris that came into the vicinity of their orbits. Debris was relentlessly assembled into planets. Some inchoate planets had molten cores, heated in part by nuclear fission. Eventually the forming planets accumulated enough mass for gravity to crush them into spheres.

Some planets were struck by large planetesimals. Such impacts were capable of knocking small, loosely assembled planets to pieces. However, the collective gravity of such a fragmented planet could reassemble the planet in time. Of the material thrown up from the impact, some would fall back, and some would escape the planet's gravity, never to return. And if the impact were a glancing blow, a moon would be created from material that neither fell back nor escaped, but which was thrust into orbit around the planet. Jupiter, Neptune, Saturn, and Uranus were large enough to capture hydrogen and helium gas in great quantities.

When the temperature and pressure reached critical levels inside the ball of hydrogen at the center of the sunless system, hydrogen began to fuse into helium and began emitting energy. The sun began to glow and to eject particles (solar wind) that swept orbiting dust beyond the outer reaches of the system. Without obscuring dust, the sun's light revealed a new solar system. During the process that took over 500 million years to complete, Earth and the other planets settled into a reasonably stable relationship with the sun and each other. However, not all of the smaller orbiting bodies were as stable.

Still orbiting the sun is debris that was not captured during the formation of the solar system. And some of it travels in Earth-crossing orbits—orbits that cross Earth's path. We know this debris as asteroids, comets, and meteors. Comets consist chiefly of ammonia, methane, carbon dioxide, and water, and it is thought that an orbiting reservoir of potential Earth-crossing comets resides beyond the orbit of Neptune to far beyond Pluto. Pluto itself is thought by some to be a large comet and not a planet. It is possible that sun-orbiting comets exist as far out as 50 times the distance from the Earth to the sun—about a fifth of the distance to Alpha Centauri (the star nearest our solar system). Comets so far from the sun could have their orbits disturbed by passing stars or other matter, and could enter the inner solar system.[15] Military defense systems intended to protect against surprise missile attack have recorded upper atmosphere impacts by comets of a few meters in diameter. The impacts average about one per month and their energy is equivalent to about one kiloton of TNT.

The debris between Jupiter and Mars failed to form a planet because Jupiter's gravity was so strong that assembling planetesimals were torn apart. That belt of debris comprises asteroids ranging up to 1,000 kilometers across. Unlike comets, asteroids are typically made of metals such as iron and nickel, silicates similar to stone found on earth, or carbon. As these asteroids are influenced by the competing gravities of Jupiter and the sun, they collide and form dust and small debris. Given the gravitational interaction of the sun and Earth, it is thought that this dust and debris form an irregular ring close enough to Earth for material to be captured by Earth's gravity.[16] The captured dust and small debris (shooting stars) are slowed by our atmosphere and fall harmlessly to Earth.[17] It is estimated that from tens of thousands to hundreds of thousands of tons of this matter fall to Earth each year.

As Jupiter's gravity dislodges asteroids from the asteroid belt, some are drawn toward the sun and inner planets. Within about 10 million years, the orbits of the larger of such asteroids will inevitably intersect those of Mars, Mercury, Venus, Earth, or the sun. Meteor Crater in northern Arizona, 1.2 kilometers in diameter, was formed about 50,000 years ago by a metallic meteor 30 meters across. Meteors larger than a kilometer across, on average, arrive once every 300,000 years. Such meteors would have energies in excess of 10 billion tons of TNT. On average, meteors about 10 kilometers across strike the Earth every 100 million years. It is this type of meteor that ended the Cretaceous period, the dinosaurs, and an estimated 70 percent of Earth's species.[18]

In this century we observed two major impacts. In 1908 a meteor believed to be made up of silicates impacted the Tunguska Valley in Siberia with an estimated energy equivalent to 12 million tons of TNT. It was about 60 meters across and did not leave a crater because the silicates were loosely connected fragments that burst apart on impact with the atmosphere. Beneath the impact point was left an area 50 kilometers across of flattened and burnt trees.[19] The second major impact was the Shoemaker-Levy 9 comet collisions with Jupiter that began July 16, 1994. The comet fragments had an estimated combined energy equivalent to 6 thousand billion tons of TNT.

Although craters on the moon are numerous, on Earth the effects of wind and water erosion, sedimentation, volcanism, and plate tectonics eventually destroy evidence of impact craters. To date, the remnants of about 160 impact craters have been found on Earth. For the next crater to be formed is just a matter of time. In 1996, an asteroid measuring between 300 and 500 meters across came within 450, 000 kilometers of Earth, the distance that such a comet would travel in less than 6 seconds.[20] It is estimated that there are about 2,000 Earth orbit-crossing asteroids larger than one-half mile across.[21]

Given the chaotic process by which clouds of matter are converted into solar systems, the arrangement of our sun and planets is clearly one of many possible *essentially* stable states a collapsing cloud of gas, dust, ice, and debris can achieve. Recent research indicates that other solar systems have evolved different arrangements of suns, planets, moons, comets, and asteroids. Given the nature of solar system formation, the stellar debris and interstellar material formed long before our sun ignited are the stuff of which the Earth is made. And inasmuch as our bodies derive from Earth, the dust from which we come and to which we return is the dust of ancient stars.

Our Planet

The Earth began to form about 4.6 billion years ago as an orbiting mass of material larger than things around it. Its increasing gravity attracted matter from farther and farther away. In time it became a small planet—a planetesimal. For over a hundred million years it grew in size as it accreted everything within reach of its gravity or that crossed its path at a relative speed slow enough to permit capture. Collisions with planetesimals, perhaps the size of the moon, knocked the infant Earth apart, only to be brought together by its collective gravity, and crushed once again into a sphere. Under the influence of its gravity, the denser materials such as iron sank to form the center core as lighter materials such as basalt and granite rose to the surface. As radioactive material decayed to more stable forms, its radiation converted to heat and raised the temperature of the Earth. Countless meteor and planetesimal impacts turned dust and debris into a layer of molten magma hundreds of kilometers beneath the surface. For millions of years volcanoes poured lava onto the surface and into newly formed impact craters.

Computer simulations show that a mass larger than Mars probably collided at a shallow angle with the Earth's mantle about 4.5 billion years ago. The collision ejected material into space and some into Earth orbit. By the time gravity resettled the debris, Earth had acquired a moon. The impact was apparently slightly off center resulting in the moon's orbital plane being about 5 degrees different from the Earth's. Were the orbital planes exactly the same we would have solar and lunar eclipses each month at the new moon and the full moon. When the moon first formed, its distance from Earth was about half what it is today, resulting in much greater lunar tides than we experience now. Although our present lunar month is about 29.5 days, the first lunar month was considerably shorter. Fossil records of tidal activity contained in "tidal rhythmites" formed about 1 billion years ago indicate that the Earth rotated about 30 percent more rapidly, completing a day in just over 18 hours and a year in 481 days. As the moon slows the Earth's rotation, its own velocity and orbital diameter increase. Ergo, the moon moves away as our days grow longer.[22]

About 4.4 billion years ago, the Earth began to retain its atmosphere and create its core. Continents would form later. By about 4.2 billion years ago, the Earth reached its present diameter of about 8,000 miles. In the center is an iron and nickel core over 4,000 miles in diameter. Heat from the core churns convection currents in the less dense mantle between the core and the Earth's crust. The crust is typically no more than about 20 miles thick and the slowly churning mantle recycles all but the lightest crustal material. Our continents are made of this low-density material that is floating on and being driven by the slow moving mantle current below; which motion we perceive as continental drift. The continental crustal material is too light to be drawn into the churning mantle and can preserve some of the Earth's oldest rocks. However, when mantle currents stretch and shear continents they form rift valleys and fault zones. When continents are driven to collide without one continental plate slipping beneath the other, mountain chains form, as the light crustal material has nowhere to go but up. When one plate slips beneath another during a collision, crustal rock melts from heat generated as the plates scrape past each other. Upwellings of molten rock at these boundaries break the surface as volcanoes. These forces together with erosion from wind and water (from melted comets) have destroyed most of Earth's earliest rocks. Some of the oldest known rocks are Australian (zircons), about 4.3 billion years old.

It is thought that the early atmosphere formed when the iron core coalesced and volcanic activity vented gasses from the interior to the surface of Earth. This process could have produced over 80 percent of our atmosphere within one million years. The earliest known atmospheric composition was nitrogen, hydrogen, carbon dioxide, water vapor, sulfur dioxide, hydrochloric acid, methane, and ammonia. Condensing atmospheric water vapor formed the oceans. Atmospheric oxygen, primarily a byproduct of photosynthesis, would not begin to appear in the atmosphere in significant quantities until about 2.5 billion years ago and would take about 600 million years to reach present levels. In time, comet and asteroid impacts diminished on an Earth thick with clouds in an orange sky. Although the sun's energy output was perhaps 25 percent less than it is today, some believe that greenhouse gases in the early atmosphere (methane, ammonia, and carbon dioxide) trapped solar radiation to a greater degree than does our atmosphere today. As the sun's energy output increased over the ensuing billion years, Earth's surface temperature did not rise proportionately because heat-trapping greenhouse gasses gradually diminished.[23]

As Earth cooled, complex molecules delivered to Earth by comets and asteroids were no longer destroyed by intense heat. Some theorize that single-celled microorganisms incubated on other planets could have arrived on Earth as well if impacts on other life-supporting planets ejected organism-containing fragments (tektites) that ultimately reached Earth. Such organisms would have been released into the oceans and atmosphere. Countless combinations of compounds found each other in the churning oceans and waters heated by geothermal activity. It was now about 3.8 to 3.5 billion years ago, and Earth was in the final stage of meteor and comet bombardment. Without oxygen, the atmosphere had not formed the ozone layer that today filters out the sun's ultraviolet radiation. This is pivotal to the evolution of life because ultraviolet radiation can damage molecules such as DNA. However, while the sun's damaging ultraviolet radiation could reach Earth's surface, it could not penetrate water. After some nine billion years of evolving since the Big Bang, the universe had produced one of perhaps countless planets whose primordial chemistry was ready to produce self-organizing and self-replicating molecules.

You may recall that in the Preface, I found it necessary to inquire into a number of knowledge disciplines to ferret out a clear understanding of the biology of belief. I also mentioned in the Preface that it might be unsettling for those accustomed to dealing with less broad subjects to read about seemingly disparate knowledge categories.. I expect that even the most persistent readers may be wondering, by this time, how these initial chapters will coalesce into a consilient explanation of the biology of belief. Thus far, we have considered processes by which we acquire beliefs without having considered their merit, and how our beliefs, assumptions, misperceptions, and evolved brain traits distort our perceptions of reality. We have considered how our biological nature makes it easier for some of us to believe in miracles, and for some of us to have our beliefs manipulated. We examined the idea that knowledge, both genetic and psychogenetic, is self-organizing, to understand how beliefs and belief systems are formed. We have endeavored to understand the origin of beliefs we inherited from our ancestors by attempting to reconstruct our ancestors' world. We examined how dreams and hallucinations influenced our ancestors' perceptions, and considered their planning-assumption-based predisposition to animism and to emotionally satisfying belief systems. This most recent chapter has described our scientific understanding of how the universe evolved from its apparent beginning to its present state—a story of creation inconceivable to our primitive ancestors. It follows that, inasmuch as our ancestors could not comprehend it correctly, today's creation-myth-based belief systems are inherited ancestral imaginings about the early universe.

To achieve a clearer understanding of the biology of belief, the following chapters examine how DNA self-organized to create the conflicted thinking organs in our heads, and how psychogenes in those thinking organs influence our perceptions, behaviors and social evolution. Using successive periods of Western history as an example, we will demonstrate the process by which psychogenes evolve over time. Philosophers and shamans have attempted, in their own ways, to deal with the consequences of the evolved, conflicted nature of our brains. We will review their successes and failures, and examine methods they used to control our beliefs. We will examine modern belief-management technology, along with examples of how it is being used to shape our beliefs today. Finally, we will present a consilient merging of the foregoing elements, together with a few logical implications the biology of belief holds for our global future.

Chapter 7

Brain Evolution at the DNA Level

The purpose of Section 1 of this chapter is to explain how DNA could have self-organized and thereafter progressed through a continuous sequence of increasing complexity, resulting in genetic code that defines the structure and functions of our brains. In Section 2, particular attention is paid to how our evolved DNA biases our perceptions and beliefs by predisposing our minds to an uneasy balance between emotion and rational thought. Readers familiar with this field of science may choose to skip or skim Section 1.

Section 1

DNA Self-organizes

Thousands of years ago, some of our ancestors believed that life could generate spontaneously from non-living matter virtually overnight. This view probably resulted from observing insects emerging from nonvisible, microscopic eggs. Microscopes made the microscopic eggs visible, and, in the 18th century, a number of ingenious experiments put the idea of spontaneous generation to rest.

The process by which self-organizing non-living matter evolved to form living matter over eons of successive random events is another matter. The Greco-Roman view of how life began spontaneously (autogenesis) was recounted by the Roman philosopher and poet Titus Lucretius Carus (99-55 BCE):

> Life does not differ essentially from other matter; it is a product of moving atoms which are individually dead. As the universe took form by the inherent laws of

matter, so the earth produced by a purely natural selection all the species and organs of life.

Nothing arises in the body in order that we may use it, but what arises brings forth its own use....[1] It was no design of the atoms that led them to arrange themselves in order with keen intelligence ... but because many atoms in infinite time have moved and met in all manner of ways, trying all combinations.... Hence arose the beginnings of great things ... and the generations of living creatures....[2] Many were the monsters that the earth tried to make: ... some without feet, and others without hands or mouth or face, or with limbs bound to their frames.... It was in vain; nature denied them growth, nor could they find food or join in the way of love.... Many kinds of animals must have perished then, unable to forge the chain of procreation ... for those to which nature gave no [protective] qualities lay at the mercy of others, and were soon destroyed.[3]

We have pondered the origin of life on Earth for, perhaps, more than 5,000 generations. It is the subject of our creation myths and our religions. It has been the subject of scientific inquiry since a few early Greek philosophers pondered marine fossils and concluded that we evolved from fish.[4] Today, we know that RNA and DNA are the molecules of life that store the information that defines every life form. DNA (deoxyribonucleic acid), the now famous double helix, consists of two long, twisted chains of nucleotides made up of the amino acids adenine, thymine, cytosine, and guanine (ATCG). It is capable of replicating itself and of synthesizing RNA. RNA (ribonucleic acid), a molecule found in all living cells, consists of a long, usually single-stranded sequence made up of phosphate and ribose and the amino acids adenine, uracil, cytosine, and guanine (AUCG). Both DNA and RNA manufacture proteins such as enzymes, hormones, antibodies, muscle, and other tissues, the essential components of living organisms. The kind of protein produced is determined by the nucleotide sequences (genes) engaged in the protein's production.

The importance of DNA cannot be overstated. While shamans look to myths to explain the creation of life, scientists investigate DNA. Even though DNA is presently capable of making RNA, some scientists theorize that the first DNA derived from RNA, and that RNA may have derived from an even earlier and simpler molecule that RNA ultimately replaced.[5] Whatever the process was, scientists engaged in researching the prebiotic chemistry of Earth are theorizing that the first self-replicating system was either simple or could be generated simply. One reason for this theory is that self-organizing molecules appeared soon after the Earth formed and cooled. Although the sequence of events that gave rise to DNA are presently unknown, that sequence does not appear to be unknowable. Given the amount of knowledge accumulated in recent decades by molecular biologists, chemists, and biochemists, it is probably just a matter of time before self-replicating molecules that reproduce the origin of life are manufactured in someone's laboratory.

It is not likely, however, that the process that gave rise to the first self-replicating molecule is taking place somewhere in Earth's biosphere today. Reactions that create complex organic molecules do not fare well in the presence of oxygen. Earth's atmosphere contained little if any oxygen 4.5 billion years ago, when the process that led to self-replication probably began. In addition, lightning, meteorites, comets, and interstellar dust could have provided more than enough amino acids for Nature to assemble them into the first self-replicating organic molecules in Earth's prebiotic environment.[6]

Once the first self-replicating molecule formed out of the primordial soup, well before 3.7 billion years ago,[7] the mechanism for retaining trial and error knowledge was in place. Between 4.5 billion and 3.7 billion years ago, DNA strands had evolved to perhaps 256 genes—sufficient to produce the equivalent of modern bacteria or archaea.[8] Primordial microbes would have lived in an atmosphere without oxygen and some would have derived their energy from sulfur compounds, perhaps near volcanoes or hydrothermal vents. Early DNA strands were circular loops attached to cell walls. These early cells had no nucleus and their membranes or cell walls were rigid, providing both protection and structural support. They took nourishment from their surroundings by secreting enzymes to dissolve nearby debris and absorbing the nutrients. By about 3 billion years ago, DNA in some organisms had evolved to become much more complex. By this time, some DNA defined a cell that had lost rigidity in its outer cell wall. This type of cell was like a flexible blob. To support itself it had developed rigid internal structures. This cell was like an amoeba with a flexible cell wall that enabled it to increase in size. It was 10,000 times the volume of a small bacterium. Its outer membrane could fold and it had evolved a nucleus, perhaps formed by the outer membrane folding a pouch where DNA attached, and the pouch then detaching from the outer membrane to move freely within the cell. This cell could consume entire bacteria by enfolding them, sealing off the pouch at the other membrane, and, having ingested the prey, discharging enzymes into the pouch that would digest the prey. This cell could eat. Some prey with protective characteristics settled into a symbiotic relationship with its host. They became cell organelles. The unique DNA of such acquired bacteria eventually migrated to the nucleus and became part of the ever-growing DNA strands of the cell's genetic code. By now, the cell contained several thousand organelles the size of small bacteria. One such plant-like organelle contained plastids (chlorophyll) capable of using the energy of sunlight to produce a source of energy for cell function. Another organelle, *peroxisomes*, which contained enzymes that catalyze the production and breakdown of hydrogen peroxide, helped in the conversion of food into energy and metabolized fatty acids. It is thought that this organelle in particular assisted its complex cell in dealing with the toxins created by the rising level of oxygen in the environment between 2 billion and 1.5 billion years ago. However, the organelle that energized cells to take advantage of newly available oxygen was the chondriosome (mitochondria). It contained enzymes important for cell metabolism, and particularly those enzymes responsible for the conversion of food to usable energy in the form of ATP (adenosinetriphosphate). *ATP* is the molecule that energizes muscle contraction and sugar metabolism. It was a pivotal event in cell evolution. Between 3.7 billion and 1.5 billion years ago, DNA had grown to produce complex single cells. The modern equivalent of such a cell contains about 12.5 million nucleotide base pairs.[9]

These large single-celled creatures stored all their eating, survival, and reproduction knowledge in their DNA as ATCG nucleotide sequences. However, for multicellular animals to evolve, functions normally carried out completely by a single cell must be carried out by different groups of cooperating cells. For example, reproduction by cell division carried out by a unicellular organism must be performed by a specialized group of cells in a multicellular organism. The information necessary for reproducing the entire organism must be contained in and implemented by the DNA of the cells representing the reproductive cells or organ of a multicellular organism. Unlike the more or less fully utilized DNA of the unicellular organism, only portions of the DNA of multicellular organisms are used by specialized cells to accomplish their limited functions. Developing these specialized cells is called "differentiation." Clearly, single cell DNA had to develop a means of intercellular communication to enable multicellular differentiation to occur.

If functions are to be divided successfully among groups of specialized cells, they must be able to coordinate their activities. To accomplish this, the DNA of one cell type must be able to regulate the activity of DNA in other cells. Such regulation can be accomplished if the DNA of one cell manufactures messenger molecules or proteins capable of regulating the activity of DNA in other cells. For example, in our bodies the fight or flight response to fear involves the release of adrenaline and noradrenaline. The adrenal glands secrete these molecules into the blood stream to increase the heart pumping rate, blood pressure, metabolic rate, blood sugar concentration, and blood flow to the muscles and to the primitive "reptilian" part of the brain. Blood flow to the thinking cerebral cortex decreases and other essential bodily functions are slowed down.[10]

DNA Enables Cells to Cooperate

What took place in early unicellular evolution to set the stage for multicellularity? A clue may be found in the behavior of the Dictyostelium amoeba (commonly referred to as "Dicty"), which has a cellular structure similar in many ways to our own. Multicellular organisms such as plants, fungi, and animals evolved from what is called the "eukarote" line of organisms. We are multicellular eukarotes and Dicty are unicellular eukarotes. At some point in our ancestry, a unicellular eukarote mutated to form multicellular eukarotes. It is possible that our first multicellular eukarote ancestor had functional characteristics very similar to the present day Dicty. What is interesting about Dicty is that they communicate with and influence each other on a grand scale to ensure their survival. Dicty normally eat bacteria and reproduce asexually by dividing. When bacteria become scarce and a colony of Dicty is in danger of starving, the first to detect the scarcity begins to release waves of messenger molecules. When the messenger molecules reach other Dicty they begin to move toward the source and also begin emitting their own waves of messenger molecules. As this process ripples out through the colony Dicty accumulate into a mound. Once in a mound, the concentration of messenger molecules is high enough to trigger other changes. The Dicty attach to each other by means of cellulose and other proteins and travel as a mass by jostling past one another. The mass begins to take on a slug-like form and it appears that the Dicty that most recently divided rise to the top of the mass and move it through the soil by heading toward heat and light. Next the cells at the tip rise up as different genes activate at different distances from the tip. After rising, cells at the tip travel down through the mass to form a stalk that supports the remainder of the colony that, by now, is acquiring a somewhat spherical shape. Some Dicty form a cup at the top of the stalk that supports the sphere while others form a disk at the bottom, anchoring it to the soil. By this time, the entire mass has taken on a spore-like appearance. In time the sphere of Dicty may be carried away on the feet of animals or by some other means to be relocated to a possibly bacteria rich environment. Keep in mind that the entire process began with the prospect of starvation. It is likely that each genetic mechanism employed by the Dicty accumulated over time in a trial and error process of avoiding predators or adapting to changing environmental conditions.[11]

What might we learn from these unicellular organisms about the evolution of multicellular animals? We know that Dicty can communicate, change their cellular properties (differentiate), and function in a coordinated way—all this without a common skin or a common first cell (egg). These independent cells contain DNA that evolved the capacity to manufacture messenger molecules capable of triggering all these effects. Is it possible that the first multicellular organism mutated from a unicellular organism that had already evolved DNA capable of triggering complex coordinations, behaviors, and physical differentiations?

Even if DNA can manufacture messenger molecules, how would a unicellular organism create extra cells that are not simply copies of itself? And even if a cell can make extra cells, how would the extra cells become different? DNA mutations had to occur that enabled a single cell to divide a number of times. Unlike cancers, which are clusters of continuously dividing cells, a multicellular organism stops dividing at some point. In addition, the extra cells produced had to respond to each other's messenger molecules as well as differentiate their functions in a way useful to the survival of the organism.

How did the extra cells differentiate into useful organs? By this stage in biological evolution, DNA sequences were getting to be quite long. Long sequences or strands of DNA are called "chromosomes." Nucleotide sub-sequences within chromosome strands that create specific proteins are called "genes." The complex arrangement of DNA with its messenger molecules was prerequisite to the development of cell differentiation. Messenger molecules have shapes that fit into specific sections of a DNA helix. Once in place, the molecules regulate the DNA's protein production by activating or deactivating nearby genes. The process becomes richly complex as molecules regulate genes that produce proteins that, in turn, regulate genes on the same DNA or on DNA in other cells that in turn produce other messenger proteins, and so on. For cell differentiation to occur, differentiation development genes must be activated to produce messenger molecules, and other genes must be deactivated in the proper ongoing sequence until differentiation is completed. In some cases the presence of protein from one development gene can inhibit the function of protein from another development gene.[12]

A hierarchy of development genes acting sequentially accomplishes differentiation. Development genes that determine an embryo's overall characteristics, such as the head, thorax, and abdomen, are supplemented by development genes that determine specific characteristics within those primary domains. As development genes manufacture regulating proteins, the concentration of those proteins decreases with distance from the originating genes: this is called "a concentration gradient." A minimum concentration of regulating proteins is required for regulation to take place. For example, imagine that development genes in an oval embryo were to activate at each end of the oval's long axis as well as on opposite sides of the center of the oval. Messenger molecule gradients from those genes would spread throughout the embryo with protein concentrations greatest at their points of origin and progressively weaker away from those points. The different proteins would combine at various concentrations throughout the embryo. As the development proteins in high enough concentrations promote and inhibit gene activity in cells of the embryo, DNA in those cells creates its own local protein gradients. The overlapping gradients would provide a very complex matrix of DNA activation and inhibition capable of producing very complexly differentiated cells.[13] One way of visualizing this process is to imagine two stones being dropped simultaneously into a still pond. As their ripples meet and overlap, a complex pattern of interacting ripples would develop. Now imagine the stones to be of different sizes. Although the pattern of interacting ripples would change it would still be symmetrical in one axis, as symmetrical as the body patterns of complex differentiated organisms. A more robust and internally asymmetrical analogy would be created if you could imagine three-dimensional or spherical waves from two stones that spawn secondary spherical waves from a few asymmetrically placed pebbles, which in turn spawn tertiary spherical waves, *et cetera.* The mathematical function that closely mimics this kind of sequential execution of multiple DNA instructions is the fractal or Mandelbrot set. *Fractals* are simple mathematical expressions that, by repeating each calculation beginning with the result of the previous calculation, can produce extremely complex irregular shapes and surfaces similar to those found in Nature.

A Small DNA Mutation Makes a Big Difference

Research indicates that very early in the evolution of multicellular organisms, the most fundamental development genes inverted their differentiation functions: this was a DNA mutation. The result was that the placement of the gut and central nervous systems in vertebrates was reversed relative to organisms with segmented bodies (lobsters, crabs, and shrimp).[14] We humans are vertebrates and we have our spines at our backs with our intestines in front. A shrimp has its gut in back (opposite its legs) and its nervous system in front. It should be apparent that relatively small variations in developmental genes can produce large differences in body patterns. However, the complexity of large animals requires long DNA sequences (many genes) to provide the necessary code. This, combined with an unlimited potential for cell division, can produce all sorts of creatures.

How many genes does it take to produce different types of body patterns? Peter Holland, a molecular zoologist at the University of Reading in England made the following observation:

> You might expect that as you look at a range of different animals, you would see widely varying numbers of genes. If you looked through the vertebrates, you would expect mammals to have more genes than reptiles and reptiles to have more genes than fish. But that turns out to be wrong.
>
> What our preliminary data suggest is that all the vertebrates have roughly the same number of genes, and all the invertebrates have roughly the same number of genes. But there was a jump [in the number of genes] between invertebrates and vertebrates.[15]

Holland suggested that a mutation in invertebrate reproduction could have doubled the number of chromosomes in its offspring and made the evolution of vertebrates possible. Inheriting an extra copy of one chromosome is common. It is the cause of Down's syndrome and other birth defects. Doubling all of an organism's chromosomes would be extraordinarily rare. Rare or not, given hundreds of millions of years and innumerable reproduction opportunities, it may have happened twice. The first time is thought to have been prior to the appearance of vertebrates, about 520 million years ago, and the second just prior to the appearance of jaws in vertebrates, about 460 million years ago. It is thought that the extra DNA, and, in particular, the doubling of developmental genes, made it possible for more complex body plans to evolve.

At about 520 million years ago, even though our DNA was producing differentiation proteins needed for our present fundamental body plan, our ancestors had no skeletal structure. It is theorized that a constant need for calcium in an environment with a changing availability of calcium led our fresh-water marine ancestors to evolve a calcium storage capacity. In time, these calcium storage structures were put to good use by evolution and became our spinal columns and related skeletal parts. In addition, chromosome doubling provided sufficient genes to support the formation of a very complex head with paired sensory organs and a three-part brain. An alternative theory suggests that the first calcium concentrations evolved to protect sensitive neural structures and progressed to provide the protective armor seen in the fossils of bony fish.

As these few inch-long, fish-like invertebrates were evolving into vertebrates, they developed bony arches which evolved from the forward-most rib that supported their gills, but they had no jaws. They ate by swallowing without biting or chewing, much like lamprey eels. It is theorized that, just prior to 460 million years ago, things changed with the second chromosomal doubling. The additional genes would have supported a number of complex innovations, including adapting the bony gill arches to close the mouth and allow water to oxygenate the gills more quickly. This trait would have improved breathing performance and speed, and as an added benefit it would have enabled these new vertebrates to suck in and clamp down on prey. The clamping became adapted with stronger muscles and various means to hold prey securely.[16] It was a development that would define much of the world as we know it today. In time, plant and flesh eaters would evolve extraordinary capacities to maximize the benefit of their highly efficient jaws. These marine vertebrates gave rise to amphibians, birds, reptiles, and mammals. No evidence of chromosome doubling after 460 million years ago has been found.

In the intervening 460 million years, mutations and natural selection pressures caused branching of DNA evolution that resulted in an enormous variety of life forms, most of which are now extinct. In that time DNA base pairs assembled into ever-longer helixes as life forms became more complex. Representative of the complexity of early bacteria, the DNA of E. coli bacteria of today comprises about 5 million nucleotide base pairs. Yeast DNA comprises about 12.5 million base pairs. Fruit fly DNA comprises about 160 million base pairs, while the DNA of humans comprises about 3 billion base pairs.[17] Those 3 billion nucleotide base pairs make up about 100 thousand genes, about half of which are involved in some way with our central nervous system.

Section 2

DNA and Brain Evolution

Understanding how our DNA structures and maintains our brains is essential to understanding the biological imperatives underlying how our minds work. Given a common DNA ancestry, it should not be surprising that brain DNA of different species have some fundamental similarities. Fruit flies, mice, and humans, for example, have identical DNA sequences that produce a protein required by each for permanent memory formation.[18] DNA produces proteins by assembling on the DNA a protein component chain that reflects the ACTG sequence of the DNA. If a portion of the DNA nucleotide sequence that assembles the amino acid glutamine, for example, was repeated incorrectly when the DNA was being formed (a kind of DNA reproductive stutter), extra copies of glutamine would be added to the protein that DNA segment produces. In the case of Huntington's disease, the resulting defective protein will cause neurons to malfunction and degenerate.[19, 20] In this case, 40 or more repeating cytosine, adenosine, and guanine (CAG) nucleotide sequences create extra copies of glutamine that stick to glutamine in other proteins. The resulting clumps in affected neurons may cause neural dysfunction and eventual death. Repeats of CAG are suspected of interfering with the flow of potassium ions into brain cells resulting in schizophrenia.[21]

In another example, there are two types of brain cells, neurons and glia, both starting from the same kind of undifferentiated brain cell. In humans, for every neuron there are 9 glial cells. What determines whether an undifferentiated brain cell becomes a neuron or a glia? Research using fruit flies (which are ideal subjects for DNA research) has shown that a DNA sequence in an undifferentiated brain cell determines which type of cell it will become. If that DNA sequence switches on briefly as the cell is differentiating, a glial cell is produced—if not, a neuron is produced. The molecule or molecules that determine whether that DNA sequence switches on determine the ratio of neurons to glia. Researchers are looking for that DNA sequence in humans.[22]

Once neurons form they must connect to each other by growing thin, at times meter long, connecting threads called "axons." By interconnecting, neurons can act in concert as a neural network. How axons connect to some neurons and not to others is determined by surface molecules that either attract or repel axons. The DNA process that determines which surface molecules to produce and when to produce them is responsible for part of the intricate process by which our brain neural networks self-assemble.[23] A typical adult human brain has an estimated one trillion neurons that are interconnected by some 100 trillion axon terminals or synapses.[24] Although connections are made during gestation, the process of axon growth continues after birth and is influenced by brain activity during early life. For example, as young children are exposed to a spoken language, neurons become connected to process the particular sounds of that language. If sounds not needed for that language are not heard while axon formation for that function is taking place, subsequent efforts to develop fluency in a new language requiring recognition of new sounds would be virtually impossible. You may learn to speak the language, but you will not sound like a native speaker because your brain cannot now learn to "hear" (recognize) the nuances. For this reason some parents expose their young children to foreign language recordings. Learning the meaning of what children are hearing can come later. It is believed that the "learning window" for discerning word component sounds remains open up to about year three; developing motor control up to about year five; emotional control, vision, and social attachment up to about year two; and ability with mathematics and logic from about year one to about year four.[25]

The brain components of particular interest are the amygdala, hippocampus, brainstem, thalamus, and the neocortex.

Hundreds of millions of years ago, when the less complex DNA of our ancestors produced less complex brains, we had only one of these components. Knowing which components evolved first and how they work together is essential to understanding how our minds function today. We know that evolution did not replace the brain's oldest parts with newer ones. The structure of our brains reflects a step by step process of adding new capabilities to old ones. The old parts kept on doing what they did, perhaps growing larger, while newer parts evolved if their capabilities enhanced our ancestors' likelihood of survival.

It started with a brainstem that was one step above a rudimentary nervous system. The brainstem surrounded the top of the spinal cord and controlled basic body functions such as breathing, metabolism, reflexes, and coordinated movement. It could react to stimuli, but it could not reason. An olfactory lobe evolved that could process and identify the smells of prey, enemies, danger, sex partners, and the like—a capability with great survival value. As it was evolving to become better at discerning water-borne and air-borne molecules, the olfactory lobe was growing larger and beginning to encircle the top of the brainstem.

Organizing the body to respond to things in the environment was becoming more complex and more specialized. The few neurons that orchestrated emotional responses gradually evolved into large almond-shaped structures (amygdalae) on either side of the brainstem. *Amygdala* is the Latin word for "almond." Similarly, neurons, which began to recognize and "remember" the factual information associated with smells and other sensory information, evolved into the hippocampus. The combination of remembering factual details and their associated emotions enabled the amygdala and hippocampus, in a crude way, to recognize patterns in incoming sensory information and to reproduce the remembered emotional response appropriate to the pattern. It was the beginning of learning, and the process was fast enough to initiate an attack or avoidance response in a few milliseconds (*milli-* is .001). Dreaming began at some point during this evolution. If dreaming is associated with forming permanent memories from experiences stored in short-term memory, it is possible that the brain began to dream when it began to remember.

By this time, sensory information flow was becoming complex and the few neurons that converted sensory information into a useable form for processing within the brain evolved into the thalamus. Smell information, for example, was received by the thalamus, converted into a form useable in the brain, and then sent to the amygdala and hippocampus. As this team of organized brain parts was evolving, the olfactory bulb was beginning to form into a ring shape around the brain stem. The word *ring* in Latin is *limbus,* and the ringed brainstem became known as the "limbic system."

The additional neurons of the limbic system provided enhanced emotional capabilities that improved survival. In addition to rage and sex drive, the limbic system had enhanced learning and memory. Smells could be remembered, compared, and recognized, and emotional responses appropriate to the sensed smell could be implemented. Our ancestors were beginning to perceive their environments, and what they perceived was a competitive and dangerous place with extreme evolutionary pressure. As other sensory capabilities evolved to provide more complex vision, sound, taste, and touch information, the limbic brain was evolving into the reptilian brain.

Feeling vs. Thinking—How DNA Evolved Our Paradox

As brain evolution continued, the amygdala and hippocampus, which today are primarily responsible for our emotions, learning, and remembering, became the underlying basis of the neocortex— the large mass of convoluted neurons and glia capping the old limbic brain. This occurred about 100 million years ago, when mammals were becoming established. As the neocortex formed, neural pathways linking it to the thalamus provided it with information necessary to enable its prefrontal lobes to analyze what should be done about incoming sensory information. The thalamus now fed sensory information directly to both the amygdala and the neocortex. However, studies using rats show that information moves from the thalamus to the amygdala in about 12 milliseconds, while information from the thalamus to the neocortex and then to the amygdala takes about 24 milliseconds. What this means is that the amygdala can respond to a situation before the neocortex has a chance to override the amygdala's decision. In other words, the reasoned response of the neocortex is not fast enough to prevent the emotional response of the amygdala from being implemented. From a survival perspective, the quick amygdala response was and is essential to avoid being killed in sudden attacks by predators. The amygdala screens all incoming sensory information, looking for any threat. It stands ready to mobilize the body (including the neocortex) to respond in milliseconds with very strong, primitive, reflexive actions. Even if some of our ancestors' "knee-jerk" amygdala responses were inappropriate, there was no apparent evolutionary penalty. The supremacy of the older emotional amygdala over the more recent rational neocortex has remained undisturbed.

In an experiment that first destroyed the auditory cortex of rats and then shocked them each time a particular sound was made, the rats learned to fear the sound. Even though they could not consciously perceive the sound (in the neocortex) the thalamus fed the sound and shock information to their amygdalae. The amygdala and hippocampus learned to fear the sound as it would have in the brain of a reptile without a neocortex. In addition, before the prefrontal lobes have time to sort out incoming sensory information, the faster amygdalae have already assessed it and formed an emotional opinion about it. The neural circuitry of our amygdalae did not lose its capacity for emotional learning with the addition of the neocortex. Evolution has overlaid and interconnected our emotional brain with prefrontal lobes in the neocortex capable of reasoning. We have two ways to relate to the world, and our emotional amygdalae are "wired" to commandeer our rational prefrontal lobes.

What would change if our amygdalae were disabled? Without an amygdala we would be without joy, anger, passion, fear, rage, competition, cooperation, social awareness, tears, and sorrow. We would be ill equipped to respond to threatening situations. We would have no emotional memory, and events would be activities without meaning. How would your life change if you lost your amygdala?

> One young man whose amygdala had been surgically removed to control severe seizures became completely uninterested in people, preferring to sit in isolation with no human contact. While he was perfectly capable of conversation, he no longer recognized close friends, relatives, or even his mother, and remained impassive in the face of their anguish at his indifference. Without an amygdala he seemed to have lost all recognition of feeling, as well as any feeling about feelings.[26]

In another case, after a woman had her amygdala removed to control seizures, she was observed to have lost the ability to perceive signs of fear and anger in other people's voices.[27] In other research, the sight of frightened faces, which induces a fear response in normal subjects, produced no such fear response in people whose amygdalae were damaged.[28]

What would change if our prefrontal lobes were disabled? In 1848, Phineas Gage, a congenial 25-year-old railway foreman, was directing rock blasting during construction of a railway line in Vermont. In an accidental explosion a spear-like three foot long tamping iron was driven cleanly through his head. Although he regained consciousness quickly and remained able-bodied and intelligent, his personality changed. He began to use profanity and to otherwise behave offensively and irresponsibly. He lost his job and, until his death in 1861, his personality never recovered from the injury to his brain. At the request of his physician, his skull and the tamping iron were preserved. A recent computer analysis of X-rays of the entry and exit holes in the skull indicated that the rod damaged his prefrontal lobes. Contemporary patients with similar brain damage display irresponsible behaviors and difficulty with expressing and interpreting emotions. A neurologist who studied the Gage case said, "The damage involved left and right prefrontal [areas] in a pattern that, as confirmed in Gage's modern [brain-damaged] counterparts, causes a defect in rational decision-making and the processing of emotion."[29]

A prefrontal lobotomy severs the neural fibers that connect the prefrontal lobes with the limbic system. The procedure was once performed to control intense anxiety and violent behavior, before medications became available. Unfortunately, what resulted from performing a prefrontal lobotomy was usually a Pyrrhic victory. Although their distress was relieved, most patients became irreversibly passive and unemotional. Similarly, cerebral strokes can disable portions of the brain by blocking blood flow, thereby killing neurons in the area of the blockage. Unlike lobotomy damage to the pathways linking the prefrontal lobes to the limbic system, damage to the left or right prefrontal lobes themselves can occur with very specific and different results. Stroke patients who experience damage to the left prefrontal cortex are prone to extreme worries and fears. Stroke patients with damage to the right prefrontal cortex are prone to being happy without cause and unconcerned about things normally deserving of concern.

When we consider changes resulting from damage to specific parts of the brain, it appears that emotional impulses originating in the limbic system are processed by the right prefrontal lobe, where they are enhanced. Before action is taken, however, the left prefrontal lobe applies a rational test to the impulse and can mediate all but the most extreme impulses. Daniel Goleman, in *Emotional Intelligence,* described how the limbic and cortex systems coordinate in a hierarchical relationship.

> In a very real sense we have two minds, one that thinks and one that feels.
>
> These two fundamentally different ways of knowing interact to construct our mental life. One, the

rational mind, is the mode of comprehension we are typically conscious of: more prominent in awareness, thoughtful, able to ponder and reflect. But alongside that there is another system of knowing: impulsive and powerful, if sometimes illogical—the emotional mind. ... There is a steady gradient in the ratio of rational-to-emotional control over the mind; the more intense the feeling, the more dominant the emotional mind becomes—and the more ineffectual the rational. This is an arrangement that seems to stem from eons of evolutionary advantage to having emotions and intuitions guide our instantaneous response in situations where our lives are in peril—and where pausing to think over what to do could cost us our lives.

These two minds, the emotional and the rational, operate in tight harmony for the most part, intertwining their very different ways of knowing to guide us through the world. Ordinarily there is a balance between emotional and rational minds, with emotion feeding into and informing the operations of the rational mind, and the rational mind refining and sometimes vetoing the inputs of the emotions. Still, the emotional and rational minds are semi-independent faculties, each, ... reflecting the operation of distinct, but interconnected, circuitry in the brain.

In many or most moments these minds are exquisitely coordinated; feelings are essential to thought, thought to feeling. But when passions surge the balance tips: it is the emotional mind that captures the upper hand, swamping the rational mind.[30]

These evolved parallel and inherently conflicted brain structures are the biological genesis of the human paradox. Even with the grief we sometimes experience from their never ending competition for control of our actions, is there a shaman who would reject dispassionate reason if it meant living eternally with chaotic emotions, or a philosopher who would embrace the solitary beauty of reason without the capacity to experience joy in its accomplishments?

As we have seen, our barbaric as well as our reasoned behavior is the result of hundreds of millions of years of brain evolution. In short, our brain physiology is the source of our unreasoned emotions. However, the neural circuitry of our amygdalae and prefrontal lobes only partly influences the balance between our capacity for reason and our emotions. To a substantial extent our psychogenetic inheritance and socialization determine the remainder. Absent civilizing influences on the learning-based circuitry of our neocortex, we are not well suited to live among civilized people. Given a proper formative socialization and an appropriate psychogenetic inheritance, our neocortex can filter out the amygdala's misplaced defensive reptilian influences while delighting in their uplifting emotions. Philosophers and theologians have attempted in their own ways to influence this balance. Philosophers have tried to use reason to convince us that emotion must be controlled by reason. Their conundrum is that emulation and blind acceptance, not reason, are the primary means by which our neocortex circuitry is shaped during our formative years. This is the source of philosophers' frustrations with our uncontrolled reptilian behavior. It is also the reason theologians use emotion-influencing myths, methods and dogma in our formative years, to inculcate their beliefs, to protect us from life's anxieties, and to help us avoid reptilian (sinful) behavior. For over two millennia it has been this aspect of the biology of belief—the uneasy balance between our amygdalae and prefrontal lobes—that has been the driving force of the struggle between our myths and our philosophies, and in today's context, between religion and science. And it may underlie the paradox represented by Newton's fascination with the Apocalypse, Kepler's belief in witchcraft, and Hawking's reference to "the mind of God."

Chapter 8
The Overt Process of Brain Evolution

The visible results of DNA evolution are what I refer to as the "overt process." Section 1 of this chapter describes the likely, continuous evolution of organisms from single celled creatures to mammals. Pivotal-organism level increases in complexity, resulting from events in DNA evolution described in the previous chapter, are noted. Readers familiar with this field of science may choose to skip or skim Section 1. Section 2 examines how psychogenetic evolution logically follows from our evolved high intelligence, capacity to communicate, and increasing social complexity.

Section 1

Evolution before Darwin

In the 19th century, Darwin was able to piece together the missing elements of biological evolution. Before Darwin, the early Greeks envisioned elements of the theory of evolution. Anaximander (610-546 BCE) thought that organisms arose by gradual stages and that land animals were once fish.[1] Empedocles (500-430? BCE) believed that Nature produces every kind of organism with some capable of propagating themselves and meeting the conditions of survival. Anaxagoras (500?-428 BCE) said that all organisms were originally generated out of earth, moisture, and heat, and thereafter from one another,[2] and that the upright posture of humans freed their hands for grasping and enabled them to develop beyond other animals.[3]

Unfortunately, Aristotle preferred his concept of "entelechy" to the natural selection of Anaximander, Empedocles, and Anaxagoras.

> He [Aristotle] rejects Empedocles' notion of the natural selection of accidental mutations; there is no fortuity in evolution; the lines of development are determined by the inherent urge of each form, species, and genus to develop itself to the fullest realization of its nature. There is design, but it is less a guidance from without than an inner drive or "entelechy" by which each thing is drawn to its natural fulfillment.[4]

In 1756, Karl von Linne (1707-78) placed humans in the primate-order classification of animals in his work *Systema Naturae*. George de Buffon (1707-88) suggested an ancestor common to all living beings in his work *Natural History*. Erasmus Darwin (1731-1802), the grandfather of Charles Darwin, proposed that "animals vary and transform through behavior which is provoked by need." Jean-Baptiste de Lamarck (1744-1829) proposed that an animal that travels on all four limbs may evolve to travel on two. The preface to *On the Origin of Species by Way of Natural Selection* presents a more complete review of theories leading up to Charles Darwin's work. In the text itself, Charles Darwin offers the fundamental question and the fundamental answer, repeated here for the convenience of the reader:

> How do those groups of species, which constitute what are called distinct genera, and which differ from each other more than do the species of the same genus, arise? All these results, ... follow inevitably from the struggle for life. Owing to this struggle for life, any variation, however slight and from whatever cause proceeding, if it be in any degree profitable to an individual of any species, in its infinitely complex relations to other organic beings and to external nature, will tend to the

preservation of that individual, and will generally be inherited by its offspring. The offspring, also, will thus have a better chance of surviving, for, of the many individuals of any species which are periodically born, but a small number can survive.

In addition to observing accurately the result of DNA's incessant refinement of genetic knowledge, to which he refers as "from whatever cause proceeding," Darwin realized that the competition for life begins with abundant offspring competing with each other for limited resources. A most extreme version of this was recently observed in a species of shark in which fully functioning siblings cannibalize each other during gestation. One might describe it as a kind of prenatal survival of the fittest. Another of Darwin's contributions to our understanding of biological evolution is his realization that offspring with genetic variations, which coexist with related offspring absent the variations, constitute branching in evolution's tree of life.

Early Life

In an attempt to reconstruct how the accumulation of slight variations over more than 3.5 billion years has produced the human brain, visualize in your mind's eye, if you will, the unseen changes in DNA that underlie overt changes in the fossil record we are about to consider. There are three main branches on the tree of life. The bacteria branch, which includes cyanobacteria; the eucarya branch, which includes plants, animals, and fungi; and the archaea branch, which are bacteria-like organisms identified as distinct from bacteria in 1977. Archaea are the least understood of the three branches.[5, 6] Research shows that archaea differ from bacteria in the makeup of their DNA and in the fact that they derive their energy using, e.g., hydrogen and carbon dioxide. Bacteria employ, e.g., sulfates (anaerobic) and oxygen (aerobic) in their energy generating processes. Whether archaea self-assembled prior to bacteria is unclear. What is clear is that self-assembly happened before 3.8 billion years ago. At that time, about 200 million years after the last meteorite bombardments, primitive organisms left their remains in what is now Greenland.[7] Within another 300 million years, however, bacteria that derived their energy from sulfate reactions encountered what to them was an ecological disaster. Bacteria much like today's cyanobacteria adapted to use sunlight to convert water and carbon dioxide into glucose while producing oxygen as a byproduct. This began a process that displaced sulfate reactions as a dominant driving force of life. Inasmuch as oxygen readily combines with many mineral compounds, newly evolving cyanobacteria began to create what would become our biosphere. Although oxygen to varying degrees was toxic to anaerobes, they were not destroyed. Instead, they were relegated to live in places where oxygen levels were low enough for them to exist—away from oxygenated water and atmosphere.

Primitive cyanobacteria thrived in the surface waters of the Earth's oceans, which, at that time, were filled with dissolved iron compounds. As oxygen was produced it combined with iron compounds, forming precipitates of iron oxides, and eventually transforming the oceans. Red deposits of iron rich sediments layered the ocean bottoms, leaving behind the clear water we see today. In time, with virtually no iron compounds remaining with which to combine, oxygen bubbled up from the oceans to transform the atmosphere.

Early life forms survived a glacial episode that reached almost to the equator 2.2 billion years ago,[8] and by about 1.3 billion years ago, simple bacteria had experienced an enormous number of mutations. These mutated descendants had acquired nuclei, were thousands of times larger than simple bacteria, and assimilated various bacteria symbiotically as organelles. It is possible that these single-celled organisms developed the cooperative capabilities of present-day Dictyostelium amoebae, or "Dicty." Another 200 million years of mutations produced rudimentary multicellular organisms without nervous or circulatory systems. This line of cells gave rise to anemones and corals.

Multicellular life survived another glacial episode about 700 million years ago. Some believe very low levels of atmospheric carbon dioxide during that time indicate that the planet surface froze completely for about 10 million years.[9, 10] This is also about the time that a developmental gene inversion is believed to have occurred. Such an inversion would have made possible body patterns with the central nervous system and intestinal tract reversed relative to the direction of the limbs. Thereafter, about 50 major body patterns evolved, including segmented bodies, invertebrates, and vertebrates. Among these were the first jellyfish. Although the Burgess shale deposits in the Canadian Rocky Mountains contain many fossils from this period, the dearth of hard parts in these squishy life forms makes the fossil record incomplete and difficult to interpret. What is very clear is that life was proliferating dramatically, perhaps with the aid of two gene doublings at about 520 and 460 million years ago.[11, 12] It is theorized that gill arches evolved into jaws. Heads and sensory organs became more complex. Three-part brains began to appear along with calcium-storing spines and skeletal parts. Filter feeders such as starfish and sea urchins evolved. Ammonite descendants of jellyfish developed well-defined tentacles, shells and eyes. In turn, descendants of ammonites, such as the nautilus, retained the shell, while other descendants such as the cuttlefish, octopus, and squid successfully adapted without shells. Plant life was coevolving and generally preceded animal life in exploiting new environments. Plants and animals had become symbiotically dependent in an oxygen–carbon dioxide cycle.

By 550 million years ago, while the ocean was supporting evolving plants and animals, the land was lifeless. Plate tectonics, wind, and rain had created and reshaped continents and mountain ranges. The roughly 10,000 species that had evolved by this time were adapted to living in salty ocean water, not in fresh water runoff from the continents. Although rivers, lakes, wetlands, bays, and dry land were devoid of animals, plants were beginning to adapt to fresh water.

There were two fundamental changes needed for ocean creatures to adapt to living in fresh or brackish water. The first was to evolve a capacity to excrete water that accumulated in their cells in the absence of sufficient salt. The second was to evolve a capacity to store calcium that was not consistently available in fresh-water environments. Without calcium, muscles cannot function. By about 530 million years ago, soft-bodied vertebrates had evolved. The cartilaginous vertebrae of their rudimentary spinal columns were calcium repositories. Within 30 million years, vertebrates living in brackish water evolved fresh-water-adapted kidneys, calcium-regulating bone, and blood-salt-level-regulating circulatory systems. By 500 million years ago, proto-fish vertebrates with scales or thin bony plates and the beginnings of a limbic brain had evolved. With no pectoral or pelvic fins they swam erratically, and, with no jaw, it is likely that they were filter feeders or scooped up nutrient-rich mud to sustain themselves.

About 440 million years ago, when trilobites dominated the oceans, when sharks were making their debut,[13] and when much of Earth's land was predominantly in the southern hemisphere, terrestrial plants evolved from aquatic plants and took root along the water's edge. By 390 million years ago, fish with jaws and fins evolved, some with eyes and some without. They had well-developed spinal columns, jaws with teeth, and pectoral and pelvic fins suitable for swim control. Within another 10 or so million years, bottom-dwelling fish began to use their pectoral fins to push themselves along the bottom of plant-thick, shallow, fresh and brackish waters. Getting enough oxygen became a problem for fish living in waters that became oxygen depleted.

Venturing onto Land

The next adaptations enabled them to supplement their gills by taking in oxygen from the air with a primitive lung organ associated with, and perhaps evolved from, the gills. Sturdy pectoral fins enabled them to "walk" over land in search of oxygen-rich water, to escape water-bound predators, and to partake of the insects, plants, worms, snails, and other invertebrates and segmented body creatures that had already adapted to living on land. Within another 10 million years, a shallow water vertebrate, much like a salamander, evolved with complex bony limbs for locomotion and lungs adapted to breathing air. This vertebrate could walk over obstacles in its shallow water environment while breathing air. However, gravity presented a problem.

A spine was fine, but, to enjoy the benefits of venturing onto land, more substantial protection was required to prevent soft organs from being crushed by gravity—a problem that does not exist for water dwellers. By 360 million years ago, strong rib cages evolved to protect vital organs and adapted what were pectoral and pelvic fins into limbs suitable for "walking."[14] These walkers were marine amphibians and the first vertebrates able to sustain terrestrial activity. Although a few of their present day descendants are newts, salamanders, toads, and frogs, one ancient South African amphibian grew to 13 feet in length. The demise of these large amphibians probably resulted from competing with the reptilian branch of the family.

Reptiles evolved a number of adaptations that gave them numerous advantages over their amphibian ancestors. Amphibian reproduction in water enabled their tiny offspring to move about their environments in search of food and prevented them from dehydrating. Reproducing on dry land was another matter. Amphibian reproduction was accomplished in two stages. When first born, their offspring enjoyed the benefits of a water birth, but, when they were large enough to survive on land, they discarded their aquatic characteristics and acquired appropriate land characteristics. Frogs have a tadpole stage before they become recognizable as frogs. By comparison, reptiles evolved a leathery egg that provided nourishment, prevented dehydration, and protected the developing offspring long enough for them to grow to a size suitable for survival on land. In addition, amphibians lost moisture through their skins and gulped air to breathe. Reptiles evolved moisture-resistant scales and a suction breathing system.

Air intake for reptiles was not limited by the size of their mouths, but by the size of their lungs. The limbic brain that reptiles inherited evolved into the more capable reptilian brain with an amygdala and hippocampus. With all their neural improvements, however, they were still driven by instinctive responses and learned emotional behaviors. Other adaptations in leg and foot structure provided reptiles with greater speed in seeking food both at the water's edge and in the nearby growths of grasses and ferns.

In time, plants evolved into tree ferns that used spores to propagate along the wet margins of land and water. As their roots and other features adapted to more arid conditions, tree ferns propagated inland, taking with them evolving vegetarian animals and their predators. The fossil record shows that by 320 million years ago, when the present continents were all part of the super-continent Pangea, conifers and cycads (pine and palm-like trees called "gymnosperms") had evolved. As with modern conifers, their seeds are enclosed in cones, but unlike modern conifers, they had soft leaves. Fruit-bearing flowering plants were to evolve later. Slowly, conifers began to cover the land. Their wind-blown pollen fertilized nearby trees, and seeds appeared a number of months after fertilization. Conifers had no insects that assisted in fertilization. Even so, they were better adapted than tree ferns and in time became the dominant vegetation. Eventually, great conifer forests covered the land. By 300 million years ago, the first flying insects evolved—the first of a number of events that would change the world again.

Early mammal-like reptiles appeared about 280 million years ago and evolved over about 210 million years from egg-laying to marsupial births, and eventually to full-term gestations. Many changes were required to evolve reptiles into mammals. For reptiles to function properly, their body temperatures must be high enough to support the biochemical processes that enable them to function. Without the ability to create and regulate their own body temperatures, reptiles had to wait for the sun to heat their bodies before they could perform effectively. For reptiles to become independent of the sun's heat they had to produce their own. To do this reptiles required a number of evolved adaptations.

Heat is produced as oxygen combines with hydrocarbons from food. To produce more heat, one must take in more oxygen and food, and combine them rapidly. To take in more oxygen, larger lungs that could be filled and emptied rapidly were required. This would both provide more oxygen to the muscles and make more heat available by speeding digestion. The evolution of a breathing diaphragm made respiration more efficient and, if required, more rapid. To take in more food required better teeth and jaws, better locomotion, and a way to prevent eating from interfering with breathing—a constant supply of oxygen is much more important to high-oxygen-consumption mammals. The evolution of a bone shelf separating the nose from the mouth made it possible to take in oxygen while chewing. Three types of teeth evolved, permitting grasping, cutting, and grinding in a precision bite. Finely chewed food is more easily digested and more quickly available for use. With intense predation by reptiles, small size became an advantage, as early mammals sought protection by hiding. However, small animals have higher surface areas per unit of body weight. All the effort required to produce heat would be compromised if it could escape readily. In time, efficient insulating pelts evolved from scales, as mammal-like reptiles evolved into mammals. Compared with cold-blooded reptiles, typical contemporary mammals are more agile, more intelligent, able to run faster, and have their all-important higher body temperatures regulated automatically, day and night. Although merely representative, these differences indicate the degree of adaptation mammal-like reptiles experienced as they evolved into higher performing mammals. It took time and good fortune.

About 250 million years ago, before mammal-like reptiles began to evolve, disaster struck the Earth. Although the mechanism is not clear, during a period of perhaps 5 to 10 million years, reef and shallow-water environments were devastated. Over 75 percent of reptiles, over 60 percent of amphibians, 8 of 27 orders of insects, and more than 90 percent of all ocean species became extinct. It is thought that volcanic eruptions in what is now Siberia and China occurred over a period of at least 600,000 years. Ocean levels dropped, parts of the ocean became depleted of oxygen, and fungal growth suggests widespread terrestrial plant devastation.[15] Mass extinctions were not new to the Earth. This extinction was the third to occur. The first occurred about 438 million years ago, about 60 million years after the first vertebrates evolved. The second occurred about 367 million years ago, after plants and arthropods (insects) adapted to living on land. Other mass extinctions followed. The fourth at about 208 million years ago occurred a few million years before mammals evolved. The dinosaur age ended about 65 million years ago with an extinction that cleared the way for the evolution of our early primate ancestors.

During the Triassic period, beginning about 245 million years ago, the super continent Pangea had moved further north, the percentage of atmospheric carbon dioxide was at least four times what it is today, and the average surface temperature was considerably warmer. It was an excellent time for plants and for animals that ate plants. While conifers were evolving, so too were reptiles. One branch of the lineage became the terror of the oceans when it readapted to aquatic life. The dinosaur branch of the reptile family was enormously successful, both as plant and meat eaters. Two general types of dinosaurs are distinguished by their pelvic structures, those described as lizard-hipped and those described as bird-hipped. Among the adaptations that distinguished some dinosaurs from their reptilian ancestors was the ability to walk and run on their pelvic legs. The dinosaur branch that adapted to flight are the ancestors of modern birds.[16]

Some contend that high-speed dinosaurs had to be warm-blooded. Whether they were warm-blooded or cold-blooded is not clear. Today's warm-blooded creatures consume energy 12 times faster than cold-blooded creatures, an energy-consumption rate that would have been unsustainable given the dinosaur's rate of food intake and body size. It is possible that at least some dinosaurs were warm-blooded, but with lower body temperatures than are possible today. To the extent that dinosaurs did not possess adaptations that mammal-like reptiles evolved, it is not clear how dinosaurs could have achieved high body temperatures.

From about 300 million to 250 million years ago, small dinosaurs evolved into many forms, including the enormous, long-necked, leaf-eating sauropods. While these evolutionary events were taking place, the center of Pangea had moved to the equator. As plant-eating dinosaurs (herbivores) evolved and flourished in a conifer-rich environment, so too did meat-eating dinosaurs in their new herbivore-rich environment. It was the dinosaur's golden age. But, as meat eaters chased plant eaters through ancient conifer forests, a small change was taking place in plant evolution. It was a change that would dramatically alter the lush environment that supported the assent of the dinosaurs.

By about 200 million years ago, flowering plants (angiosperms) had evolved. Flowering plants differ from conifers in that their seed is enclosed in fruit. Another difference is that flowering plants rely more on insects than on the wind for pollination. As they coevolved, insects and flowering plants adapted to each other's shapes or other characteristics. This meant that flowering plants had insect partners capable of delivering pollen to distant plants. Early mammals also played a role in speeding the propagation of flowering plants. Mammals at that time[17] were the size of tree shrews and probably foraged at night to avoid being eaten by small meat eating dinosaurs. In addition to eating insects and perhaps other small creatures, these mammals ate flowering-plant fruit and dispersed the seeds with their droppings. Fertilization in flowering plants was extraordinarily fast. These new genetic traits, together with the coevolution of pollen- and seed-spreading animals, accounted for enormous variety among flowering plants and for their capacity to out-compete and displace conifers in temperate regions. This is not to say that conifers did not evolve as well. Over millions of years of ravaging by dinosaurs, conifers began to evolve defensive poisons and needle-like leaves. Unfortunately for conifers, they were still slow propagators and less well adapted. As you would expect, where flowering plants displaced conifers they displaced conifer-eating dinosaurs as well. At about 180 million years ago, Pangea separated near the equator with what would become North America and Eurasia moving north, and South America and Africa moving south. An equally significant change was taking place in the structure of reptilian brains. Additional brain capacity was forming as the neocortex began to grow larger. It provided the reptilian brain with improved memory and with the beginnings of a capacity to reason.

The First Mammals

About 160 million years ago the first fossil record of mammals appeared.[18] By 140 million years ago, our mammalian ancestors were evolving jaws with high flanges at the back of the jaw and larger jaw muscles connecting the jaw to the skull, permitting a more forceful bite. In time, to further the business of getting to and acquiring food, and avoiding predators, limb bones elongated or shortened and adapted toes with claws, nails, feet, or hoofs. Some adapted for speed, others for climbing, and others with hoofs were suited for grazing. Grazing limbs lost their ability to turn to the side and found two primary toes (cloven hoofs) well suited to the task of grazing and escaping predators. Other limbs adapted for swimming, climbing, running, digging, walking, flying and seizing. All of these adaptations placed new survival demands on the brain for speed and information processing. A larger brain began to evolve that could process large volumes of information from the senses and could provide fine control over the nervous system.

By 120 million years ago, Africa and South America separated, as did Eurasia and North America. The Atlantic Ocean was in its infancy. By about 70 million years ago, our mammalian ancestors probably weighed about 150 grams, had long tails, a body length of about 7 inches, walked on all fours, had long snouts and ate fruit and insects. They shared their environment with dinosaurs, but this would change soon.

By 90 million years ago, conifer-eating dinosaurs were forced to regions where colder temperatures gave conifers an advantage over flowering plants. The cycle was now complete. Those dinosaurs whose success followed the success of conifers over tree ferns were now experiencing hardship as conifers lost ground to flowering plants. It is ironic that the fate of many awesome dinosaurs would be affected so profoundly by the evolution of fragile flowers. Triceratops, a dinosaur with a large head plate and three horns, was an exception. It was able to eat flowering plants, and survived in great herds until about 65 million years ago. At that time, the Cretaceous period ended: a meteor about 6 miles across, traveling at about 50,000 miles per hour struck at a location that we know today as the town of Chicxulub in Mexico's Yucatan peninsula. Its energy was equivalent to about 100 thousand billion tons of TNT. Although the crater ultimately reached about 150 miles in diameter, within 10 seconds after impact the crater was already 30 miles across, 15 miles deep, and was spewing molten rock in ballistic trajectories all over Earth. The impact fractured the Earth's crust and created earthquakes and tsunamis. The sky was filled with molten ejecta and fires started everywhere. And, because the impact area was rich in limestone and sulfur,[19] vast quantities of carbon dioxide and sulfur dioxide were released into the atmosphere. This was doubly unfortunate. The first result was that sulfur dioxide combined with atmospheric moisture to form sulfuric acid droplets. Such droplets block sunlight, cool the Earth, and cause acid rain, possibly as strong as battery acid. In addition to the smoke and dust that blackened the sky for months, volcanic eruption studies tell us that the effect of sulfur dioxide might have been to cool the Earth as much as 10 degrees Celsius for a decade. The second result was that carbon dioxide released by the impacted limestone could have caused the atmosphere to warm as much as 15 degrees Celsius for centuries.

From computer simulations and actual measurements, we now know that the Chicxulub impact in the Yucatan caused a wave about five kilometers high to sweep over what is now Cuba, and a layer of sea floor rubble about three feet deep to cover parts of

Texas. Ocean bed core samples taken 320 kilometers east of Jacksonville, Florida recorded the event very clearly. Prior to impact, the core sediments were rich in fossil remains, characteristic of a healthy ocean ecosystem. Deposited on top of that layer is about ten centimeters of gray-green impact debris topped by a thin red layer rich in iron. The iron is probably the remains of the meteor, since the Yucatan site had little iron. On top of the red layer is about five centimeters of sediment with no evidence of fossils. It is estimated that this 5-centimeter layer took 5,000 years to deposit. Sediments above the 5 centimeter layer show the return of fossils and evidence that the ocean near Florida had reestablished an ecosystem.[20] Virtually everywhere on land, a layer of iridium containing soot about 1/2 inch thick marks the end of the Cretaceous period. Iridium is an element uncommon on Earth's surface, but commonly found in meteors. It was iridium in the dark global shroud covering Cretaceous period soil that, in the late 1970s, led Luis and Walter Alvarez to unlock the mystery of how the Cretaceous period was ended.[21]

Presently it is estimated that 6 million years before the Chicxulub impact there were about 60 kinds of dinosaurs. That number dropped to less than 20 by about 2 million years before the impact. The impact caused about 90 percent of Earth's biomass to burn, and some believe that all remaining dinosaurs starved. Of the other species then on Earth, about two-thirds were destroyed. Whether the demise of dinosaurs was due solely to an "impact winter" is not clearly understood. It is said that some dinosaur species survived the impact and later became extinct for other reasons. What is clear is that their demise changed the status of our mammalian ancestors from dinosaur snacks to precursors of apes that would dominate the Earth. Blockage of sunlight would have devastated animals dependent on fresh vegetation or on animals that ate fresh vegetation. Insects survived on the remains of decomposing plants and, at that time, our ancestors ate insects.

When the meteor struck, North and South America were not yet joined at Panama, and where the Mediterranean would be was open water from the Atlantic to the Pacific. By about 50 million years ago our ancestral mammals' limbs had grown longer, their snouts had become shorter, they lived in trees, developed protruding ears, weighed about 300 grams (about 10 ounces), and had long tails. Small though they were, their tiny neocortexes were providing them with enhanced mental capabilities, well suited to ensure their survival in a meteor-altered world. The dinosaurs as such were gone and tapir-like mammals weighing about 200 pounds shared the habitat. About 55 million years ago, when the Himalayan Mountains formed as present-day India collided with Asia, huge limestone formations were exposed to the weather. As carbon dioxide in the atmosphere combines with rain it forms carbonic acid. Although weak, carbonic acidic rain would have reacted with the exposed limestone of the Himalayas to form carbonate particulates, trapping atmospheric carbon and washing it into the sea. Eventually, carbon dioxide, a greenhouse gas, diminished, and that is thought by some to have contributed to global cooling and may have precipitated glaciation. Although in its more ancient history it experienced infrequent glaciations and a generally higher global surface temperature, Earth has experienced about 12 glaciation cycles in the past 20 million years.

Between 40 and 20 million years ago, the Mediterranean was formed as Africa collided with Eurasia. Salt domes found at the bottom of the Mediterranean, deep cuts in the rock at the bottom of the Nile and other rivers feeding the Mediterranean, and other evidence suggests that the Mediterranean went dry when the Gibraltar Strait was dammed by natural forces. Rivers flowing into the Mediterranean did not (and still do not) provide enough water to equal its evaporation, and it gradually went dry. About five million years ago, Gibraltar was breached by the Atlantic. Water from the Atlantic (less salty) now flows in at the upper portion of the Strait, and saltier (heavier) water flows out in the lower portion. Phoenician sailors discovered this and lowered drag devices into the lower out-flowing water to pull their ships against the surface current into the Atlantic.

By about 30 million years ago, our ancestors looked monkey-like, weighed about 7 kilograms (about 15 pounds), had

32 teeth (as do we), were arboreal, and ate fruit. They coexisted with an herbivore that looked like a rhinoceros with side-by-side horns. By 17 million years ago, they evolved a chimp-like appearance and weighed about 18 to 50 kilograms. They were apes with no tails, a more substantial jaw, shortened faces, rounded skulls that were rotated to look forward while standing, but with an unimpressive brain size. An elephant-like mammal shared their environment. A large mammal with a horse-like head and gorilla like legs shared its environment with our primate ancestor 14 million years ago. This ancestor began to stand on its pelvic limbs and was functioning with a neocortex that was increasingly sharing decision-making with the older amygdala and hippocampus. By 4 million years ago, our hominid ancestors had shortened arms, could walk with a waddle, and had a brain slightly larger than a chimpanzee's. Fossil remains of one of these Australopithecus afarensis ancestors found in Ethiopia were named Lucy. By 3.5 million years ago, hominids left their footprints in the volcanic ash of Tanzania.

About 2 million years ago, some time after the Straits at Gibraltar filled the Mediterranean, North and South America were joined with the formation of present day Panama. It is theorized that, in creating this formation, tectonic forces cut off warm ocean currents that flowed to the Arctic. Similarly, flow through what is now the Bering Strait was reduced, as North America moved closer to Asia. Over about 300 million years, the internal hydrodynamics of Earth had moved the continents by plate tectonics from an essentially north-south mass concentrated mostly in the southern hemisphere to a distributed east-west arrangement centered closer to the equator. In addition to influencing biological evolution in other ways, it is thought that this massive reforming of the continents resulted in the restriction of warm currents flowing to the Arctic and may have contributed to recent periodic glaciations or ice ages.

By 2 million years ago, what was probably the first human, Homo habilis (handy man) weighed about 40 kilograms (88 pounds), had an upright stance, was about 4 feet tall, had a brain about half the size of ours, and was able to make tools. By 1.7 million years ago, Homo erectus (the standing human) had a less massive jaw and a much larger brain (from 900 to 1000 cubic centimeters). Homo erectus built shelters, made flint tools, and hunted and gathered food. By 1 million years ago the ability of Homo erectus to make fire provided access to previously uninhabitable territory.

Homo sapiens archaic lived 200 to 100 thousand years ago. They looked like stocky humans, weighed about 50 to 70 kilograms (110 to 154 pounds), and some lived in caves and as hunting nomads. Some contended with cave hyenas, which were much larger than their present-day relatives. By 35 thousand years ago, some Homo sapiens sapiens (the thinking human) lived in tents made of wood frames covered with animal hides. Isolated groups had evolved traits suited to their environments. Long noses, skin with varying degrees of pigmentation, and flat noses were a few of the obvious adaptations. They organized, tanned hides, made flint and reindeer-antler tools, created cave and rock paintings, buried their dead, and believed in the existence of a spirit world. And most importantly, they thought with the same evolved, inherently conflicted reptilian brain and neocortex that we inherited.

Section 2

Large-scale Social Evolution Begins

The first coming together of scattered Western settlements occurred in the Middle East. Why in this region? Perhaps the following happened. In a process similar to the drying of the Mediterranean, the Black Sea is thought by some to have been a brackish-water lake dammed off from the Mediterranean at the Bosporus strait at what is presently Istanbul, Turkey. It is possible that tectonic forces raised such a dam. It is also possible that earthquakes and rising ocean levels after the last ice age might have played a part in breaching the Bosporus. Today, saline water from the Mediterranean flows into the Black Sea at the Bosporus through what is now a strait about 20 miles long and 1/2 mile wide at its narrowest. By comparison, the Strait at Gibraltar is about 40 miles long and 9 miles wide at its narrowest point. Before the Bosporus strait was formed, the Black Sea was thought to be perhaps one hundred meters below present sea level. When the strait first formed, flood water that began flowing from the Mediterranean into the Black Sea region would have destroyed the existing brackish-water-lake ecosystem, which had been receiving water primarily from the Danube, Kuban, and other rivers. The breach would have flooded what is believed to have been an inhabited region of considerable size. Given the volume of the Black Sea basin, pre-flood inhabitants would have been relentlessly forced to higher ground during the time it took to bring the Black Sea to its present level. Appendix F shows inferred Black Sea migrations. Based on discoveries of submerged pre-flood shorelines and related findings, some scientists believe that Black Sea flooding occurred about 7,600 years ago and that the cataclysm may be the source of Middle Eastern myths involving disastrous floods.[22] It has been reported that scientists are planning sea-bottom explorations to confirm the existence of pre-flood settlements.

If a pre-Sumerian culture lived on the shores and in the marshes of a pre-flood Black Sea, they would have been displaced and traumatized by the deluge. Water could have risen more than 9 inches per day, on average, and completely flooded the region within about 12 months. In their common plight, people from small scattered settlements may have combined and built large villages or cities away from the rising sea. Such a process would have been contemporaneous with the appearance of "city-kings" in the history of the region. If events occurred in this way, pre-Sumerians who migrated south through the high ground of the Turkish mountains and into the fertile crescent of the Tigris-Euphrates region would have built their cities in what is present-day Iraq. Cities dating to about 5,000 BCE have been found in this region. Such a traumatic flood would have been recorded in the oral history of the survivors.

Stories about the flood would have filtered through many generations, and may be the source of the sages' description of the great flood in the Sumerian story of Gilgamesh. The Sumerians believed the flood to be retribution for the sin of an ancient Sumerian king,[23] Apparently, the same story subsequently made its way through—and was reinterpreted by—the Babylonian and Hebrew cultures, and in turn became part of the Christian tradition involving Noah. By 5,000 BCE, after settling in the Fertile Crescent, ancient Sumerians— equipped with their large brains— were evolving language, writing, technology, and social organization. They created social hierarchies, irrigation farming, currency, law, sophisticated scripts, libraries, schools, literature, poetry, cosmetics, jewelry, sculpture, palaces, temples, arches, columns, slavery, and ecclesiasticism.[24]

After billions of years of evolving by accumulating molecular knowledge in the form of DNA, self-organizing knowledge had crossed a threshold with the Sumerian culture. From a reflexive emotional brain suited to survival in a hostile environment, trial and error evolution had produced a thinking organ capable of evolving knowledge in the form of organized beliefs, instead of organized nucleotides. A few millennia later, the early Greeks invented natural philosophy, employing a rational thought-process to organize beliefs. In just over two millennia from the death of Aristotle, that process evolved into a scientific method of analysis that has enabled us to discover the history of life on Earth and to begin to understand the biology of belief. After eons of evolving organic life by refining DNA using Nature's test of survival value, the process of self-organizing knowledge began to evolve human culture and wisdom by refining human beliefs, not by selecting for their survival value, but by selecting based on their perceived value to those who would inherit them.

Chapter 9

Where Darwinian Evolution Ends and Psychogenetic Evolution Begins

In Edward O. Wilson's book *Consilience*, during a consideration of cultural traits that confer Darwinian advantage to the genes that predispose them, he states that

> The epigenetic rules [hereditary regularities in development, including mental] that guide behavioral development are also largely unexplored, and as a result the exact nature of gene-culture co-evolution can in most cases only be guessed. ...
>
> These shortcomings in behavioral genetics and development are conceptual, technical, and deep. But they are ultimately solvable. Unless new evidence commands otherwise, trust is wisely placed in the natural consilience of the disciplines now addressing the connection between heredity and culture, even if support for it is accumulating slowly and in bits and pieces. The resolution of the difficulties awaits the further expansion of biology and its coalescence with psychology and anthropology.[1]

This chapter examines the evolutionary mechanism that limits genetic influence on cultural evolution, and further examines how that same self-organizing knowledge mechanism in a psychogenetic environment is able to influence cultural evolution in ways that genes cannot.

Technologically advanced societies measure time in increments of less than a billionth of a second (a nanosecond) because events they deal with begin and end within such small spans of time. By contrast, some tropical island cultures would have considered an hour to be uselessly small given the events necessary to their way of life. The absence of words in their language to describe small increments of time reflects the level of their interest in and therefore their understanding of short-lived events. If language reflects interest and understanding by the presence or absence of words, then what can we say of ourselves regarding the depth of our understanding of how essential information is passed from generation to generation? Our words for this essential process include breeding, culture, tradition, legend, roots, lore, parables, mythology, philosophy, heritage, inheritance, legacy, and the like. All are equivalent to an hour, and none is a nanosecond. What is a quantum of tradition; an irreducible unit of legacy? If a quantum is the smallest amount of a thing that can exist independently, then what is our word for a quantum of culture?

The Gene-Psychogene Boundary

Richard Dawkins proposed that memes, self-reproducing ideas in the form of tunes, bird songs, catch-phrases, modes of dress, ways of building arches, and ideas in general[2] are the cultural analogs of genes. Cavalli-Sforza and Feldman, in *Cultural Transmission and Evolution,* accept a cultural unit or trait as "[T]he result of any cultural action (by transmission from other individuals) that can be clearly observed or measured ..."[3] They make the following observation regarding a unit of cultural transmission:

> It is perhaps a pity that the objects of cultural evolution lack an appropriate collective name. Terms like "cultural traits," or more specific words, such as behaviors, skills, values, rules, tools, technologies, connote such different phenomena that any essential similarities are lost in the absence of more detailed discussion.[4]

154

As I understand the definition of memes, they are products of mental activity within social organisms that behave much like genes. They are units of heredity that determine particular characteristics of social organisms and are represented or formed in the mind as thoughts, notions, intuitions, concepts, and the like. Richard Dawkins describes them as ideas that collect people. As a class of memes, psychogenes replicate and experience a form of genetic evolution. They are characteristic phenomena of social organisms that influence social structure, function, growth, evolution, and so on. However, in addition to this meme characteristic, psychogenes require a mental act, perception, condition, habit of acceptance or conviction that something is true, actual, or valid. What I have not been able to find in reading about the nature of memes is an explanation of the mechanism that predicts which members of a group are likely to "be acquired by" a given meme, and which members are unlikely to be acquired by the meme. In this regard I have defined psychogenes as self-replicating beliefs with perceived inheritance value. The qualification that inheritance of psychogenes is a function of the recipient's perception recognizes the importance of the recipient's perceived value of the psychogene to the process of acquiring it. In my view, it is the potential meme recipient's perception of the meme that determines who will be "acquired" by the meme. Such perceptions are not always rational and involve a labyrinth of thought-influencing biological predispositions as well as the perception-altering nature of the perceiver's existing beliefs. In attempting to understand this labyrinth and its influence on how we inherit beliefs, this work addresses the evolution of our brains, the effects of neurotransmitters, the interdependence of belief and perception, and other factors that collectively influence and constitute the biology of belief.

Although my path to the question of cultural evolution is different from that of evolutionary biologists, to a degree my quest raises similar questions. Beginning with the premise that people act in ways consistent with their beliefs, it appears that skills, bodies of knowledge and actions are evidence of underlying beliefs that motivate the actor. The word *technology* derives from the Greek word *teckne*, which means skill. Cultural differences in behaviors, skills, *et cetera*, reflect different cultural beliefs, and the continued transmission of those beliefs makes possible the similarity of acts from generation to generation. In this regard, the evolution of skills (behaviors based on beliefs about cause and effect relationships) can be viewed as belief refinement. It would seem that addressing behaviors without examining their underlying beliefs would make analysis of cultural characteristics extremely difficult. How one determines, from myriad possible beliefs, which belief motivated a particular behavior in a long dead civilization is another matter.

Values and rules in themselves do not involve acts, but they are social behaviors that reflect the relative importance of beliefs in the minds of individuals and cultures. Keeping in mind that zoologists consider instinctive behaviors in examining cultural evolution, as the term is used herein, cultural evolution in animals capable of neocortex-level thinking begins where Darwinian behaviors reach the limit of their capacity to shape culture. The pivotal question seems to be whether Darwinian natural selection, which works at the genetic level, operates to determine higher-level social behaviors. Inasmuch as basic human urges are a matter of biological predisposition, one can understand how genes can affect individual behavior at the rudimentary levels of survival and reproduction. However, the jump from individual genes controlling some individual behaviors to individual genes adapting to determine group behavior has a few problems. The DNA feedback loop that determines individual survival does not translate easily to the determination of group survival except on a rudimentary level, and even then only for small groups or for groups with simple structures. Social insects have DNA that defines specific morphic and behavioral characteristics of each type of member in the colony. Working together, combined types such as workers, soldiers, queens, and drones, with simple sets of genetic instructions, perform synergistically as a group. And Darwinian modification of their genetic instructions can be determinative of future group behavior. However, baboon groups with their guards, nurturers and infants differ in that they have more complex and subtle genetic behaviors as well as a behavior-modifying cerebral cortex. Does a baboon act out of DNA-driven predisposition or out of neocortex-derived altruism, ego, or whatever, when it risks its life to attack a leopard it finds stalking its group? Interposing a neocortex, albeit small, interferes with a DNA feedback loop that might determine complex group behaviors. Consider what influence DNA-derived behavior would have on human group behavior with our large neocortex (at least four times larger than that of a baboon) overriding our DNA feedback loop. Darwinian evolution requires a repeatable survival-related result from changes in DNA. In other words, the Darwinian feedback loop of DNA survival is closed. For example, a fear and flight reaction in response to seeing someone's frightened face has survival value. That is why our brains respond with fear on seeing a frightened face. Our ancestors whose DNA provided them with a fear response survived, while those without it did not, and we descended from the survivors. However, the influence of a reflexive DNA response becomes uncertain to the extent that it can be overridden by thinking. For example, assume that only one out of many faces shows fear, and the flight response, perhaps resulting from a specifically evolved brain cell arrangement or module,[5] is overridden by reasoning that the sole expression of fear may be unjustified. Perhaps the observer was taught that the person with the fear expression belongs to a group that overreacts in such situations. In this case, the Darwinian feedback loop would not be closed. The DNA possessor's judgment—based on his or her belief about the person with the fear expression—is an indeterminate factor. Darwinian feedback is overridden in this example by a belief that stereotyped the person with the fear expression. In a life and death decision based on response to the sight of a frightened face, it is conceivable that twins with identical physical genes could have opposite psychogene-based responses. The twin that responded correctly and survived would pass on the same genes as the one that made the wrong survival decision and Darwinian evolution would not have been relevant. However, it is likely that the surviving twin would pass on the successful psychogene to his or her offspring.

Given its knowledge-accumulating nature, it appears that Darwinian biological evolution is a special case of what I refer to as the principal of self-organizing knowledge. Darwin's is a theory of self-organizing molecular knowledge. By adding molecular adaptation resulting from slight intergenerational variations, Darwin added the third element of self-organizing knowledge, i.e., adaptation, to the theory of evolution—the other elements of recording and reproduction having already been understood. Setting aside the argument that things psychological are actually biological, human cultural evolution, unlike Darwinian evolution, appears to be driven by the mechanism of self-organizing knowledge in the form of psychogenes or beliefs with perceived inheritance value.

One might conclude that a population of humans that experiences mostly reflexive behaviors with little intellectual intervention is likely to experience cultural change that reflects Darwinian closed-loop evolution. A family unit would be the smallest human reproductive population and would maintain cohesion through mother-child bonding, male-female bonding, and other similar genetic behaviors perfected by Darwin's closed-loop DNA feedback. These would be equivalent to genetically derived pack behavior in other animals. For this reason, family culture appears to be defined largely by Darwinian closed-loop behaviors that promote cohesion and survival of the family group, especially where intellectual intervention is rudimentary. It follows that Darwin's closed-loop influences on cultural evolution would attenuate as the significance of reflexive behaviors diminishes. This is what occurs in large groups. Large groups maintain cohesion through common dress and rituals and by establishing common beliefs that provide a basis for common ties, providing family-bonding-like cohesion at the large group level. If large groups do not rely on Darwinian closed-loop evolution as such, then

Darwinian closed-loop evolution alone cannot be determinative of human cultural evolution. Otherwise stated, psychogenes determine in large part the social evolution of groups of self-directed animals with sufficient mental capacity to override the mechanism of Darwinian closed-loop feedback.

The Nature of Psychogenes

While individual human actions are driven partly by reflexive behaviors, what humans learn to believe during their enculturation accounts for the vast majority of their complex actions. Our common beliefs—in the form of intellectual and artistic preferences, rituals, and symbols—create the social bonds responsible for our various forms of social organization. It is not Darwinian genes but heritable and transmittable beliefs, or psychogenes, changing by perceived inheritance-value-driven selection, that determine human social evolution.

Psychogenes cease to be transmitted between or within generations when they are perceived by the prospective recipient to have no relevance or are not believable. As with folk wisdom proven false by science, once something is no longer believed it fails to be transmitted, is forgotten, and no longer influences culture. For this reason, the oldest of our psychogenes do not relate to matters of passing interest; they relate to matters of common interest to all generations.

The key to genetic evolution is that genes have the capacity to change the way we interact with our environment, and the trial and error process of natural selection determines which genetic changes survive. By acting in ways consistent with our beliefs, we change something or prevent something from being changed. And that belief-driven act provides Nature, others, and subsequent generations opportunities to select from alternatives, and thereby effectuate cultural evolution. For this reason, heritable or transmittable beliefs are the intellectual analogs of genes. It follows that if acting in a manner consistent with our beliefs is the impetus that drives cultural evolution, then information must be believed if it is to influence cultural evolution.

Collective social adaptation to changing conditions is not inevitable. Many societies have maladapted over time, as beliefs that were true for their time caused social problems later, when circumstances changed and beliefs failed to adapt. Beliefs once established are difficult to change. In addition, because we defend our beliefs, they tend to be self-protective. Therefore, to the extent that an influential subgroup's beliefs are different from those of the group, that subgroup's beliefs are not protective of group beliefs. It follows that social evolution from within often comes from newly influential sub-groups with beliefs different from the group, at a time and in circumstances favorable for their acceptance. In these times, new beliefs replace old ones. Reform movements are an example. Examples of externally induced social evolution would be from being conquered, failing in some way to adapt to Nature, or by contact with and emulation of other cultures. To the extent that one or a few individuals control society, their psychogenes and DNA-based behaviors will influence social evolution. In this case, propaganda and information control would be used to influence social evolution by manipulating group beliefs in ways consistent with the beliefs or objectives of those in power. The more control becomes a group activity, the more the controlling group's common psychogenes will influence social evolution.

In the following description of Greek superstitious beliefs, some psychogenes are recognizable today, while others, which are no longer believed, can be found only in historical references. Those early Greek superstitions you recognize, perhaps in a new context, are examples of successful psychogenetic evolution. The ones that, by today's way of thinking, appear to be arcane or peculiar are merely psychogenes that did not survive, at least in our culture. It should also be noted how little if at all some superstition psychogenes have changed.

> Between these upper and nether poles of Greek religion
> ... surged an ocean of magic, superstition, and sorcery;

behind and below the geniuses whom we shall celebrate were masses of people poor and simple, to whom religion was a mesh of fears rather than a ladder of hope. It was not merely that the average Greek accepted miracle stories—of Theseus rising from the dead to fight at Marathon, or of Dionysus changing water into wine:[6] such stories appear among every people, and are part of the forgivable poetry with which imagination brightens the common life. ... What oppressed the pious Greek was the cloud of spirits that surrounded him, ready and able, he believed, to spy upon him, interfere with him, and do him evil. These demons were always seeking to enter into him; he had to be on his guard against them at all times, and to perform magical ceremonies to disperse them.

... Madness was possession by an alien spirit; the madman was "beside himself." In all these cases a ceremony of purification was considered necessary. Periodically homes, temples, camps, even whole cities were purified, and very much as we disinfect them—by water, smoke, or fire.[7] A bowl of clean water stood at the entrance to every temple, so that those who came to worship might cleanse themselves,[8] perhaps by a suggestive symbolism. The priest was an expert in purification; he could exorcise spirits by striking bronze vessels, by incantations, magic, and prayer; even the intentional homicide might, by adequate ritual, be purified.[9]

... Out of this belief in an enveloping atmosphere of spirits came a thousand superstitions, which Theophrastus, successor to Aristotle, summarized in one of his *Characters:*[10]

Superstitiousness would seem to be a sort of cowardice with respect to the divine.... Your Superstitious Man will not sally forth for the day till he have washed his hands and sprinkled himself at the Nine

Springs, and put a bit of bay-leaf from a temple in his mouth. And if a cat cross his path he will not proceed on his way till some one else be gone by, or he have cast three stones across the street. ...[11]

The simpler Greeks believed, or taught their children to believe, in a great variety of bogies. Whole cities were disturbed, at short intervals, by "portents" or strange occurrences, like deformed births of animals or men.[12] The belief in unlucky days was so widespread that on such days no marriage might take place, no assembly might be held, no courts might meet, no enterprise might begin. A sneeze, a stumble, might be reason for abandoning a trip or an undertaking; a minor eclipse could stop or turn back armies, and bring great wars to a disastrous end. Again, there were persons gifted with the power of effective cursing: an angered parent, a neglected beggar might lay upon one a curse that would ruin one's life. Some persons possessed magic arts; they could mix love philters or aphrodisiacs, and could by secret drugs reduce a man to impotence or a woman to sterility.[13] Plato did not consider his Laws complete without an enactment against those who injure or slay by magic arts. Witches are not medieval inventions; note Euripides' Medea, and Theocritus' Simaetha. Superstition is one of the most stable of social phenomena; it remains almost unchanged through centuries and civilizations, ...

Although beliefs are generally described in static terms (something is believed or not), they are much like genes in the way they can be inherited, adapt, evolve over time, and determine characteristics of their possessors. Since our beliefs influence our perception of reality, what we are taught to believe we become. Unlike genes, psychogenes are transmitted from individual to individual and group to group, as well as from generation to generation. They define our organizations, our governments, our religions, our ethnic groups, and the like. And, real or imaginary, psychogenes determine characteristics of culture. Each generation, by education, by ritual, or by neglect passes to the next a unique and altered combination of psychogenes that influences and perhaps defines the next generation.

Nietzsche's *The Three Metamorphoses* in *Thus Spake Zarathustra*, presents an allegory that addresses the process by which psychogenes might be changed. In the allegory, the human spirit metamorphoses by first becoming a camel, then a lion, and then a child. As a camel, the spirit bears many burdens, among them are: "To humiliate oneself in order to mortify one's pride," and "To exhibit one's folly in order to mock at one's wisdom." When the spirit metamorphoses into a lion, it confronts a great dragon that symbolizes God. And each golden scale of the dragon represents a religious belief to which Nietzsche refers as a "Thou shalt!"

> The values of a thousand years glitter on those scales, and thus speaketh the mightiest of all dragons: All the values of things—glitter on me.
>
> All values have already been created, and all created values—do I represent. Verily, there shall be no "I will" any more. Thus speaketh the dragon.

The purpose of the spirit's metamorphosis into a lion was to use its strength to make the creation of new values possible.

> My brethren, wherefore is there need of the lion in the spirit? Why sufficeth not the beast of burden, which renounceth and is reverent?
>
> To create new values—that, even the lion cannot yet accomplish: but to create itself freedom for new creating—that can the might of the lion do.
>
> ... As its holiest, it once loved "Thou shalt": now is it forced to find illusion and arbitrariness even in

the holiest things, that it may capture freedom from its
love: the lion is needed for this capture.

Neitzsche's final metamorphosis of the spirit into the form of a
child symbolized a means of breaking with the past and beginning
anew.

Innocence is the child, and forgetfulness, a new
beginning, a game, a self-rolling wheel, a first
movement, a holy Yea.

Aye, for the game of creating, my brethren,
there is needed a holy Yea unto life: its own will, willeth
now the spirit, his own world winneth the world's
outcast.

A psychogenetic interpretation of Nietzsche's *The Three
Metamorphoses* would be that some inherited psychogenes
denigrate wisdom to discredit rational challenges to religious
psychogenes, which use the past to define the future with
immutable "Thou shalt" beliefs. Each of the dragon's scales
represents a religious psychogene, and to change those
psychogenes requires first, a lion's strength—for society to admit
their arbitrary nature—and second, society's courage, to pass on to
the next generation a new and presumably better psychogenetic
inheritance. The point at which the psychogene changes is when
the altered psychogene is passed to a receptive child. Nietzsche's
allegory demonstrates the strength with which psychogenes
replicate with little alteration from generation to generation, and the
means by which to change them. We become what we are taught to
believe as children. As adults we protect our beliefs because they
have become "self," and any challenge to our beliefs is a challenge
to self. Since our young experience many of the same fears and
hopes their ancestors experienced, they willingly inherit their
ancestors' beliefs, which deal with those same fears and hopes. In
addition, reward, shame, repetition, and so on replicate our
psychogenes quite effectively. Our customs, religions, myths,

habits, traditions, and superstitions, although ostensibly modern, are all essentially beliefs we inherited from our ancestors as surely as we inherited their genes. Perhaps celebrations of the winter solstice, when winter days begin to grow longer, may result from memories of ice-age hardship and the joy our ancestors felt knowing that winter would soon end. Austrians still include winter-solstice demons of darkness with their celebration of Christmas. Holding on to rituals whose meaning has been long forgotten is a measure of the strength of psychogenetic transmission.

Given the persistence of psychogenes, it is easier to redirect them than to terminate them. For this reason, missionaries convert native rituals and celebrations to their own use. In 601, Pope Gregory I instructed his missionaries as follows:

> Let the shrines of idols by no means be destroyed but let the idols which are in them be destroyed. ... let alters be erected ... so that the people, not seeing their temples destroyed, may displace error, and recognize and adore the true God ... And because they were wont to sacrifice oxen to devils, some celebration should be given in exchange for this[.] [T]hey should celebrate a religious feast and worship God by their feasting, so that still keeping outward pleasures, they may more readily receive spiritual joys.[14]

The Encyclopedia Britannica describes the selection of the anniversary of Christmas as follows:

> The exact day and year of Christ's birth have never been satisfactorily settled, but when the fathers of the Church in C.E. 440 decided upon a date to celebrate the event, they wisely chose the day of the winter solstice which was firmly fixed in the minds of the people and which was their most important festival.[15]

Nietzsche identifies the minds of the yet unindoctrinated as the most malleable link in the chain of psychogenetic inheritance. Inasmuch as belief alters perception, as we grow older, the earliest psychogenes we inherited cause us to add selectively to our model of reality, in ways consistent with those psychogenes. This gives disproportionate value to those early beliefs and is the genesis of the education-based battle for our psychogenes. The same process that replicates culture in new generations is used to "program" followers of all kinds for political, religious, and other causes.

Creationists object to biological evolution being taught in public schools because it conflicts with their belief that creation as described in the Bible is literally true. Knowing that their belief system would lose credibility were biological evolution to be accepted by their young, they attempt to control exposure to it by preventing the teaching of it. Failing that, creationists have tried to have creationism taught along with biological evolution, as if mythology and science were in some way equivalent. The effort expended, by those who believe in Creationism, to control the psychogenes of their children is a clear measure of the importance placed on the uninterrupted transmission of psychogenes to the young. In contrast, Roman Catholicism is reinterpreting its mythology to deal with biological evolution. In 1953, Pope Pius XII acknowledged biological evolution with the proviso that it is guided by God. In 1996 Pope John Paul II endorsed evolution as "more than just a theory." To integrate the reality of biological evolution, the Papacy cannot interpret Genesis literally. According to its present view, the soul is said to have entered into humans when we had evolved to the likeness of God. Unlike the Creationist Christians, whose interpretations of their mythology are literal, the Roman Catholic Church interprets its mythological scripture symbolically, not literally.

In his work *Tractatus Theologico-Politicus* the Dutch philosopher Baruch Spinoza (1632-77) wrote:

> All Scripture was written primarily for an entire people,
> and secondarily for the whole race; consequently its

contents must necessarily be adapted, as far as possible, to the understanding of the masses.[16] Scripture does not explain things by their secondary causes, but only narrates them in the order and style which has most power to move men, and especially uneducated men, to devotion. ... Its object is not to convince the reason, but to attract and lay hold of the imagination.[17] ... The masses think that the power and providence of God are most clearly displayed by events that are extraordinary, and contrary to the conception which they have formed of nature. ... They suppose, indeed, that God is inactive so long as nature works in her accustomed order; and *vice versa*, that the power of nature, and natural causes, are idle so long as God is acting; thus they imagine two powers distinct from one another, the power of God and the power of nature.[18]

Middle Eastern peoples thought and wrote allegorically. Therefore, the Scriptures should be read as one reads poetry and not as one reads literal accounts of events; otherwise, the Bible is full of errors, including the description of the Creation in Genesis.

Karen Armstrong, a former Catholic nun who now teaches at the Leo Baeck College for the Study of Judaism and the Training of Rabbis and Teachers, wrote the following in *A History of God*:

When some Western Christians feel their faith in God undermined by the new science, they are probably imagining God as Newton's great Mechanick, a personalistic notion of God which should, perhaps, be rejected on religious as well as on scientific grounds. The challenge of science might shock the churches into a fresh appreciation of the symbolic nature of scriptural narrative.

The idea of a personal God seems increasingly unacceptable at the present time for all kinds of reasons: moral, intellectual, scientific and spiritual.

Feminists are also repelled by a personal deity who, because of "his" gender, has been male since his tribal, pagan days. Yet to talk about "she"—other than in a dialectical way—can be just as limiting, since it confines the illimitable God to a purely human category. The old metaphysical notion of God as the Supreme Being, which has long been popular in the West, is also felt to be unsatisfactory. The God of the philosophers is the product of a now outdated rationalism, so the traditional "proofs" of his existence no longer work. The widespread acceptance of the God of the philosophers by the deists of the Enlightenment can be seen as the first step to the current atheism. Like the old Sky God, this deity is so remote from humanity and the mundane world that he easily becomes *Deus Otiosus* and fades from our consciousness.

The God of the mystics might seem to present a possible alternative. The mystics have long insisted that God is not an-Other Being; they have claimed that he does not really exist and that it is better to call him Nothing. This God is in tune with the atheistic mood of our secular society ... Instead of seeing God as an objective Fact, which can be demonstrated by means of scientific proof, mystics have claimed that he is a subjective experience, mysteriously experienced in the ground of being. This God is to be approached through the imagination and can be seen as a kind of art form, akin to the other great artistic symbols that have expressed the ineffable mystery, beauty and value of life. Mystics have used music, dancing, poetry, fiction, stories, painting, sculpture and architecture to express this Reality that goes beyond concepts. Like all art, however, mysticism requires intelligence, discipline and self-criticism as a safeguard against indulgent emotionalism and projection.[19]

In addition to the influence of theology on our early beliefs, some so-called education experts are engaged in the business of controlling formative psychogenes. Their apparent objective is to reform society by teaching their beliefs to the young under the guise of psychological research. It is a view that sees education as teaching what to think instead of how to think. Their effect on American culture will be interesting to observe as they attempt to stamp out incipient homophobia in two-year-olds and teach the evils of competition to children who must make their way in an increasingly competitive world.

According to an Associated Press story published in *The Daily Progress* of Charlottesville, Virginia on June 30, 1996, R. Jefferson Garnett, chairman of the state Child Care Council, in a letter to the Governor of Virginia, advised that the council had been quietly infiltrated by national groups pushing a radical ideology that is "contemptuous of and antagonistic to the traditional values of Virginia." Garnett wrote that the national groups were trying to shape child day-care services on several fronts, and said that the groups were promoting a college curriculum aimed at turning out "politically correct" day care professionals. They also were pushing "a politicized core curriculum for day care providers ... to be used to form the minds of our children with a radical ideology before they enter the public schools." Garnett said in an interview that state groups were the unwitting pawns of the national organizations. His letter dealt with an investigation of alleged contract steering of a federal block grant by the national groups.

When does education degenerate to indoctrination? George Bernard Shaw's thought: "What we want is to see the child in pursuit of knowledge, and not knowledge in pursuit of the child." Although psychogenes define and perpetuate our culture, we find ourselves in a curious situation. Even though our knowledge of the things of life is greater than that of our ancestors in great part, we accept our ancestors' psychogenes without challenge, indeed, with veneration. These immutable beliefs, fashioned to satisfy the needs and prejudices of people long dead, reach into the future where they may serve a fitting purpose, or perhaps cause great harm.

Compounding the difficulty is that persons held in high social esteem, the shamans and sages of ritual and cultural identity, whose livelihoods and institutions rely on perpetuating our ancestors' psychogenes, are responsible for interpreting and dispensing our fundamental beliefs.

Perhaps part of the agenda of the political correctness movement is directed to preventing and reversing social damage done by the ancient writers of what has been assembled into the Bible. Although prejudice against homosexuals was not unique to biblical times, the psychogenetic power of the prejudice that was written into and is now enshrined in such an influential work makes daunting the task of reversing that psychogene. Equally daunting is dealing with mythological opposition to the Supreme Court's Roe v. Wade decision, which balances the rights of both mother and fetus by gradually diminishing the mother's rights and increasing the fetus' rights as gestation progresses. Here again, if a biblical psychogene interprets destroying a human egg the second after fertilization as equivalent to destroying a human being, the balanced rights achieved by the Roe v. Wade decision would be irrelevant. Notwithstanding the allegorical nature of biblical writings, the narrow belief systems of some mythologists cause them to interpret scripture in the same literal, mindless way that computers perform program instructions. On the other hand, overstating how many people are homeless, or demonizing or belittling people who happen to disagree with something deemed politically correct, suggests that at least some advocates of political correctness may be as emotion-driven as some mythologists.

Our psychogenes determine what we are. They influence our attitudes, expectations, behaviors, and decisions. They give us a view of the world through the lens of belief-altered perception. They become self, and contradictions to them are perceived as personal challenges to ourselves. This reality-distorting process, however, is not tolerated in systems we build to serve us. We rely on computers every day for all sorts of decisions, from aircraft navigation to economic forecasting. Imagine a computer that is influenced by its own reality-altering requirements. How much trust would you place in its decisions?

When criminals justify their acts and condemn their imprisonment, many of us respond with incredulity—they cannot possibly believe what they are saying. But they do. We all perceive and act in a way consistent with our beliefs, and we believe we are correct when we do so. Criminals are no different. Their beliefs are what cause them to act as they do. That is why criminals are "reformed" when they accept an ethical-religious belief system in place of their own.

Challenges need not come from competing beliefs. Prozac, a mind-altering drug, increases the availability of serotonin, a neurotransmitter that gives us positive feelings. Prozac can convert some introverts into extroverts. Because it chemically changes fundamental characteristics of personality, Prozac is seen by some as a chemical threat to "self." It requires us to acknowledge that we are biochemical beings with less control over what we are than we thought. For some, Prozac's capacity to alter our attitudes, expectations, behaviors, and decisions has upset their view of themselves. Self has collided with a mere chemical. Similarly, it was confirmed recently that we respond to pheromones emitted from other people. It is thought we have pheromone receptors in vomero nasal organs (VNO) in our nasal passages. A study was undertaken to determine why college women living in dormitories had synchronized menstrual cycles. In a series of tests at the University of Chicago it was shown that most women exposed to chemicals emanating from other women had their menstrual cycles sped up or slowed down.[20] Other research indicates that pheromones emanating from the skin of persons of the opposite sex can cause us to "feel good." Does our free will in choosing a mate have much in common with that of moths?

If Prozac and pheromones can be disquieting, what will happen when we face the first thinking computer? Attempts to bolster belief in our uniqueness by using creation myths to distance ourselves from the other animals will be dwarfed by the effort required to rationalize "inorganic thought." Then again, unlike the response to Copernicus, the discovery of what some believe may be fossilized life on Mars has thus far been interpreted by the keepers of mythology as compatible with their creation myths. I wonder how the news would have been received if the world were less secular and the Inquisition were still active.

Psychogenes and Organized Ignorance

Reality is what is real to Nature. For us, correct belief about reality is an ideal. What we believe reality to be we assemble into belief systems in which our psychogenes encapsulate the truths of our time—such as they are. The degree to which our reality models fail to conform to or predict reality is the degree to which our psychogenes are defective. That we all perceive reality in our own ways is not to say that we cannot agree on anything or that all models of reality derive from self-serving assumptions or prejudices. If we put aside what we want reality to be and objectively test our beliefs to eliminate personal or other biases, we are more likely to perceive reality as it is. To do this we must expose our beliefs about reality to rational criticism. Scientists do this every day, and their models of reality have been refined well enough for us to rely on them when we fly to distant places, trust the results of computer-processed information, and expect to be cured by medical treatments and devices they created that are consistent with their reality models.

However, that words are used to describe reality makes it easy to mistake words for reality or to equate subjective opinion with objective observation. For some time, social reformers have been redefining social values to be more inclusive of minority views and rights. This is not unique. Contemporary reformers are standing on the shoulders of previous generations of reformers who fought for women's rights, unionism, abolition of slavery, and so on. What is interesting about the present approach is that traditional standards and models that resulted from the efforts of previous reformers are being attacked as totally subjective. This appears to be an attempt to dismiss everything, *en masse*, and to replace it with an egalitarian, politically correct system of beliefs and values. The postmodernist view that everyone is free to define his or her own reality and that we cannot know reality is the philosophical basis some social engineers are using to deny the validity of traditional values and beliefs. Because they feel free to deny the validity of traditional reality models, it appears that some social engineers feel free to dismiss the values and beliefs derived from those reality models. This postmodernist ultra-subjective view perceives science in the same way. Reality for some postmodernists is that the science of mechanics (the behavior of rigid bodies) has more status in science than the science of fluid dynamics (the behavior of gasses and liquids) because men do science and their sexual parts are rigid. Conversely, as this description goes, women are more fluid, and the prejudices of male scientists have relegated fluid dynamics to a position of lesser importance. I have never heard an intelligible statement of this premise. If anything, fluid dynamics relies on more complex mathematics than does simple mechanics. Perhaps those who believe this nonsense are more rigid than they know.

In literature and philosophy, white European males are the culprits.[21] This postmodernist approach to perceiving reality is like that of 18th century solipsists who believed they could destroy the world by going to sleep. If social policy were not being influenced by this kind of self-serving and sometimes paranoid thinking it would be laughable. I wonder how many postmodernist social engineers are rejecting medical treatment for their cancer or heart disease because the treatment technology in great part derives from white European male scientists' reality models. I mention these matters because I do not want my views to be confused with or considered supportive of this kind of political thinking, masquerading as philosophy. When I state that correct belief about reality is an ideal, I presuppose a reality common to us all. The idea that everyone's different subjective realities are equally valid representations of reality, to me, is unintelligible. It appears to be a misguided analogy of the cultural relativist belief that although cultures are different they are equal.

Not only are differences in cultures reflective of differences in their psychogenes, their psychogenetic differences influence how each perceives reality in its own way. In the 19th century, Western colonial governments established trading posts in Melanesia and New Guinea. The indigenous populations were pre-industrial and could not comprehend that the cargoes of goods they coveted were produced by an economic system vastly different from their own. Acting in a manner wholly consistent with their belief system, they turned to their tribal deities and ancestral spirits to deliver cargoes to them. Westerners referred to them as cargo cults. In the 20th century, during the war with Japan, cargoes arrived on the islands once more. This time they were brought by aircraft that landed at newly constructed military airfields. This time their deities and ancestors were prevailed upon to direct the cargo-carrying silver birds to land on airfields they built in forest clearings (small dirt strips with control towers made of lashed logs). Of course no silver birds landed in their clearings, and their efforts to attract cargoes eventually ceased. For the condescending among us, is there any difference between their behavior and ours when we thank our deities for medical "miracles" that, in reality, are delivered to us through the hard work of countless men and women in science and medicine whose knowledge of medical science is to most of us as knowledge of Western manufacturing was to the natives of New Guinea?

Culture is a structured social organism with beliefs and behaviors unique to its time and place, and it evolves with each generation. Its language embodies much of its psychogenetic heritage. Over time, words that represent evolving psychogenes are created, appropriated, or emphasized while other words that represent psychogenes that are falling out of favor become archaic. Star-crossed is a phrase that appears to be gaining in popularity. If so, it may suggest that more of us are deriving comfort from astrology, perhaps owing to disenchantment with or ignorance of science or traditional religions. Words used by different segments of society reflect psychogenetic differences among classes, regions, and the like. Consider the beliefs behind the phrases "filthy rich" and "social Darwinism." Evidence of psychogene migration among cultures can be found in the way our languages evolve. Incorporation of foreign-belief-based words and phrases suggests adoption of the foreign psychogenes those words represent. When societies interact, as during immigration, the minority population is assimilated and much of its psychogenetic inheritance becomes mere stories to its young. In time, succeeding minority generations learn the dominant psychogenes and, if numerous enough, alter the culture as they become part of it. When Incas invaded Ecuador in 1493, they erased Ecuadorian culture. When small groups of Ecuadorians were transported to widespread parts of the Inca Empire, Ecuadorian cultural psychogenes did not survive for lack of "critical mass" in the size of the transplanted Ecuadorian groups. *Critical mass* would be a minimum population sufficient to retain its psychogenetic inheritance by mutually self-validating belief reinforcement. Without Ecuadorian psychogenetic critical mass, Ecuadorian children inherited Incan psychogenes and became Incas.

Changes in climate, technology, population, economic power and the like determine which centers of power and psychogenetic influence will most influence the world. It is as if humanity is a global organism with the psychogenes of different cultures switching on or off over time, causing the influences of different cultures to rise or fall, their interacting psychogenes altering, being altered, and combining, and continually redefining global humanity.

If the psychogenes we inherit are receptive to new beliefs, such beliefs will likely influence our psychogenetic evolution for better or worse. Conversely, those of us who inherit psychogenes that compel rejection of new or foreign beliefs will become inflexible if such beliefs are perceived as a threat to traditional psychogenes. We can be enlightened or stunted by our psychogenetic legacy, and most of us can do little to change it. Modern telecommunications and commerce, by their pervasive nature, tend to spread the psychogenes of foreign cultures. In response to a perceived dilution of French culture, France has established the French Ministry of Culture to prevent foreign influences from making France less French. Similarly, for about two decades a number of Islamic countries have been making an effort to remove Western cultural influences and to strengthen traditional Islamic beliefs. In June of 1998, nineteen countries were represented at a meeting in Canada. The U.S.A. was not invited. The meeting's focus was American cultural dominance. Participants specifically dealt with ways of exempting cultural goods from treaties that lower trade barriers, on the grounds that free trade threatens national cultures. The Ottawa meeting followed a similar gathering in Stockholm, sponsored by the United Nations. The Stockholm meeting resolved to press for special exemptions for cultural goods in another global trade pact, the Multilateral Agreement on Investment.[22]

Although Luddites rioted in opposition to technological change in early 19th century England, attempts to freeze what is thought by some to be an ideal culture are typically seen in religious sects. The Amish are an orthodox Baptist sect that has retained 17th century methods, clothing, and customs as part of its religious belief system. Hasidic (from Hebrew meaning pious) Jews have beliefs that proscribe changes in their dress and appearance, which reflect 18th century Eastern Europe, where and when the sect was founded.

Mass beliefs form a consensus reality that can be quite different from actuality. During 1636 and 1637, almost the entire population of Holland believed that tulips were so valuable that the price continued to spiral upwards as they outbid each other for tulips and tulip futures. This is called the tulip bubble. The bubble burst when illusion exceeded credulity. When prices fell, many were badly damaged financially. A similar event took place in England in the 18th century. The South Sea Company represented that it had special trading access to markets in Central and South America, and sold stock to begin operations. Stock prices rose and continued to rise, with the help of a little manipulation by the company's directors, even though the company never sent a ship to the South Seas. When the bubble burst, Isaac Newton was among the losers.

The tulip bubble and the South Sea Company bubble are examples of highly focused, short-lived, mass psychotic beliefs. While the bubble exists, those inside the bubble cannot see it for what it is. One way of looking at such a phenomenon is to think of each of us as having our own bubble. It is likely that we each have beliefs equivalent to the tulip and South Sea Company bubbles, but because they are not sufficiently commonly held in our immediate communities, they are not cross-validating. Were enough of us to believe the same unreality, our individual bubbles would combine synergistically to form a significant social bubble. As the Internet makes it easier for us to find others of a similar mind, for the first time in history it is facilitating the formation of cyber-bubbles of geniuses, fanatics, and everything in between. Whether a bubble will burst depends on the nature of the believed unreality. Financial bubbles burst because economic reality is material and must balance in the end. Incorporeal or metaphysical psychogenetic bubbles by their nature are not directly subject to objective bursting, and can survive indefinitely or until some consequence of their unreality bursts them. For example, the Salem witch-trial bubble ended abruptly when a highly respected citizen was accused of being a witch.

Psychotic psychogenes accumulate and combine in populations within and over generations. When cross-validation accelerates, a new bubble forms. It might take the form of a utopian political movement or simply a new common perception that some aspect of culture is no longer fashionable. Whatever form it takes, it will be based on unreality and is likely to burst in time, either as it collides with reality or as changes occur in the underlying reasons that created it. And while the bubble persists, those on the inside will denigrate or persecute those on the outside who are audacious enough to suggest that the bubble is not real.

Even though they may understand their deficiencies, at times societies are unable to adapt to changing conditions. Why do we fail to adapt to circumstances that are detrimental to society or even threaten our collective future? The American War Between the States changed the law regarding slavery but did not change the attitudes (beliefs) of a portion of American society. Beliefs cannot be legislated; they must evolve. For some, it would take almost a century before African-Americans began to be seen as equals, and it would take a similar passage of time for some African-Americans to free themselves from the negative psychogenes of slavery.

Individuals act in ways consistent with their beliefs, and so do societies. If adapting to the changing world requires actions that conflict with the core beliefs of those in power, change will take place one funeral at a time. If the funeral rate is too slow relative to the world's rate of change, and if internal stress does not force a change in leadership, such societies will suffer the consequences of their leaders' beliefs. This has been the fate of social experiments such as communism; the 18th century Enlightenment, wherein reason was to prevail in guiding social evolution; and countless political, religious, and utopian movements. The historical record demonstrates how natural selection chooses which psychogenes or psychogenetic organisms survive. The core psychogenes of dead civilizations are not likely to be replicated in a totally different civilization. As "real" as they were in their day, they were the product of unique times and places, and they were often built on largely baseless linkages of cause and effect. To a great extent, they were organized ignorance. Our core psychogenes will probably fare no better. Only the most hubristic among us would think that our own psychogenes will be exempt from this process. What remains to be seen is which of our cherished psychogenes will survive and for how long.

Organized ignorance is an all-too-common manifestation of the biology of belief. We have seen that, although knowledge can self-organize, there is no natural mechanism impelling psychogenetic knowledge to organize in ways consistent with reality. Evolution's fiat is that knowledge be suited to its environment, not that it be correct. For this reason, assemblages of ignorance can survive indefinitely if they are not challenged to adapt. We can live quite comfortably inside bubbles of psychogenetic illusions, given the way in which we acquire our beliefs and the way those beliefs alter our perceptions of the world. To us, the illusions are real. And coping with those illusions is part of the reality experienced by those of us who make every effort to require that our beliefs reflect reality.

Inasmuch as our beliefs can be based on reality or illusion, our belief-altered perceptions necessarily reflect the underlying reality or illusion of our beliefs. Those of us who make every effort to ensure that our beliefs are consistent with objective reality would logically assume that that is the best thing to do. It is necessary if you intend to do quality science, but is it the best assumption for the non-science part of our lives? Are our lives best lived when we have no illusions? Is being correct the same as being content? If the process of living and dying is difficult and even frightening if we perceive it for what it is, then would perceiving life through illusory beliefs provide insulation from psychological traumas and stresses that might otherwise shorten our lives? Are those of us whose psychogenetic inheritance includes believing that myth is reality better off than those of us who perceive reality more clearly? If it were possible to guarantee that an ideal system of mythical beliefs would be socially beneficial, without the destructive consequences common to actual myth systems, would believing in such a myth system not be more comforting and enjoyable than facing cold reality at every turn? For those of us who find ourselves dismissing illusion, these questions may seem odd, as if we have a choice between believing or not believing in illusion, when, in fact, we don't. In addition, accommodating believers of myth who behave ethically for fear of spiritual punishments or in anticipation of spiritual rewards, i.e., out of self-interest, is made no easier when they condemn ethically altruistic nonbelievers as ethical inferiors. What these questions are intended to suggest is that, setting aside the damage that illusory belief systems have done throughout history, it seems apparent that those of us who believe in a comforting myth may live happier and possibly more productive lives by living the illusion and rejecting, perhaps by forced beliefs, the unpleasant realities of life.

The questions we are considering are ageless, and logically flow from the nature of our belief biology. How philosophers and theologians have dealt with them is considered in a subsequent chapter.

Chapter 10
Psychogenes and Cultural Evolution

Cultures do not spontaneously self-assemble. They evolve through the efforts of generations to create the complex of coherent commerce, communications, and institutions for which each society is known. Each new generation must be educated to receive the culture and to pass it on. It can be lost if just one generation fails to sustain it. So too, reversals of fortune may damage or destroy it. The sustaining bounty of Nature can change with the weather or with a more abrupt natural disaster. Harbors can choke with silt. Natural resources can be depleted or squandered. Trade routes can change, leaving prosperous civilizations to wither. New technology in the hands of competitors can lead to economic or military ruin. Institutions essential to social organization may evolve to serve themselves instead of society. The failure or corruption of religious, social, political, or economic leadership can lead to social decay, class conflict, disunity, or destructive wars. Whether written or oral, symbolic or explicit, the essence of any society can be found in its psychogenes. Japanese psychologist Shinobu Kitayama of Kyoto University observed that "[L]argely unspoken, collective assumptions about appropriate social behavior vary greatly from one country or geographic region to another..."[1] While Westerners value personal independence, Easterners value social interdependence. A few relevant Western psychogenes emphasize individuality, independence, and personal achievement. Counterpart Japanese psychogenes subordinate individuality to an interconnected social web and stress sensitivity to the expectations of others concerning right and wrong behavior. Shinobu Kitayama thinks that

> This cultural perspective appears in various forms throughout East Asia. Its adherents tend to write off the

> European-American pursuit of self-esteem as an
> immature disregard for the relationships that nurture
> self-identity. ...[2]

Although psychogenetic evolution is faster than biological
evolution, it often takes a number of generations to observe
fundamental psychogenetic change. From about 750 BCE to 1600
CE Italian beliefs experienced many fundamental changes as Italy
evolved from a republic phase to an empire phase starting with
Julius Caesar, then through decline to Christian domination in the
Dark and Middle ages, and then to the Renaissance and the
beginnings of modern philosophy and science. We will consider
the psychogenetic influences that gave rise to the Roman state, the
consequences of conquering Greece and assimilating its culture, the
psychogenetic influence of the rise of Christianity, and the
influence of Greco-Roman beliefs on Italian psychogenes during
the Renaissance.

Early Roman Psychogenes

In about 753 BCE, Rome began as a small town in central Italy
about 20 miles from the sea. Although it may have begun as an
Etruscan town, it is said that Latins used it as a defense against
Etruscan expansion. Its origins are not clear. Eugene Weber of the
University of California at Berkeley described early Roman core
beliefs as follows:

> The virtues the Romans admired were all related to
> discipline and self-discipline. They believed in
> "Pietas"– respect for established authority and tradition.
> They believed in "Fides" – being true to your
> responsibilities; in "Religio" – the common belief[s]
> that bind men together; and above all in "Gravitas"– the
> sober seriousness that marks a real man. Even the word

"Virtus" means manliness. … True virtue subordinates
the person to the city, the individual to the state. … The
Romans were a conservative people and so they wanted
strong leaders, but not too strong.[3]

Armed with Pietas, Fides, Religio, and Gravitas they encountered
the world, and more by evolution than design, they conquered it. In
the process, Roman practices changed the agriculture, settlement
patterns, and interregional economics of conquered lands. Formerly
independent regions conformed to the Roman model. Large
farming estates replaced smaller farmsteads. Roman economic and
military considerations dislocated populations and altered
traditions, as selected cities became bureaucratic and commercial
centers. As new administrative centers and trade routes brought
some old cities into the republic, other cities withered. Change
created wealth for some and new tax burdens for others. As with
assimilation at other times in human history, old boundaries,
beliefs, traditions, and cultural identities were transformed.[4]

The Assimilation of Early Greek Psychogenes

While this was happening Roman culture was itself evolving. In
conquering Greece, austere, militant Rome took into its culture a
Trojan horse. With Greece came Greek religion, morality, and
philosophy, which had in turn been influenced by older cultures,
including those of Egypt, Phoenicia, Judea, Crete, India, and
Babylonia. The Roman statesman, philosopher Marcus Tullius
Cicero (106-43 BCE) observed that "It was no little brook that
flowed from Greece into our city, but a mighty river of culture and
learning."[5]

Whether the austere discipline of the early Roman Republic
would have remained unchanged as wealth and power concentrated
in Rome is unlikely. That notwithstanding, it is clear that within
about one hundred years of conquering Greece, Rome had been
influenced significantly by the experience. As Rome assimilated its

Greek gifts, Roman psychogenes evolved into Greco-Roman psychogenes, leaving behind the severe beliefs that fostered the Republic. The Greek Trojan horse contributed to the disengagement of the militaristic engine that drove the Roman Republic. Austere Roman gods were replaced by enlightened and self-indulgent Greek gods. With the strength of the Roman State rooted in a combination of mythology, superstition, nationalism, and self-discipline, these changes went to the core of Roman psychogenes. The Greek historian Polybius (200?-118? BCE) wrote:

> The quality in which the Roman commonwealth is most distinctly superior is, in my judgment, the nature of its religion. The very thing that among other nations is an object of reproach – i.e., superstition – is that which maintains the cohesion of the Roman State. These matters are clothed in such pomp, and introduced to such an extent into public and private life, as no other religion can parallel. ... I believe that the government has adopted this course for the sake of the common people. This might not have been necessary had it been possible to form a state composed of wise men; but as every multitude is fickle, full of lawless desires, unreasoned passion, and violent anger, it must be held in by invisible terrors and religious pageantry.[5]

And as government could no longer appeal to the Pietas and Fides of its citizens, increasingly it appealed to their fears through their superstitions and myths. By so doing the government no longer reflected Roman psychogenes; instead, it attempted to manage them. However, government controlling what people believe so that they act in their own best interest is a small step away from having them act in the government's best interest. Wealth and governmental power concentrated as the vigorous psychogenetic inheritance of Rome's creators found fewer and fewer adherents. The tribune Sallust (86?-34? BCE) observed:

As soon as wealth came to be a mark of distinction and an easy way to renown, to military commands, to political power, virtue began to decline. Poverty was now looked on as a disgrace, and a blameless life as a sign of ill nature. Riches made the younger generation a prey to luxury, avarice, pride. Squandering with one hand what they grabbed with the other, they set small value on their own property while they coveted that of others. Honor and modesty, all laws human and divine, were alike disregarded in a spirit of recklessness and intemperance.[7]

The government was making decisions driven by the desire to concentrate power and wealth in the hands of a few. It was alienating its citizens and was becoming accountable only to itself. Power had long been concentrated in a limited number of powerful families and the constant battles for wealth and power eventually took their toll. The republic eventually saw the struggle for power played out in battles among its generals. Not long after Sallust's death, Julius Caesar won the battle of the generals for control of the government. Julius Caesar's assassination was a futile attempt by the Roman Senate to recapture power, but too much had changed for that to be possible. The psychogenes that built the Republic were no longer fashionable. The empire phase had begun.

Within a century, the empire would end its conquests and begin the slow loss of its colonial economic base. Influences that would set the stage for reshaping Italian psychogenes over the next few centuries include class struggle, failing trade, bureaucratic abuses, over-taxation, countless wars, depletion of mineral resources, deforestation, soil erosion, plagues, malaria, dependence on provincial grain production, the loss of markets to provincial competition, balance of trade problems, currency devaluation, the unavailability of capital due to confiscatory taxes, the emigration of capital and labor, rising serfdom, rising costs for armies, doles, public works, and an expanding bureaucracy. The most insidious change was the gradual loss of allegiance to what had become an imperial government. Increasingly, Italians saw their new government as less responsive to and less representative of those who fought to preserve and protect it.

Italy's population of about 6 million represented less than 10 percent of the empire. Its centuries as a colonial economy made it expert at taking and distributing wealth, but left it with little industry. It could no longer support a population dependent on its dwindling colonies. Its middle class suffered from the economic decline and from increasing taxes. Roads and other infrastructure fell into disrepair. Government corruption and bureaucracy increased and its *raison d'être* increasingly became to collect taxes to support and perpetuate itself. Many of the wealthy lived in villas, avoiding the crime and strife in the city. Some left the empire altogether to preserve their assets. Available labor diminished as family size decreased and owning slaves became uneconomic. Farmers in Italy and the colonies were caught between raiding barbarians and the government's tax collectors. As they conveyed their farms to landlords in exchange for protection and a share of the farm's production, they were sewing the seeds of feudalism. With all its problems, Rome remained the intellectual and cultural center of Western Europe, where professors taught literature and philosophy to students from across the increasingly unstable empire. Barbarians at the borders had no interest in such things.

The Assimilation of Early Christian Psychogenes

By the time Christianity began to establish itself in the second century, the Roman Empire had already been weakened. Population decline in the Western empire necessitated importing large numbers of Germanics. They had insufficient time to acquire Greco-Roman psychogenes and could not transmit them to their offspring. Imported Orientals (Middle Eastern peoples), on the other hand, did not acquire or transmit Greco-Roman psychogenes because they wanted to destroy Roman culture. Germanic and Oriental populations increased within the empire as Italian and

Romanized cultures experienced declining populations. Simply by the sizes of their populations, Germanic and Oriental psychogenes were sufficient to dilute and weaken Greco-Roman culture.

What may have been more significant was the effect increasing despotism and declining religious fervor had on the Roman's sense of patriotism. The conquest of Greece marked the beginning of religious decline, as the old gods became less and less relevant. With patriotism and religion so intertwined, patriotism declined along with the old religious fervor. The source of the Roman character—and in turn the stability of the Roman state—was gone. In time, it was replaced by Christian pacifism, which would pray for Rome, not fight for it.

The transition to Christian psychogenes was not pleasant. Roman emperors were treated with the respect accorded deities. For a Roman patriot, burning incense before the emperor's statue was equivalent to an American pledging allegiance to the flag. It was a matter of God and country. Americans during World War II and Romans in the first century would have found much in common in their fusions of religion and patriotism. General George Patton's request that his chaplain write a prayer for God to grant clear weather so he could kill the enemy would have made perfect sense to Patton's Roman counterparts. Christians, on the other hand, rejected the Roman belief that religion was subordinate to the state. To a Christian, treating the emperor with the respect accorded a deity represented polytheism and idolatry. In addition, Christians were advised by their leaders to refuse military service. Their allegiance was to Christ, not to Caesar.

What was the underlying cause of this turn of events? It was a time when national and tribal identities were subordinated to the central government, and when non-Romans had little power in dealing with the Roman State. The individual was powerless and this powerlessness was fertile ground for a new, fortifying mythology. Christ's new mythology acknowledged that their lives were veils of tears and promised an eternal and idyllic life after death for those who believed. By promising eternal life, Christianity overcame the fear of death. It gave power to the powerless by claiming moral victory through love and tolerance. That myth created strength was not new. However, in a time of God-kings this mythology empowered Christians to defy the state. This mythology provided a God who supported his worshipers and not Caesar. By separating church and state, the new mythology denied Caesar the power of myth as a governing tool, and in particular as a means to rally the population to defend the borders. Roman Christianity kept church and state apart until Emperor Constantine recombined them by embracing Christianity.

The average Roman saw Christian disinterest in earthly matters, including defending the Empire, as shirking civic duty, unpatriotic, and a threat to the future of the Empire. In contrast to other mythologies of the day, Christianity was perceived by the common Roman as aloof and condescending. In time, dislike for Christians permeated the Empire. The government was encouraged to punish them for insulting the state and the gods.

Although there was an orthodox state mythology, other mythologies were generally tolerated provided they paid at least token respect to orthodox gods and the emperor. Jews were exempted from emperor-worship. Christians, initially thought to be Jews, received the same exemption. Eventually, growing popular hostility toward Christians was joined by resentment in government for overt Christian disrespect for the emperor and the state. Inevitably, persecutions began when the government came to perceive Christians as subversives. The level of persecution varied over the years. It was particularly severe during barbarian attacks. As the population, stirred by patriotism and fear of invasion, increased their religious fervor, they were confronted by Christian pacifism and disdain for the Roman military and Roman gods.

Near the end of the second century, some Romans attempted to revive the old Roman faith by attacking Christian myths with reasoned arguments. They realized that the Empire could not protect itself from barbarian threats if Christian pacifism were to become dominant. These attempts notwithstanding, Christian ranks continued to grow. Early converts were mostly working-class Romans.

As persecutions became more violent, initial popular resentment of Christians turned to sympathy and respect, as persecuted Christians accepted their fate with calm certainty. Some Romans risked their lives to protect Christians, instead of condemning them as unpatriotic. In 311, Galerius, Emperor of Rome (305-311 CE), promulgated an edict of toleration that recognized Christianity as a lawful religion.

Accelerating decline of the Empire during the third century caused many to find comfort in the fortifying myths of Christianity. With its ranks swelling, the Christian Church built cathedrals, and, with the Christians' new status, their resentment of non-Christians diminished. The Christian prohibition against marrying non-Christians was eased. Christians, earlier called atheists by their Roman theological adversaries, now referred to pre-Christian Romans as "pagans" from *pagani* (peasants), possibly because the peasant class was the last to convert to Christianity.

Emperor Constantine (285?-337 CE), a statesman first and a supplicant second, realized that, although Christianity was a minority religion, it was replacing the old faith. He saw that Christians were strong, brave, and united by strong beliefs while the non-Christian majority no longer had the zeal of their fathers that derived from confident belief in myths of a simpler time. He personally had seen Christian ranks grow despite three persecutions.

In 312, Constantine prepared to battle Maxentius for control of the Western Roman Empire. From his youth to this time in his life, Constantine had worshipped the Roman sun god Sol, as did his father.[7] The day before battle, he claimed to have seen a flaming cross in the sky with the inscription "in this sign conquer."[9] On the day of battle, he claimed to have dreamed that a voice commanded him to have his army's shields marked with a symbol representing Christ. His partly Christian army carried these symbols into battle. Constantine defeated Maxentius at the battle of the Mulvian Bridge, nine miles from Rome. In so doing, he became emperor of the Western Roman Empire. Eleven years later, by defeating Licinius, Constantine became emperor of both the Eastern and Western Empires.

The Christian Rejection of Greco-Roman Psychogenes

When Constantine declared himself a Christian, the metamorphosis of Roman religious psychogenes was complete. In about three hundred years, Christianity had grown from a persecuted minority religion to the orthodox religion of the Roman Empire. There is reason to believe that, at the time of his conversion, Constantine was performing the act of a statesman.[10] In *The Historia Augusta,* Constantine is quoted as saying "It is Fortuna that makes a man emperor."[11] Before he converted to Christianity, Constantine had appointed non-Christian scholars and philosophers to his court.[12] After his conversion, he paid little attention to Christian ritual and theological concerns, unless they influenced matters of state. His relationship with the bishops of the Church was as a statesman with his administrators. His relationship with Christianity was symbiotic. In acquiring the political influence of the Church, which now taught the divine right of kings to its flock, Constantine consolidated and expanded his power. The Church, in endorsing Constantine, inherited the ecclesiastical administrative structure and mystical ritual of pre-Christian Rome. The business of governing perfected by Rome passed to the Christian Church. It would be used to spread Christianity throughout the fading empire. Rome, thereby, would become the center of Christian Europe for the next twelve centuries. But unlike Roman polytheism, Christianity was not tolerant of competing mythologies. Constantine's pact would lead to Christian repression of competing mythologies and of the science, philosophy, literature, and art of Greco-Roman culture. Acceptance by the Church of certain high-living aspects of pre-Christian Rome led a few devout Christians to initiate the monastic movement to bring the Church more in line with the teachings of Christ. Early arguments about whether the trinity represented polytheism were settled to the satisfaction of Church bishops with the help of Constantine. The Christian Church was now ready to create a Holy Roman Empire. Salvian, a priest of Marseilles, said this of the time, perhaps with some expected exaggeration:

> [A]dultery and drunkenness are fashionable vices, virtue and temperance are the butts of a thousand jokes, the name of Christ has become a profane expletive among those who call Him God.[13] The Roman world is degenerating physically, has lost all moral valor, and leaves its defense to mercenary foreigners. How should such cowards deserve to survive? The Roman Empire is either dead, or drawing its last breath, even at the height of its luxury and games. *Moritur et ridet*—it laughs and dies.[14]

After deriding Roman values, Salvian went on to extol Christian Germanic tribes whose psychogenes seem to include an improbable combination of Pietas, Fides, Religio, Gravitas, and benevolence. With *Pax Romana* a distant memory, barbarians sacked Rome while Christians used Roman roads and governance to spread Christianity and purge Greco-Roman psychogenes from the former empire. For the next nine hundred years, Christian psychogenes permeated Italy, and early attempts to resurrect Greco-Roman psychogenes were thwarted by Christian Popes in Rome. However, at its peak, the Roman Empire extended from the Crimea to Gibraltar and from the Euphrates to Hadrian's Wall. Greco-Roman psychogenes were passed on to Arab scholars who later reintroduced them into Europe in the 12th century.

> To understand the Middle Ages we must forget our modern rationalism, our proud confidence in reason and science, our restless search after wealth and power and an Earthly paradise; we must enter sympathetically into the mood of men disillusioned of these pursuits,

standing at the end of a thousand years of rationalism, finding all dreams of utopia shattered by war and poverty and barbarism, seeking consolation in the hope of happiness beyond the grave, inspired and comforted by the story and figure of Christ, throwing themselves upon the mercy and goodness of God, and living in the thought of His eternal presence, His inescapable judgment, and the atoning death of His Son.[15]

The Christian Dark and Middle Ages experienced their own peculiar psychogenetic evolution. In 1513, sixty years after the death of the last Caesar, with the fall of the Eastern Roman Empire to the Turks, and four years before Martin Luther's theses, Italian political theorist Niccolo Machiavelli wrote the following prophecy, reminiscent of Salvian's prediction for the Romans of his day:

Had the religion of Christianity been preserved according to the ordinances of the Founder, the state and commonwealth of Christendom would have been far more united and happy than they are. Nor can there be a greater proof of its decadence than the fact that the nearer people are to the Roman Church, the head of their religion, the less religious are they. And whoever examines the principles on which that religion is founded, and sees how widely different from those principles its present practice and application are, will judge that her ruin or chastisement is near at hand.[16]

The intervening events that brought Christian Europe to the threshold spoken of by Machiavelli were examined in part in *The Columbia Encyclopedia's Crimes Against The Truth*, written by Joseph McCabe in 1950. As a young Englishman of 19 years, Joseph McCabe (1867-1955) became a Franciscan monk. Unlike the Catholic priest Jean Meslier, whose disagreement with Church teachings became public only after his death, McCabe left the order after ten years and expressed his disagreement with the Church in a long career as an author and lecturer. In his lifetime, he wrote about 250 books and gave perhaps 4,000 lectures on the subject.

In fairness to the Columbia Encyclopedia, we should note that Joseph McCabe also wrote *Lies and Fallacies of the Encyclopedia Britannica*. As it presents Joseph McCabe's analysis of aspects of Christian history from the Roman era to the Renaissance, his writing demonstrates in particular how belief management can be used to shape and perpetuate our psychogenes. Inasmuch as *The Columbia Encyclopedia's Crimes Against The Truth* may be difficult to obtain, the relevant portion follows:

> In view of all this [McCabe's analysis of the politics of publishing encyclopedias] we know what to expect in the field of history, which today is more dreaded by the Church than science because in its own version of European history it rivals Baron Munchhausen. Articles of an historical nature show generally—history. In my criticism of this I complained in the first place of the way in which it slighted the most notable advances, from the modern angle, in the Greek-Roman civilization—the Ionic-Epicurean line of thought and its fine results in the science of Alexandria and the social-welfare schemes of the Roman Empire—and later attempts, foiled by the popes in the Dark Age, to bring the race back to this line. The objection applies in full force to the new encyclopedia. The growth of a sound conception of the universe and life in the ancient world is ignored, and the work of the Ostrogoths, the Lombards, and particularly the Arabs is miserably undervalued.
>
> On the other hand the Catholic myth that their Church, instead of bringing darkness upon civilization, brought light into a dark world and made heroic efforts to preserve it after the collapse of the Roman Empire is

sustained in hundreds of articles. In the list of the popes, which is obviously borrowed from the Catholic Encyclopedia, 40 out of the first 50 are described as saints. The halo decorates even Victor I (friend of the most brazen concubine in the harem of the debauched Emperor Commorlus), Collistus (ex-slave and, imprisoned for theft, and a corrupter of the church), Damasus (who got elected by his followers murdering 150 of those of his rivals, an acknowledged forger of lies and myths, and the only pope who was indicted by the civil authorities for adultery), Boniface I (who, fought his way to the throne), Zosimus I (whom some historians think as bad as Damasus,) Symmachus (repeatedly accused of adultery), and Hormisdas (whose son, "St." Silvarius, succeeded to the papacy). The Church, moreover, gives the first 30 popes their halo on the ground that most of them earned the crown of martyrdom, whereas, even the Catholic experts on the martyrs like Duchesne, Delehaye, Ehrhard, *et cetera*, admit that only one Pope ever died for his faith. Even the ancient legend of the seven persecutions of the early church finds place in this up-to-date encyclopedia. History has recognized for the last hundred years that there were only two.

The Dark Age, it seems, has been so completely abolished by the new historians that it has not here been considered worthy of a special entry. It is explained in the article on the Middle Ages that at one time the phrase Dark Age was applied to the whole of the Middle Ages. No historian ever did this, so the encyclopedia's little joke—that we now see that the darkness was not so much in the period as in the mind of those who considered it—falls flat. Nor is the encyclopedia more impressive when, following the new historians, it gives the Carolingian Renaissance as one of the great discoveries that make the Dark Age light. Our encyclopedia even says that "the preservation of classical literature was due almost entirely to his initiative"—which is more daring, even than the myth that "the monks preserved the classics"—but it admits that he is "scarcely to be considered educated by later standards." In point of fact his secretary tells us that though he tried hard, he never learned to write. However, the encyclopedia tells us that he was a man of such "simple manners" and led such a "frugal existence" that the Church declared him "Blessed" (or a semi-saint). I should not have thought that any cultivated person was unaware that he was a savage in war (the Saxon war), and that he and his daughters and court had a notorious contempt for the Church's supreme virtue, chastity.

As I showed in the earlier volume, it is now generally agreed in history that the work of Charlemagne has been greatly exaggerated and that it was in any case wiped out in the next generation. I admit that the Columbia could quote in its support practically the whole of the historians, but listen to this. In its article on Pope Nicholas I, who became Pope 54 years after the death of Charlemagne, the Catholic Encyclopedia says about the time of his accession: "Christianity in western Europe was then in a melancholy condition. The Empire of Charlemagne has fallen to pieces. ... Christendom seemed on the brink of anarchy. ... There was danger of a universal decline of the higher civilization." Contemporary with Charlemagne was the Lombard civilization in Italy which did make a permanent impression. Our encyclopedia barely mentions it. The pope and Charlemagne (who got most of his teachers from it) did their best to destroy it.

The article on "Education" (which is shorter than the following article on King Edward I) has not a single word about the system of universal free schooling for the sons of the workers in the Roman empire which had no equal in history until the French Revolution. Thus the reader who has been inoculated with the monstrous lie that "the church first gave the world schools" is encouraged to persevere in it. Much the same is the impression given by the article "Libraries." There is a reference to the "great public libraries of the Roman Empire," of which it is lightly said that as they were "filled with pagan learning" they were destroyed or burned. We are told also that the Arabs "collected and preserved many libraries." Not a word is said about the burning of the Alexandrian Library and others by the monks and Christian mobs long before the Middle Ages began, and, as no figures are given, the reader gets a totally false perspective. He might be less disposed to surrender the phrase Dark Age if he were told that the Alexandrian Library had about 500,000 books, and the Arab royal library at Cordova (in the 10th century) had the same number, but no monastic library in the whole of Europe had as many as 2,000 books (99 percent religious), and very few had 500 throughout the Middle Ages. Yet this is what the chief of the new historians, Professor Thompson, has established in his defense of medieval culture.

The article on Roger Bacon says of his 30-year confinement in monasteries of his order, which is fully substantiated in the most reliable biography of him, in the Dictionary of National Biography:

"Bacon would seem to be involved in some obscure trouble with the authorities of the Church, but there is no evidence that his difficulties were caused by his interest in science, and it would seem more likely that they were due to his notoriously pugnacious disposition."

Instead of explaining that, as is now well known, his remarkable scientific learning was derived entirely from the Spanish Arabs through a school of their science at Oxford, it is scurvily granted only that he was "acquainted with Arab Aristotelianism." Aristotle's share in his science was like a single pebble in a truck-load of ballast.

The article on the Arabs is just as inadequate, and in the article on Sylvestus II (Gerbert) not a single word is said about the Arab character of his learning and his studies in Cordova. Under the title Canossa we get the discredited myth that the Emperor Henry stood or knelt three days barefoot in the snow begging absolution of the pope; a legend that Professor Thompson himself refutes. Under "Chivalry" we get the full flavor of the Catholic myth of the Age of Chivalry.

My readers will have noticed that in the field of historical lies this is my pet aversion, for this purely mythical moral splendor during three centuries is still generally believed outside serious history (and by most of the new historians) and regarded as one of the best redeeming features of the Middle Ages, while every historical expert on any country in Europe during the period (1100-1400) shows that it is the exact opposite of the truth. Yet here in the Columbia you get the myth in all its virginal freshness. There is not even a hint that it was ever disputed. The "ethical code" of the knights, who were almost entirely on the moral level of Hitler's worst troops, is said to be "Still the basis of the ethic of gentlemanly conduct." We get unctuous passages like this: "The cult of the Virgin, with which chivalrous love is intimately connected, was the supreme expression of the glorification of womanhood."

That is as flagrant a defiance of the facts as the saying of a Jesuit writer that the Inquisition was a model court for the administration of justice. For the overwhelmingly greater part of the women of the Age of Chivalry were "viragoes," as Professor Luchaire calls them, who despised tenderness and chastity. It is only when the Inquisition got busy that we find a few pious sonnets; and Bayard, who is here given as a type of chivalry, does not belong to the age of chivalry at all. The standard work of Leon Gautier is given as the chief authority, yet he says, often in violent language, just the opposite of what the dreamy writer of the article says. I notice that peculiarity in several places.

The Donation of Constantine, the blatant forgery by which the popes claimed that the Emperor Constantine had bequeathed nearly the whole of Italy to the papacy, may seem an awkward document to mention when the Catholic Encyclopedia acknowledges that it was a forgery. But Our encyclopedia glides gracefully— much more easily than its Catholic colleague—over the thin ice. It seems that it was "never of great practical value." In point of fact, as I pointed out 30 years ago, Pope Hadrian, in whose court it was forged, expressly reminds Charlemagne (Ep. LX) that it was the basis of the swollen territorial claims of the papacy, and this makes it clear that the forged document was shown to the Frank monarch when he was taken, melodramatically, to the "tomb of St. Peter," to sign the document which, by the way, mysteriously disappeared, in which he awarded nearly the whole of Italy to the pope. The Columbia adds that "it was not, as is sometimes asserted, universally accepted in the Middle Ages." The undisputed fact is that from the date of Charlemagne's award (774) to within a few years of the end of the Middle Ages (as fixed by this encyclopedia) it was universally accepted. To the great anger of the papacy, which severely punished him, Lorenzo Valla then exposed the forgery, but the Church insisted that it was genuine and up-held it until the 19th century. Equally false is the statement that the pope's temporal power did not rest on the Donation of Charlemagne but on that of his father, Pepin. That monarch awarded the pope only the territory he had conquered in Italy, which was far smaller; and Pepin, an entirely ignorant and boorish soldier, was duped by a forged "letter from St. Peter in heaven," which we still have, just as Charlemagne was duped by the forged Donation of Constantine.

For the errors and misleading statements in the devout article on the Crusades I should require an essay and must refer my readers to my discussion of these piratical expeditions in my earlier volume. Our encyclopedia regards them as an outcome of "the highest point which religious devotion had reached in Western Europe," though it does admit an infiltration of less august motives. The description of the knights of Europe at the beginning of the 12th century as very devout is humorous. They were then in the most brutal and licentious stage of the so-called Age of Chivalry. In calling for the first crusade the pope, whose sermon we still have, held out to the knights the prospect of rich loot, and all experts on the crusades acknowledge that, except in a few cases, the motives were greed, love of fighting, and liberation from the heavy feudal burdens at home. Historians admit also that the Turks did not hinder pilgrimages as the Columbia says, and a crusade was unnecessary. The pope chiefly aimed at bringing the Greek Church under Rome. Naturally the perfidy and horrors of the Fourth Crusade, which I described in the earlier volume, do not appear in this article.

Just before the Fourth Crusade the Knights whet their appetites for loot in the massacre of the Albigensians, and this foulest episode of the 13th century is gravely misrepresented. The reader has not the least idea of its magnitude. It was not the people of Albi (one city) but a population of hundreds of thousands all over Southeastern France that defied the church: not because they all embraced what is called the Albigensian creed, which few strictly adopted, but because of the corruption of the church. The article does not tell that it took 300,000 soldiers several years to reduce the region, so numerous were the rebels. The article says that the action of Pope Innocent III in sending a body of preachers to them was decisive—they notoriously accomplished nothing and that is why the Pope turned to violence but their efforts were hampered by "the war which soon broke out." and this war was "overshadowed by political interests from the first." This is a miserable sophistication of the whole ghastly story in order to conceal the guilt of the pope. Not a word is said about the duplicity with which he engineered the "war," and the reader has no suspicion of the mighty volume during three or four years of rape, loot, and murder, as described by contemporary Catholic writers.

Out of it all, as the encyclopedia rightly says, emerged the Inquisition; for even after the appalling carnage and the ravishing of the most civilized part of Christendom large numbers continued to reject the faith. So this grim institution was, says the encyclopedia, just "an emergency measure"—it lasted in Catholic countries until the 19th century—and in the usual fashion of Catholic propagandists it tells the reader that the worst evils were due to the civil authorities and the people, who, in their horror of heresy, compelled the gentle papal authorities to act. "Burning of heretics was not common in the Middle Ages" the writer says. The editors have overlooked the fact that in the article on Witchcraft we read, "Burning, as for heresy, was common." He omits also to remind the reader that until the 11th century the population was too ignorant, the clergy generally too illiterate, and sensual, and the middle class too scanty for heresy to spread, and that burning began as soon as heresy began. But the chief fault of the article is to exonerate the clergy at the expense of the laity. The inquisitors, it says, were always anxious to avoid the extreme penalty but the civil rulers were sterner. All the greed and sacrifice of the innocent was, the writer says, because the confiscated property of the heretic went to them. It did not. It was divided between the informers, the Inquisitors, and the civic power. The writer does not perceive how much he (or she) gives away in saying that the civic authorities got the loot. It was just because civic rulers were so reluctant to persecute that the papacy tempted them with this loot, besides threatening them with excommunication. The writer also says that torture was used against "a long-standing papal condemnation of torture (e.g. by Nicholas I)." When a writer says "e.g." he means that he is quoting one out of many others he could quote. He not only could not quote any others but Nicholas I himself never issued a general condemnation of torture. Neither that fanatical historian of the early medieval popes, Father Mann, nor the Catholic encyclopedia credits him with this. And at the close of this remarkable article the writer warns the reader against Lea's scholarly work on the Inquisition as out-dated and inaccurate, and recommends instead a zealous French Catholic and two other works that I cannot trace.[17]

As we learned from the evolution of Roman government, any organization that becomes accountable only to its administrators will eventually serve their purposes while paying lip service to the organization's ostensible purpose. In the case of faith-based organizations, accountability disappears when members are required to have faith in the judgment of their administrators. This is a particularly dangerous arrangement, since faith-based belief systems are, by their nature, subjective and are not inclined to objective standards. By denying reason and requiring faith as payment for peace of mind, administrators of the faith are free to indulge their prejudices, define anyone as an enemy, and commit any act—all justified in the name of their faith.

The Rebirth (Renaissance) of Greco-Roman Psychogenes

In itself, the corruption referred to by Machiavelli was not enough to bring change. The 12th century was a time when the splendor of Moorish culture in southern Spain contrasted sharply with the enforced Christian unenlightenment of Europe. By introducing his commentaries on Aristotle, the Moorish physician-philosopher Averroes reawakened European philosophy that had been relegated by Augustine and others to searching for rational support for theological dogma. As the 13th century began, William of Ockham and philosopher Marsilius of Padua (1290?-1343? CE) openly challenged Church dogma with rediscovered Aristotelian logic. By the 14th century, the rediscovery of Greco-Roman culture blossomed into the Italian Renaissance (rebirth). Life was seen once again as an opportunity and not merely as a veil of tears. Lasting some 200 years, the Italian Renaissance rediscovered humanism, philosophy, classical art, science, architecture, and literature, and returned secular learning to Europe. Among the resurrected psychogenes, intellectual freedom reappeared after languishing for almost one thousand years. Thanks to Arab scholars, the evolving culture of Italians had recaptured from their Roman ancestors the best essence of their psychogenetic heritage. By the 16th century, the rebirth of Greco-Roman psychogenes had begun to return religion to its earlier position as bishop on the chessboards of Europe, and had laid the foundation for the present blossoming of the second secular era of Western science and philosophy.

By this same process of psychogenetic evolution, each of us has inherited the evolved psychogenes of our own unique cultural heritage. And, in turn, we will play our part in their evolution. Although there are considerable differences in the ways cultures around the world have evolved, what is not different is the psychogenetic process by which they evolved. It is an evolutionary process that is fundamental to the biology of belief. Much like our biological evolution, our cultures evolve by "genetic" inheritance, creation and commingling. However, unlike the fossils Nature has preserved, which fix for all time what our ancestors were, the intangible nature of beliefs provides us with multiple histories, some based on the best objective evidence available and others based on what we would like our ancestors to have been.

Chapter 11

The Noble Experiments and Aristotle's Resurrection

Which beliefs we deem worthy of acceptance depends, among other things, on how our amygdalas and prefrontal lobes influence our perceptions. These brain structures have shaped, in large part, our history and our cultures. Both philosophers and shamans have sought—and still seek—answers to questions we assume are valid: how did the universe come to be, why does it exist, is it influenced by an intelligent force, does it have a beginning and an end, is it without limit, why do we exist, what are we, have we lived before, will we live after our present existence, are our lives predetermined, do our bodies each have a personal spirit, what rules or concepts should guide us as we live our lives, and so on. In attempting to answer these questions, philosophers are motivated by curiosity and a love of wisdom. Shamans seek to assuage fear of the unknown, to provide comfort to those who rely on myth, and to influence the spirit world of their particular mythology. The word *philosopher* is derived from the Greek words, *philo* (love) and *sophia* (knowledge or wisdom). *Shaman* is derived from the Sanskrit word *sramanah* (religious exercise). The noble experiments describe how philosophers and shamans have dealt with our most fundamental fears and our need to understand the how and why of our universe, and how they have sought to encourage us to act ethically despite our inherited primitive passions.

The Noble Early Greek Attempt to Replace Myth with Reason

Shamans appeared in our history long before philosophers. The animism of which shamans are an integral part probably began before our ancestors first practiced ritual burial—perhaps 70,000 years ago. In the West, early animistic mythologies evolved into animal-god worship, and later into the worship of gods in human form. Such mythologies evolved through the millennia until about 600 BCE. At that time the budding Greek philosophers, beginning with Thales (624?-546? BCE), began using their developing discipline of logical analysis to examine the things around them. Included among those things were Greek myths about gods, souls, and creation such as were recorded in the *Iliad*, *Odyssey*, and *Theogony*, written earlier by Homer and Hesiod. Unlike the pre-Socratic Greek philosophers, shamans approach understanding Nature through intuition and the interpretation of dreams. *The Encyclopedia of Psychology* describes the influence of dreams at the dawn of Western culture as follows:

> There can be no doubt about the salience of dreams in the ancient world. The written records provide profuse evidence of their prophetic, religious, and curative significance to the people of those times.
>
> One of the first writings of importance was the Assyrian epic of Gilgamesh, which was written in the third millennium. This half-divine hero was introduced to his companion Enkidu in two dreams. Enkidu became the interpreter of Gilgamesh's dreams, which were messages from the gods and guided the two in their human adventures. ... The cuneiform libraries of the Babylonia and Chaldean peoples contain large numbers of dream recordings and translations. ...
>
> The Upanishad writings of India from about 1000 BCE contain long passages about dreams and their importance in spiritual life. Two very familiar sources

attest to the early role and presence of dreams: Homer's *Iliad* and *Odyssey* and the Old Testament. In the opening of the *Iliad*, Zeus sends a dream figure to Agamemnon, which urged the attack on Troy. The presence of dreams directs much of the continued action and continues in the *Odyssey* with the dreams of Penelope about the return of her husband, Odysseus. It was the uncertainty of these latter dreams that led to the description of dreams that passed gates of ivory (true dreams) and those that passed through the obscure gates of horn (false dreams). The Old Testament speaks of the important role of dreams from Genesis through Zechariah. God spoke to Abraham in the night informing him of the Covenant between God and his people and reiterated his message to Jacob. ...

The important role of dreams continues in the New Testament. One need only to point to the annunciation dream of the birth of Christ: "But when he thought on these things, behold an angel of the Lord appeared unto him in a dream, saying, Joseph, thou son of David, fear not to take unto thee Mary thy wife; for that which is conceived in her is of the Holy Ghost" (Matthew 1:20).[1]

Although the primary approach of philosophers to understanding Nature is through rational, analytical thought, their perceptions are altered by their inherited beliefs. What some early philosophers believed about dreams is described in *The Encyclopedia of Psychology*.

The treatment of dreams can be found in the writing of most of the great early Greek philosophers, e.g., Pythagoras, Heraclitus, and Democritus. Plato clearly took dreams quite seriously as seen in his dialogue *Crito*. Here he describes Socrates' dream about his impending death. In *The Republic* he discusses the emergence of the dark, instinctual aspects of persons in dreams.

In this pervasively supernatural dream world there are two remarkable exceptions: the writings of Aristotle and Cicero (Webb, 1990). Each flatly denied the supernatural prophetic role of dreams. Aristotle viewed dreams as residual sensory impressions and accounted for their unusual quality in terms [of] our reduced level of "reasoning" during sleep and their uncontrolled "running" and "collisions." Cicero considered dreams to be "phantoms and apparitions." He suggests that we should pay no more attention to dreams than we do to the products of drunks or the insane. He suggested that to solve a problem, such as whether a voyage would be successful, [we] consult an expert, such as a navigator.[2]

Aristotle's work *On Prophesying by Dreams* gives us an insight into what early peoples thought dreams were. Generally, dreams were believed able to predict events.

The fact that all persons, or many, suppose dreams to possess a special significance, tends to inspire us with belief in it [dreams foretelling the future], as founded on the testimony of experience; … even scientific physicians tell us that one should pay diligent attention to dreams, and to hold this view is reasonable also for those who are not practitioners, but speculative philosophers.

Some early Greeks believed it quite conceivable that dreams might be indications and causes of future events. However, they believed that inasmuch as some lower animals and inferior humans also dream, dreams were not sent by God. Most prophetic dreams, they thought, were mere coincidences, especially those in which the dreamer was unlikely to participate in the predicted event.

They believed that dreams were distorted images of future events propagated back in time to us like ripples on water. If an event prophesied in a dream did not take place it was the result of "movement" during dreaming that interfered with propagations from the future event. They analogized propagation of motion in air or water, which continues after the cause has ceased, to sleeping persons perceiving movement propagated by future events.

Why did Greeks and others believe that fate or Gods predestined their lives? Did their belief that some dreams about the future were true force them to conclude that their future was scripted for them? Were their dreams glimpses of a future over which they had no control? Were oracles, soothsayers, and prophets as well as prophetic dreams means by which to see their destiny? Have dreaming and hallucinating shaped our mythology and our history?

For the early Greek philosophers who most influenced the evolution of Western culture, rational thought was more a goal than a reality—much as it is today. Their social and mythological psychogenes, together with the planning assumption and extra-experiential intuition, created a kind of myth-reality hybrid. Not unexpectedly, the Greek experience with myth and reason exemplifies how we have dealt with these two aspects of our nature over the intervening millennia. But when the Greeks applied reason to questions of mythology it was a new experience. For them, all things were possible, at least initially. So began the early Greek attempt to teach ethics to the masses using reason instead of myth.

Many Greek philosophers before Socrates questioned the truth of myth and found it wanting. Subsequent philosophers, such as Plato (c. 427-347 BCE) and Epicurus (341?-270 BCE), attempted to create non-mythical ethical systems to replace discredited myth-based morality. In the end, however, philosophy could not satisfy those whose lives were filled with disappointment, suffering, and fear. For the Greeks, a rational philosophical view of life was probably more an ideal than an attainable reality. After various attempts to replace myth with reason, Zeno of Citium (336-264 BCE) founded Stoicism in 308 BCE. Zeno believed that humans should be free from passion and should calmly accept life's events as the unavoidable result of the natural order. His view recognized that myth was rooted in our emotional nature and he tried to remove myth by removing emotion. His was an emotionless view of life in a very emotional world. The conquests of Alexander (356-323 BCE) in the East flooded Greece with mystic cults. Although Zeno denied the existence of gods, after his death Stoics tried to address the emotional needs of the masses by incorporating into Stoicism emotion-assuaging Asiatic and Semitic mythical beliefs. As Greek Stoicism evolved from philosophy into theology, the noble experiment of the Greek philosophers drew to a close. In the words of Will Durant,

> There were many who could not find in life the consolations that had satisfied Epicurus; poverty, misfortune, disease, bereavement, revolution, or war overtook them, and all the counsels of the sage left them empty-souled. ...
>
> Philosophy, like a prodigal daughter, after bright adventures and dark disillusionments, gave up the pursuit of truth and the quest of happiness, returned repentant to her mother, religion, and sought again in faith the foundations of hope and the sanctions of charity. Stoicism, while seeking to construct a natural ethic for the intellectual classes, sought to preserve the old supernatural aids for the morality of the common man, and, as time went on, gave a more and more religious color to its own metaphysical and ethical thought. ...[3]
>
> In this philosophy we find the sense of sin that was to play so stern a role in primitive and in Protestant Christianity, the lofty inclusiveness that as in the new religions welcomed all races and ranks, and a celibate

asceticism that derived from the Cynics and culminated in a long line of Christian monks. From Zeno of Tarsus to Paul of Tarsus was but a step, which would be taken on the road to Damascus. ...

In essentials Stoicism was one elemental phase of the Oriental triumph over Hellenic civilization. Greece had ceased to be Greece before it was conquered by Rome.[4]

The views of Plato and Aristotle (384-322 BCE) were particularly influential in the evolution of Western mythology. Plato believed that our senses enabled us to perceive mere shadows of perfect ideas and forms. To him, matter was inert until God or soul animated or empowered it, based on some perfect idea or form to which the imperfect animated matter aspired, or to which form the matter was drawn. According to Plato, the soul that moved man was part of the soul or God that moved all things. He believed that the soul could exist in consecutive incarnations and the soul's experiences during previous incarnations could be recalled in a later life. Although hell and purgatory were possibilities, the soul would arrive at paradise only after it had been purified of all wrongdoing through its various incarnations. About 200 years earlier, Plato's predecessor Pythagoras, who might have learned of reincarnation during his travels in India, believed that virtue was the means by which a soul could win release from reincarnation.

Aristotle was a student of Plato for almost 20 years. Although he was quite scientific in his approach, Aristotle's long exposure to Plato may account for some of his work. Plato's distrust of the senses and belief that memories can be recalled from prior lives, and that perfect ideas are the force behind the material world, were refuted by Aristotle. In Aristotle's view, our ideas arrive in our minds through our senses and cannot be memories from another life, and perfect ideas are not the force behind the material world. Whereas Plato saw the senses as an inconvenient and imperfect representation of the ideal forms of Nature, Aristotle relied on sensory observations and reasoning to uncover Nature's secrets. However, Aristotle rejected the idea put forth by Anaximander, Empedocles, and Anaxagoras that living things acquired their forms as a result of evolution and natural selection. Aristotle believed that

> [T]he lines of development are determined by the inherent urge of each form, species, and genus to develop itself to the fullest realization of its nature. There is design, but it is less a guidance from without than an inner drive or "entelechy"[5] by which each thing is drawn to its natural fulfillment.

Aristotle believed that a Final Cause drew living forms to their natural fulfillment. For example, Aristotle believed that the front teeth grow sharp to cut food and that molars grow flat to grind it. In other words, teeth grow as they do because they have an inherent purpose. This is much like Plato's view that imperfect matter aspires to or is drawn to a perfect idea or form, in this case a perfect tooth for cutting or grinding. In rejecting natural selection and accepting the concept of "Final Cause," Aristotle provided a bookend for Plato's concept of God as a "Prime Mover Unmoved," or "First Cause."

Plato's God, or Prime Mover Unmoved, derived from his conclusion that a mover is required for something to be moved, and the First Cause or prime motion was caused by God, the Prime Mover Unmoved, or Soul of the World.[6] His God moved and ordered the universe in a manner consistent with forms and perfect ideas. Aristotle accepted Plato's First Cause, but Aristotle's God was more a spirit entelechy.

> All causes[7] at last go back to the First Cause Uncaused, all motions to the Prime Mover Unmoved; we must assume some origin or beginning for the motion and power in the world, and this source is God. As God is the sum and source of all motion, so he is the sum and

goal of all purposes in nature; he is the Final, as well as the First Cause.

What Aristotle began as a deductive reasoning process linking motion and cause was rendered moot by his assumption that there was a First Cause. If a First Cause was the source of the universe, what was the source of the First Cause? If a First Cause were not assumed, the First Cause would have to be caused, and that cause would have been caused, and so on in infinite regression. About fifteen centuries later, William of Ockham, using Aristotle's own method of deductive analysis, rejected Aristotle's assumption of a First Cause.

> [A]n "infinite regress" of motions or causes is no more inconceivable than the unmoved Mover or uncaused Cause of Aristotle's theology.[8] ... Since nothing can be known save through direct perception, we can never have any clear knowledge that God exists.[9] ... That God is omnipotent or infinite, omniscient or benevolent or personal, cannot be shown by reason; ...

Ockham contended that ideas based on reason could be mistaken for things if reason is not based on experience. This concept is essential to scientific reasoning and explains why belief systems that depart from experience must employ faith.

Plato's was a God based on perfect ideas; it was not a God to be feared. Therefore Plato sought a basis in reason, instead of divine wrath, to induce men to ethical behavior.

> Morally "the highest good ... is the power or faculty, if there be such, which the soul has of loving the truth, and of doing all things for the sake of truth."[10] He who so loves truth will not care to return evil for evil;[11] he will think it better to suffer injustice than to do it; he will "go forth by sea and land to seek after men who are incorruptible, whose acquaintance is beyond price. ...

> The true votaries of philosophy abstain from all fleshly lusts; and when philosophy offers them a purification and release from evil, they feel that they ought not to resist her influence; to her they incline, and whither she leads they follow her."[12]

In the end Plato decided that reason was an inadequate basis for morality and that it must be subordinated to emotion. He decided that the state should determine which and how gods would be worshiped. "Any citizen who questions this state religion is to be imprisoned; if he persists he is to be killed."[13]

In the absence of a vengeful God, Plato created a vengeful state. Medieval Christianity, by creating the Inquisition, would have both. His views that the senses were not to be trusted, the body was the tomb of the soul, and his belief in transmigration, karma, sin, purification and release of the soul, based on Orphism and the teachings of Pythagoras, provided Neoplatonists and subsequently Christians with a link between philosophy and mythology. That Plato's views were clearly in the minority of Greek philosophical thought was irrelevant to the soon-to-evolve Christian faith. So ended the Greek philosophers' noble experiment to teach ethics through reason. And so began a new noble experiment—to establish an ethical society by marrying philosophy with Christian myth.

The Noble Early Christian Attempt to Merge Faith and Reason

Plotinus (205-70 CE), the Egyptian-born Roman who founded Neoplatonism, was a non-Christian philosopher whose beliefs happened to coincide with Christian thinking. Neoplatonists described Plato's Prime Mover Unmoved as the Logos or Divine Wisdom or Mind of God. The Neoplatonist view is that all existence emanates from a single source with which human souls can mystically join. Support for their view was attributed to Plato's

214

distrust of the senses and his belief that the world is our imperfect perception of an ideal eternal reality. To defeat philosophical opposition to Christianity, Augustine (354-430 CE), an early Christian Church father and philosopher, as well as others of his day, used the writings of Plotinus and Plato in an attempt to prove that Christian beliefs were supported by reason. They used Plato's distrust of the senses to argue against the Aristotelian method that used empirical data and deductive logic to pursue rational inquiry—a method that views faith as opinion. And they used writings of the Greek Christian Platonist philosopher Origen (185?-254? CE) to represent Christianity to be not merely a faith, but a philosophy whose Scriptures were supported by reason. However, by seeking the defeat of Christianity's opponents through philosophical argument, early Christians sewed the seeds of future defeat. By seeking the endorsement of philosophy, Christianity acknowledged the authority of reason.

The early Christians' forced merger of faith and reason remained unchallenged in Christian Europe primarily because the Christian Church repressed Greco-Roman philosophical writings inconsistent with the Church's mythological view.

> [T]he Alexandrian Library seems to have amassed half a million scrolls, and it continued to thrive under Roman rule. The story that Julius Caesar destroyed the Library in 48 B.C. is a myth that came about through the misunderstanding of a reference to a large quantity of papyri stored in the docks being burned during his siege of the city. The real enemies of the Library were the later Christians, who systematically ransacked the pagan centers of learning during the fourth to fifth centuries A.D. According to tradition, the Library was burned by the Arabs after their conquest of Egypt in A.D. 640, but by that time there would have been precious little surviving of this once great home of ancient science. In fact if it were not for the Arabs, who preserved much of Greek learning in their own universities, passing it on to

the Western world during the later Middle Ages, we would be ignorant of many of the scientific writings of the Greco-Roman world.[14]

The Arabs Reintroduce Aristotle to Europe

The Moors and other North African Moslems controlled Southern Spain from the 8th century to the 15th century, when they were driven out by Isabella I (1451-1504) and Ferdinand V (1452-1516), Queen and King of Castile. Arab philosophers such as al-Farabi (870-950), Avicenna (980-1037), and Ibn Bajja (1106f) preserved and continued the Greek philosophical tradition. The reintroduction into Europe of Aristotle's method of deduction using empirical information began during the Moslem occupation of southern Spain in the 12th century and was the undoing in the 13th century of Christianity's claim to rational support for its faith.

During the 12th century, Ibn Rushd (Averroes) (1126-1198), a Moorish physician and philosopher, was born in Cordoba, Spain. Averroes was as extraordinary a physician as he was a philosopher. He was the first to explain the function of the retina and the first to observe that those previously infected with smallpox acquired immunity to the disease.[15] His encyclopedia of medicine was used to teach medicine in Christian universities. When Emir Abu Yaqub Yusuf (1163-1184) wished to have a written statement of Aristotle's views, Averroes prepared a summary, a brief commentary, and a detailed commentary, each writing increasing in complexity, as was the custom. Averroes' interpretations of Aristotle from a secular viewpoint contrasted sharply with the predominant theological view of Christian Europe. The quality of his works established Averroes as among the greatest Moslem philosophers. Averroes' personal view was that

[T]hough a little philosophy might incline a man to atheism, unhindered study would lead to a better understanding between religion and philosophy. For though the philosopher cannot accept in their literal sense the dogmas of "the Koran, the Bible, and other revealed books,"[16] he perceives their necessity in developing a wholesome piety and morality among the people, who are so harassed with economic importunities that they find no time for more than incidental, superficial, and dangerous thinking on first and last things. Hence the mature philosopher will neither utter nor encourage any word against the established faith.[17] In return the philosopher should be left free to seek the truth; but he should confine his discussions within the circle and comprehension of the educated, and make no propaganda among the populace.[18] Symbolically interpreted, the doctrines of religion can be harmonized with the findings of science and philosophy;[19] ... He defines philosophy as "an inquiry into the meaning of existence," with a view to the improvement of man.[20]

As did the Neoplatonists before him, Averroes said that God is the mind that provides order and force to the universe. He believed that our minds could join with God, not through austere self-discipline or mysticism, but by perceiving truth through reason. His was a philosophical, not a mystical God, and, to reconcile Aristotle with Mohammed, Averroes avoided all but the essential theological dogmas. However, history was not on the side of Averroes as it was with the European inheritors of his commentaries on Aristotle. There was no widespread Moslem discontent with their religious leaders as there was in Christian Europe. In fact, the Moslem world was about to seek comfort in faith for a number of reasons, not the least of which would be loss of their cities in Spain, the destruction of Baghdad by the Mongols, and the capture of Jerusalem by the Crusaders. As Moslems moved away from philosophy and toward theology, Averroes, "the Commentator," would become a footnote in Moslem history.

Aristotelian Logic Ends Claims that Faith is Supported by Reason

Averroes and the Arab philosophers who preceded him made it possible for Aristotle's disagreement with Plato to be resurrected in Europe after fifteen centuries. Plato's denigration of the senses and reverence for intuitive assumptions served Christianity well. From the early Christian rise to power, through much of the 13th century, reason had been relegated to seeking rational support for orthodox Christian beliefs. That changed when the Scottish Franciscan monk and theologian Duns Scotus (1265?-1308 CE) employed Aristotle's method of deduction using empirical information. He wrote *On the First Principal,* disputing Thomas Aquinas' harmony of faith and reason. Scotus was followed by William of Ockham and by Marsilius of Padua. Ockham is famous for his writings and what has come to be known as Ockham's Razor. It was a reasoning method that employed Aristotelian logic, which Ockham used to challenge basic Church doctrine. His "razor" contended that among competing theories the simplest theory that relies on what is already known is more likely to be true. His "razor" created serious problems for mythical explanations that layered unprovable supposition upon unprovable supposition. Similarly, the Italian philosopher Marsilius of Padua wrote *Defender of the Peace,* which denied the secular authority of the Pope. These philosophers used Aristotle's method of reasoning, not necessarily what Aristotle believed. We are all products of our time, and Aristotle was no exception. Notwithstanding Aristotle's use of empirical information and deductive reasoning, his conclusions were influenced by early Greek psychogenes that he had acquired from Plato and many others. By the 14th century, Aristotelian secular reason had been delivered to the doorstep of the Reformation and consequential doctrinal and ecclesiastical disputes had sewn the seeds of the Italian Renaissance and the subsequent 18th century Enlightenment.

In the 15th century, Pomponazzi (1462-1525.), Florentine statesman and political writer Machiavelli (1469-1527), and historian Guicciardini (1485-1540) further applied Aristotelian secular reason and set the stage for Giordano Bruno and Galileo Galilei, and the present age of science and philosophy. By the time the Inquisition burned Giordano Bruno to death and placed Galileo under house arrest for their agreement with Copernicus' view that the Earth orbited the sun, the power of the Christian Church in Rome to subordinate secular philosophy to the will of the Church had all but come to an end. From Augustine to Giordano Bruno, Christianity left no significant contribution to philosophical enlightenment. Eighteen centuries after Greek philosophy evolved into theology, faith and reason parted ways and the present European secular era began. Much as the noble experiments of Plato, Epicurus, and others to divorce morality from mythology had failed, so too, the noble attempt of Christianity to marry faith and reason had failed. As the execution of Jesus Christ can be said to symbolize the reason for the demise of the physical domination of Europe by the Western Roman Empire, the execution of Giordano Bruno by the Inquisition in Rome for contending that the Earth orbited the sun can be said to symbolize the reason for the demise of the intellectual domination of Europe by Roman Catholicism.

Before the dawn of human civilization, our ancestors lived in a hostile world with little if any social structure on which to rely for protection and sustenance. They survived by relying on evolved instincts that were equal to the hostility around them. Those same instincts are in all of us and can be seen today in our natural drive for self-preservation. For society to work, those primal instincts must be controlled through moral and legal codes in exchange for the benefits we derive from being part of society. However, our nature is such that most of us require that our moral codes, and in some cases our legal codes, derive from a higher authority than man. Given our social evolution and the nature of our brains, we seem to accept moral caveats more readily if they are part of a mythology that rewards us with emotionally satisfying answers to our questions, and with a sense of purpose, dignity, and hope for the future—things which mere mortals seem unable to provide. By failing to marry faith with reason, and by failing to teach reasoned ethics to the masses without myth, these noble experiments have exposed the reality of the mental processes we inherited from our pre-linguistic ancestors. The vast majority of us perceive the world through instinctive or learned emotional responses to symbols, not through rational analysis. While the irrational majority relates to the world through emotion-evoking mythological, cultural, and other symbols, only a small minority perceives the world with the dispassionate, rational analysis of a scientist. With the majority requiring unreasoned myth to control its passions and anxieties, it should be no surprise that minorities with different myths or no myths must pay the price for the majority's irrational perceptions and actions.

Key Participants in the Noble Experiments

Some of the people who influenced the noble experiments were attempting to resolve their personal conflicts of reason and emotion. Others sought to overcome society's emotional, antisocial inclinations; some through reason, and others through controlling myths. Ironically, some were victims of mythologies intended to establish ethical societies. They all influenced the evolution of Western culture, and much of what we believe today can be traced back to them. We already know who they were. We saw how Plato's ideas were interpreted by Augustine to become part of Roman Catholicism. We also saw how Aristotle influenced Averroes, who, in turn, influenced Scotus, William of Ockham, Marcelius of Padua, and Bruno, who participated in the intellectual revolution that was the Renaissance. There were others as well. We know what they did, but why did they do it?

Plato

In Greece, in about the year 427 BCE, he was born into a wealthy aristocratic family. His mother was the daughter of a prominent Athenian lawgiver and poet, and his father descended from the early kings of Athens. His family was part of a ruling elite that had a strong dislike for democracy. At birth he was named Aristocles, not Plato. When he became an athlete, his imposing physique and broad shoulders earned him the nickname Platon (the Greek word for "broad"). Good looking, intelligent, charming, poetic, and courageous, he excelled at almost everything. When he met Socrates in his early twenties, Plato's focus turned to philosophy. As fate would have it, a revolt led by his relatives in 404 BCE began a series of events that ended in the death of Socrates, and Plato's departure from Athens. For a time he traveled and studied with philosophers in Greece and priests in Egypt. Eventually he returned to Athens and opened a school that became known as The Academy. There he taught mathematics, music, law, astronomy, and philosophy to students of both sexes from upper-class families. Aristotle was one of his students.

In his philosophy, Plato was more a poet than a logician. He believed that the world of science and philosophy was composed, not of individual things, but of Ideas;[21] that God, according to perfect and changeless eternal laws and forms, set the universe in motion. This was in stark contrast to his view that our senses were "rabble."[22] His early idealism was reflected in his approach to social ethics as well. He sought to teach ethics without relying on myth by appealing to Athenian rationality.

> The Good is neither reason alone nor pleasure alone,
> but that mingling of them, in proportion and measure,
> which produces the Life of Reason.[23]

However, he was dealing with Athenian amygdalas. In time, he realized that the mass of society is more easily controlled by myth-driven emotional constraints than by reason. His views on ethics, mythology, and politics changed. Perhaps his aristocratic heritage led him later in life to envision a utopian state we would characterize today as a communistic aristocracy.[24] In Plato's utopia, ethical behavior would be achieved through State control of morality. Education, literature, science, the arts, and all other means and institutions that contributed to forming public opinion and personal character would be controlled by the State. Acknowledging the emotional power of myth to control the behavior of the masses, the State would control religious worship as well. Religion was so important an influence in his utopia that those who refused to accept the State's religion would be killed.[25] The contrast between his perfect ideas and imperfect fellow humans resulted in his viewing humans as having an evil nature and a divine spirit.[26] This aspect of Plato's philosophy, although unappealing to his Greek contemporaries, would appeal to early Christians. Plato's image of humanity eventually shaped Neoplatonism, which added to Platonism the mystical concept of individual souls joining with their concept of God. Through Neoplatonism, Plato influenced Christianity.

In about 347 BCE, Plato attended the wedding of one of his students. Late in the evening he retired to a chair away from the festivities, where he died in his sleep. The city of Athens attended his funeral and Aristotle built an altar to honor him.

Aristotle

Two years after Plato began his Academy, Aristotle was born. Plato was then in his forty-sixth year. Aristotle's father, court physician to the grandfather of Alexander the Great, was living in a Greek settlement in what is now the southeast Balkan Peninsula. When he came of age, his father sent the young Aristotle to study with Plato in Athens. After his approach to philosophy matured, it was apparent that the student had parted ways with his mentor. Their approaches to philosophy were quite different. Plato, ever the idealist poet, imagined the world to be an imperfect reflection of perfect forms and ideas. Aristotle, the empiricist, relying on observations provided by his senses, relentlessly applied deductive reasoning to unravel the secrets of Nature. However, learning from a mentor whose thinking had no discernable system did not serve Aristotle well. Nonetheless, while Plato's reason was driven by the emotion of a poet, Aristotle was beginning to think with the dispassionate clarity of a scientist. Even though Plato's thinking lacked the reasoned structure Aristotle needed to unravel Nature's secrets, Aristotle was able to invent a systematic method to do just that. That Aristotle's own work did not always reflect systematic thinking is the result of his inheritance, and not his legacy.

At about the age of forty-one he was invited to educate Alexander (the Great), who was all of thirteen at the time. Four years later Aristotle returned to Athens and opened his own school, the Lyceum, which chiefly taught natural science. In addition to his writings on logic, ethics, poetics, politics, and metaphysics, the compendium collected by his students on every conceivable subject enabled him to formulate his theories on natural science. He defined syllogistic logic and the process of rational inquiry, which is the basis of science. For two thousand years his treatises were the textbook of logic for the Western world. He had invented the core of the modern scientific method. His influence was such that, had he accepted the view of Empedocles and others that biological evolution progressed by natural selection, Darwinism, by another name, might have predated Christianity. His persistent striving to find scientific and not mythical explanations for natural occurrences is among his greatest legacies. Much as the early philosophers extracted philosophy from a quagmire of animism, myth, and countless arbitrary linkages of cause and effect, Aristotle managed to extract science from early Greek philosophical conjectures and speculations about Nature.

Augustine

When Christianity was in the process of being formed, Augustine (354-430) was a Church father and philosopher. Although his mother was Christian, as a young man he preferred Manichean dualism to explain the good and evil he saw around him. For a time he considered the skepticism of the later Academy, but found "no answer" to be emotionally unfulfilling. He studied Plato and Neoplatonism. However, it was the Bible, and particularly Paul's symbolic interpretation of patently puerile biblical accounts, that resonated in Augustine. He related to Paul's doubts, and, as he studied, he too found an emotional comfort in faith that the skepticism of his intellect could not provide. For Augustine, his epiphany not only afforded mental peace, but a clear basis for morality, and, for him, a resolution of the dualism of good and evil. When Augustine became a Christian he brought with him his Platonism and Neoplatonism. His pagan logic and philosophy, when applied to religion, made him exceptional among theologians. His 230 treatises were foundation stones for the new Church that embedded Neoplatonism in Christian thinking. Although his passion and intellect influenced the thinking and history of Western Christianity, Eastern Christianity of his day did not care for his anti-intellectual valuing of emotion over reason. He argued that the Church should dominate both government and thought, which it did until the Renaissance.

The Arab Philosophers

Averroes adopted an Aristotelian view of religion and a scientific approach to God. His was a philosophical, not a mythical God. Realizing, as did Plato, that the mass of society relies on emotional mythology to ensure their ethical behavior and peace of mind, he felt it necessary to preserve their myths. To do this, while preserving his own non-mythical view of God, he made every effort to find rational justifications for religious dogma.

Averroes was attempting to walk the line between myth and reason by perceiving God through a rationalist theology. However, mysticism was at the core of the Islamic world. While Averroes was in Spain, one philosopher in Iran and another in Iraq, whose influence would all but eradicate that of Averroes in Islam, were attempting to fuse philosophy with mystical spirituality. They were following the writings of Ibn Sina (980-1037), known in the West as Avicenna. Avicenna, in turn, based his writings on an Arabic view of philosophy known as "Falsafah," which derived from the works of Greek philosophers translated into Arabic during the ninth and tenth centuries. Faylasufs (adherents to Falsafah) believed that rationalism was an advanced form of religion with a higher notion of God than the God of scripture. They were seeing God through the eyes of Aristotle and Plotinus. The Faylasufs believed that God and reason were one. Unlike Augustine, who found comfort in Plato's rejection of rational inquiry based on proof provided by the senses, the Faylasufs believed that Aristotle's God was actually provable. Avicenna used Aristotle's proofs in an attempt to demonstrate the existence of God. But near the end of his life Avicenna became frustrated with the rational approach to God. He sought to fuse philosophy and spirituality without using rational arguments. It was this view that was most compatible with Islam's preference for mysticism. Contemporaries of Averroes who advanced Avicenna's later approach were favored by history, as Islam underwent major changes that ushered in its present anti-secular era.

The Reformers

Two Franciscan monks, considered among the most brilliant thinkers of the 14th century, used the Aristotelian logic revealed in Averroes' commentaries to question the Church's forced marriage of reason and faith. Duns Scotus used it to dispute Thomas Aquinas' attempt to harmonize faith and reason. William of Ockham, with his Aristotelian "razor," inflicted wounds from which the followers of Augustine would not recover.

As a young man, William of Ockham was sent to be educated at the Franciscan college at Oxford. There he learned of Duns Scotus' critique of theology, which, in Ockham, was transformed into skepticism. While in his twenties, he wrote commentaries on Aristotle and a summary of all logic, *Summa totius logicae.* But his writings critical of Church doctrine came to the notice of Pope John XXII. He was ordered to appear at the papal court in Avigonon, France to account for his heresies. He was imprisoned, but soon escaped with two other Franciscans. They found their way to Pisa, Italy and the court of Louis of Bavaria. On a trip to Munich with his benefactor, Ockham met Marsilius of Padua. They wrote books and pamphlets criticizing papal heresies and abuses of power. Influenced by Marsilius' anticlericalism, Ockham used his "razor" to dissect the Church's additions to the simple Christianity of old. Ockham questioned everything, including the Apostolic Succession of the popes and papal infallibility, arguing that many popes were criminals and heretics. In time, Louis of Bavaria reconciled his differences with the Church, and, without Louis' protection, it is believed that Ockham did the same. At about sixty-four years of age, he died during a plague. However, the power of his ideas in a time of discontent with corruption in the Church ensured that he lived on in the universities of Europe. His argument that reason cannot prove the truth of the tenets of faith was widely accepted. A school of Ockhamists was formed at Oxford. When teaching Ockham's views was banned at the university in Paris, his supporters declared him a champion of free thought. Martin Luther declared Ockham the "chiefest and most ingenious of Scholastic doctors."[27] From Aristotle to Averroes to Ockham, the seeds of the Italian Renaissance had been sewn. But, as with Averroes, Scotus and Ockham feared the ruin of theology. They too used Averroes' distinction between theological truth and philosophical truth to provide a basis for skeptics to preserve morality among the masses by supporting their religion.

Giordano Bruno

Five years after Copernicus died, Giordano Bruno was born in Nola, Italy, near Vesuvius. He attended a Dominican monastery where Thomas Aquinas had taught, but, because of his unorthodox views, he soon left the monastery and Italy. He began writing. In 1581, at age 33, he moved to Paris and quickly became known to Henry III. Among his numerous books was one that refuted contentions by Lully that the dogmas of the Church could be proven by reason. Bruno contended that Christianity was irrational, is accepted through faith, and that revelation has no scientific basis.

In Bruno's time, European scholars were strongly inclined to parrot and not question Aristotle's views. This at a time when science was beginning to provide insights that Aristotle would likely have welcomed to refine and revise his thinking. It was particularly true in England. While visiting England, Bruno's support of the Copernican view of the solar system (a view not widely held at the time) fell on unbelieving ears because it did not square with Aristotle's teachings. Galileo had not yet taken up Copernicus' cause.

> Bruno had no secure place in either Protestant or Roman Catholic religious communities. He carried out his long fight against terrible odds. He had lived in Switzerland and France and was now in England and left there for Germany. He translated books, read proofs, and got together groups and lectured for whatever he could get out of it [to survive]. ... In his book *De la Causa, principio et uno (On Cause, Principle, and Unity)* we find prophetic phrases:
>
> "There is no absolute up or down, as Aristotle taught; no absolute position in space; but the position of a body is relative to that of other bodies. Everywhere there is incessant relative change in position

throughout the universe, and the observer is always at
the center of things."[28]

His writings dealt with sophistic superstition, the narrow and
tiresome focus of Catholic and Protestant cultures on trivialities,
philosophical concepts which would be taken up by Descartes
(and which were published five years before Descartes was born),
mathematics, and numerous other topics. He believed that the
Church encouraged ignorance. One of his heresies was that he
believed that God and Nature could not be separated. In addition
to contradicting the Christian dogma of Genesis, he contradicted
Aristotle. His philosophical views became an intimate part of
Spinoza's (1632-1677) thought[29] and anticipated theories of the
German philosopher Gottfried Leibniz (1646-1716). Bruno
represented a transition to modern philosophy. His radical view
of an infinite and relative universe left no room for the Church's
medieval God or its perfect heaven.

He accepted an invitation from Giovanni Moncenigo to
live in Venice. Returning to Italy, however, would be his
undoing. Moncenigo subsequently delivered Bruno into the hands
of the Inquisition. He was imprisoned in Rome from 1593 to
1600. On February 9, 1600 he was sentenced to death at the
palace of the Grand Inquisitor. When he heard his sentence,
Bruno said, "Perhaps you, my judges, pronounce this sentence
against me with greater fear than I receive it." Refusing to repent,
eight days later he was burned alive, scornfully pushing away a
crucifix offered to him as the flames ended his life.

In 1603 his works were placed on the Index Expurgatorius
and became rare. The attempt to remove Giordano Bruno from
our history almost succeeded. Although he was rediscovered in
the 18th century by English deists and German philosophers, he
remained obscure. However, in the late 19th century he was
rediscovered by Italian scholars and has been recognized as a
martyred philosopher in the intellectual renaissance that ended
the Church's anti-classical, anti-intellectual hold on European
thinking begun by Augustine in the fifth century. It might be said

that the Italian Renaissance, which began in the 14th century with the rebirth of Greco-Roman culture, was completed when Giordano Bruno championed the rebirth of free-thought, science, and secular philosophy. Although the Renaissance marked the beginning of a new secular era for Europe, it took hold unevenly. With the burning of Bruno, the house arrest of Galileo, and the intimidation of Descartes, the center of European philosophy and science moved to Protestant Europe.

The philosophers who most influenced the noble experiments fall into roughly two groups—poets and scientists. The poets' perceptions were emotional and intuitional compared with the perceptions of the more reason based scientists. Augustine and Avicenna chose emotionally satisfying myth and were instrumental in guiding their respective religions more deeply into mythologies intolerant of rational inquiry. Scotus and Ockham made decisions using their powers of reason. The question in my mind is whether all their choices were more influenced by the biology of belief than their free will. They were all intelligent. They all had detailed knowledge of both the good and evil of human nature, and the arguments for and against believing that something like a God could exist. Why did they choose as they did? Was Augustine inclined to resolve his frustration by believing what was emotionally satisfying? And, had he inherited Arabic psychogenes, would Augustine have written just as convincingly in support of Mohammed? Were Augustine and Avicenna born with a God module, and Scotus and Ockham not? How significant were their psychogenetic inheritances and planning assumptions? Were these philosophers accomplished thinkers with varying degrees of amygdala and prefrontal lobe dominance or of left and right brain hemisphere dominance? Does much of the difference simply reflect historically different myth-driven assemblages of organized ignorance? Are the volumes of well-reasoned philosophical arguments merely empty logic attempting to justify their inherited beliefs or emotional needs? These questions will no doubt exist for as long as thinking beings exist. Whatever the answers, by myth and reason the participants in the noble experiments attempted to find the truth and to convince our ancestors to control their inborn reptilian instincts. Although the experimenters chose different methods to compensate for aspects of the biology that shapes our beliefs, their common goals were clearly noble.

Chapter 12
The Battle for Our Psychogenes

Our psychogenetic inheritance and other beliefs are beset constantly by organizations, governments, causes, mythologies, and individuals who need our cooperation to achieve their goals. And, to the extent that our beliefs can be manipulated to conform to or serve the purposes of others, they can be successful. Public opinion is at the core of modern politics and commerce. In non-totalitarian governments, it is difficult if not impossible to survive politically against public opinion. Negative revelations about politicians or businesses can force them out of office or out of business. For this reason people in influential positions "power surf" by staying just ahead of the dominant beliefs of their power base. Polling public opinion provides the information they need to stay on the wave. In an earlier time the equivalent metaphor was to stay ahead of the parade, but not too far. By this mechanism, dominant public beliefs (opinions) influence those who make policy. But, as does everyone, people with power like to make decisions consistent with their own beliefs. If the public believes the "wrong" thing, public opinions can be changed. Consensus building requires that you convince people to believe in your goal. And because people act in ways consistent with their beliefs, they will act to achieve your goal. The operative word is *convince* which derives from the Latin *vincere*, to conquer.

To Convince is to Conquer

The underlying principles involved in the process of influencing public opinion are not complex. Events are merely sensory data until they become perceptions in the mind. If belief alters perception, then how we perceive something depends on our beliefs about the thing observed. And if our beliefs can be biased through propaganda, then propaganda influences our perception of events. This is why propaganda that undermines our belief about someone's motives, values, *et cetera*, destroys our ability to perceive that person's words or deeds correctly. For this reason, polls of public opinion are of questionable value. By polling what we believe today, a media strategist can contrive and deliver propaganda to influence tomorrow's polls. Otherwise stated, if today's polls reflect yesterday's propaganda, then of what value is a propagandist's claim that his or her position is supported by the polls? If the polls merely reflect the effectiveness of someone's propaganda, then they are of little value in determining the opinion of an informed public. This problem is compounded by our tendency to believe what we prefer were true—our tendency to believe what is emotionally satisfying—and our tendency to force, for example, the belief that the president is not lying, to ensure that he stays in office and that he continues to veto legislation we do not want. This is in addition to the need of true believers among us who want to be told by their authority figures what to believe. In *Spin Cycle,* Howard Kurtz said this about President Bill Clinton's media management:

> To be sure, Clinton's performance had helped create the sense that the country was doing just fine on his watch. But it was a carefully honed media strategy—alternately seducing, misleading, and sometimes intimidating the press—that maintained this aura of success. No day went by without the president and his coterie laboring mightily to generate favorable headlines and deflect damaging ones, to project their preferred image on the vast screen of the media establishment.[1]

One small example of such propaganda resulted from the president's refusal to provide the Food and Drug Administration with power to bar imports of substandard food. When a story appeared in the *New York Times* describing how federal inspections of imported food had plummeted just as scientists were finding more outbreaks of food-borne diseases,

> [T]he White House promptly staged a ceremony in the picturesque Rose Garden as Clinton proposed giving the FDA new power to ban imported fruit and vegetables, the very power he had refused to grant years earlier. Mike McCurry [press secretary] even credited the *Times* for its role in spotlighting the problem.[2]

The Rise of Secular Mythology

Have you ever heard of Edward Bernays? *Life* magazine included him in a list of the one hundred most influential Americans of the 20th century.[3] Your encyclopedia probably describes him as a nephew of Sigmund Freud and the father of public relations. In talks with his uncle, when Freud described ways to understand the workings of the subconscious mind, Bernays saw an opportunity for the social elite to retain power by applying discoveries about the workings of the mind to control public opinion. The world was approaching The First World War, and things were changing. The role Bernays would play throughout the 20th century was described by Stuart Ewen in *PR!*.

> The explosive ideals of democracy challenged ancient customs that had long upheld social inequality. A public claiming the birthright of democratic citizenship and social justice increasingly called upon institutions and people of power to justify themselves and their privileges. In the crucible of these changes, aristocracy began to give way to technocracy as a strategy of rule. Bernays came to maturity in a society in which the exigencies of power were—by necessity—increasingly exercised from behind the pretext of the "common good."… Born into privilege, developing into a

233

technocrat, Bernays illustrates the onus that the twentieth century has placed on social and economic elites; they have had to justify themselves continually to a public whose hearts and minds now bear the ideals of democracy.[4]

The human ability to reason is relatively new in our evolutionary history. It requires mental discipline and a willingness to change beliefs that reason shows are wrong. Until perhaps the past million or so years, our ancestors interacted with their surroundings, not with the aid of reason, but with subconscious, intuitive, impulsive, emotions. Those primitive, unreasoning responses are still so strong in our nature that reason plays a minor part in the day-to-day thinking of most of the population. Added to this is the fact that part of our psychogenetic inheritance provides us with culture-specific stereotypical responses and emotions. When we act in concert, those stereotypical responses satisfy an apparently inborn need we have to be part of a group. Knowing this and other aspects of our subconscious nature—knowing what people and things we fear, envy, or hate—propagandists manipulate our subconscious mechanisms to control our beliefs and behaviors. What this means in a world filled with propaganda is that forming public opinion is more analogous to herding sheep than it is to well-reasoned debate.

In addition to Edward Bernays, John Hill, Carl Byoir, Ivy Lee, Elmo Roper, George Gallup, and others, a journalist named Walter Lippmann (1889-1974) became interested in propaganda. Early in the 20th century, Lippmann reasoned that democracy presupposes a rational electorate. This was an Enlightenment view held by the framers of the American Constitution. However, if most of us use primitive emotional mechanisms and symbolism instead of reason, Lippmann thought, the government cannot function unless a rational and responsible elite shapes public opinion to support governmental policies. His books *Public Opinion* and *The Phantom Public* contain his ideas on how such a democracy could be achieved. He believed that most of humanity perceived events, not objectively, but through mental images that did not provide a correct view of reality. In addition, he thought that the average person's perception of reality became less accurate as the world became more complex and as events were perceived less through personal experience and more through the mass distribution of the perceptions of others. It followed that the ability to control the access of news media to events was the key to managing public perceptions and opinions. This is the reason public relations is such a clandestine business. If manipulation is to be effective, no one must know what the manipulators are doing. Lippmann determined that the public's stereotyped approximations of reality could be manipulated most easily through visual media, in part, because images required less thought and were better able to elicit strong responses if the viewer related personally to the subject matter of the images.

> Lippmann turned toward Hollywood, America's "dream factory," for inspiration. Never before had an American thinker articulated in such detail the ways that images could be used to sway public consciousness. Appeals to reason were not merely being discarded as futile, they were being consciously undermined to serve the interests of power. ...[5]
>
> Educated by the lessons of the media culture taking shape around him, Lippmann saw the strategic employment of media images as the secret to modern power, the means by which leaders and special interests might cloak themselves in the "fiction" that they stand as delegates of the common good. The most compelling attribute of symbols, he asserted, was the capacity to magnify emotion while undermining critical thought, to emphasize sensations while subverting ideas. "In the symbol," he rhapsodized, *"emotion is discharged at a common target and the idiosyncrasy of real ideas is blotted out."*[6]

Lippmann's formula for leadership required

> [T]he use of symbols which assemble emotions after they have been detached from their ideas. Because feelings are much less specific than ideas, and yet more poignant, the leader is able to make a homogeneous will out of a heterogeneous mass of desires. The process, therefore, by which general opinions are brought to cooperation consists of an intensification of feeling and a degradation of significance. Before a mass of general opinions can eventuate in executive action, the choice is narrowed down to a few alternatives. The victorious alternative is executed not by a mass but by individuals in control of its energy.[7] ... He who captures the symbols by which public feeling is for the moment contained, controls by that much the approaches of public policy. ... A leader or an interest that can make itself master of current symbols is the master of the current situation.[8]

Edward Bernays thought that Lippmann's *Public Opinion* was too theoretical and abstract. In Bernays' book *Propaganda* he wrote that the group mind's first impulse is usually to follow the example of a trusted leader. Bernays was particularly interested in using the details of the human subconscious to his advantage. Today, securing the endorsement of trusted public figures to sell everything from coffee machines to government policy is so common we do not consider when or why it began.

> Subscribing to Lippmann's vision of modern society and its conditions, Bernays saw the public relations counsel not simply as a person who applied modern scientific know-how to his work, but also as one of the "intelligent few" who must, within democratic society, "continuously and systematically" perform the task of

"regimenting the public mind." These "invisible wire pullers," as Bernays tagged public relations experts, would provide the skills necessary to bring about a successful negotiation between the chaos of popular aspirations and exigencies of elite power.[9]

Bernays described propaganda as "the executive arm of the invisible government" [10] and the public relations counsel as one "who was a master of creating pseudo-environments" – "creating pictures in the minds of millions" by staging seemingly spontaneous events—that would quietly induce the public to comprehend the world in a desired way." [11] An example of this process was reported in a 1993 *New York Times* article:

> Consider Bonner & Associates, which occupies an entire floor of one of Washington's pricier office buildings. ... This Company is among a new breed of Washington firms that has turned grass-roots organizing techniques to the advantage of its high-paying clients, generally trade associations and corporations. ... [T]he new campaigns are sometimes intended to appear spontaneous. ... [T]he rise of this industry has made it hard to tell the difference between manufactured public opinion and genuine explosions of popular sentiment.
>
> Bonner & Associates specializes in seizing on unformed public sentiment, marshalling local interest groups and raining faxes, phone calls and letters on Congress or the White House on a few days' notice.[12]

People in the public relations business know the organizing of these "grassroots" groups as "Astro Turf Organizing." [13] A Washington rally in support of a proposed "big government" health plan was reported to have been attended by people from the health insurance and health care industries posing as ordinary citizens.

Just as "grassroots" has its public relations "Astro Turf," science has a fictitious public relations version—junk science. The tobacco industry used junk science for decades to confuse the public regarding valid scientific research, which showed that smoking tobacco products was harmful. This is different from the junk science generated by incompetent or politically motivated research. With the willingness of public relations firms to lie so convincingly to manipulate the public's emotions and perceptions, it should come as no surprise that major corporations with "image problems" were among the first clients of public relations firms. In *PR!*, Stuart Ewen quoted part of a report to the Standard Oil of New Jersey (SONJ) 1948 Public Relations Conference. The company had recently completed a public relations film, which was the subject of company vice president Stuart Shackne's remarks. Ewen described it as follows:

> Their achievement, argued a publicity director at the [conference], was in their ability to set "an emotional tone" linking the company and the public on a psychological level, one that allowed "the Company and the public" to "*share an experience.*"
>
> This psychological communion, Schackne advised, must inform SONJ's public relations thinking overall. One could not expect the public to study and embrace the complexities of a corporate perspective. To guide public opinion it was necessary to speak to those regions of mind and spirit that religion—more than science—had customarily addressed. He [Schackne] continued:
>
>> In this connection I might cite, with entire respect, the Roman Catholic Church, which frames the imposing logic of its theology in a setting designed to stimulate the emotions by color, architectural form, music, and all the beauties of art. ... [W]e

> are trying to add to our public relations
> techniques what might be called some
> seismographic methods to probe into the
> depths of feeling as a supplement to the
> surface instruments of fact.[14]

More recently, attempts by polluting corporations to improve their images without altering their polluting ways involve something akin to whitewashing. They use the symbols and wording of environmentally responsible organizations, but the words and symbols are false. This is called "greenwashing."

In another example, prior to the Gulf War with Iraq, a fifteen-year-old Kuwaiti girl reported that Iraqi soldiers in occupied Kuwait City had removed Kuwaiti babies from their incubators and placed them on hospital floors to die. The story was widely circulated and repeated often. It clearly characterized the Iraqi military as barbarians and undoubtedly biased the American public against Iraq. The girl, a self-described hospital volunteer, had testified along with others before the Congressional Human Rights Caucus on October 10, 1990. It was stated at the hearing that the girl's identity would be kept secret to ensure her safety. Inasmuch as news stories are seldom verified, the source of this story did not become general knowledge. Had this story been investigated, the following facts described in *PR!*[15] would have come to light. The girl was the daughter of the Kuwaiti Ambassador to the United States. That she witnessed any atrocities is dubious. The meeting of the Congressional Human Rights Caucus was arranged by Gary Hymel, a vice-president of Hill and Knowlton, a large public relations firm. Hymel also provided the other witnesses. The Kuwaiti royal family in exile retained Hill and Knowlton to manufacture American public support for military action against Iraq. The hospital atrocity story was part of a larger plan to demonize Iraq and to condition the public to support U.S. military intervention.[16]

If we are marionettes with propagandists working our biological strings, then how shall we know what is true? Has a new era of secular mythology begun? Perhaps William James' vision of our reality is correct. "Truth lives ... for the most part on a credit system. Our thoughts and beliefs 'pass,' so long as nothing challenges them, just as bank-notes pass so long as nobody refuses them."[17] By selecting or eliminating specific psychogenetic beliefs, prolonged propaganda has reshaped cultures in much the same way that selective breeding has reshaped domesticated animals. It goes without saying that properly practiced public relations does much to assist various interests in getting their story before the public. However, it would be useful to remember that the Roman republic was transformed into a dictatorship after its citizen army was replaced with professional soldiers. The change that made dictatorship possible probably went unnoticed by all but a few. When the republic's professional army was formed, it was decided to permit soldiers to be compensated in booty and slaves by the general under whom they served. From that time forward, each army's loyalty was to its general, not to the Republic. This policy, which enabled Julius Caesar to become Emperor of the Roman Empire, was later reversed by Augustus Caesar, to ensure that Roman armies would remain loyal to him. What effect will blind tolerance of belief-altering propaganda have on our future if the loyalty of an army of propagandists is to the power elite that pays them, and not to our republic?

Belief management is known by many names—public relations, propaganda, disinformation, positive and negative advertising, demonization, misrepresentation, spin, half-truths, distortion, suppression (of opposing views or truthful reports), censorship, one-sidedness, fabrication (lies), exaggeration, minimization, and the like. Whatever it is called, it is still "belief management." One means of influencing public opinion is to bias people very early in a debate. We find it difficult to suspend judgment and readily accept information to reach conclusions quickly. Unfortunately, early bias damages our ability to perceive subsequent information correctly. Bias is belief, and belief alters perception. The mechanism is easily demonstrated. When a photograph of a happy face is presented following a photograph of a happy scene, we see the face as congenial. The same happy face photograph, presented following a photograph of a gruesome scene will be perceived as sadistic. The belief created by the first image distorts our perception of the second. In the two sequences, the smiling face did not change. Our belief about the cause of the smile changed. Similarly, a thing perceived when we are angry or afraid is likely to be perceived differently when we are tranquil. What we believe the future holds for us influences our perception as well. Is the glass half full or half empty? These and other influences on our perception are manipulated by propagandists to create self-serving beliefs. Their work is made easier when we want to believe the propaganda. Speech or images with strong emotional content are the stuff of which propaganda is made. Speakers who invoke God, country, children, the needy, our fears, resentments, hatreds, and so on, or who demonize their opponents, are attempting to bias our thinking through our emotions while avoiding discussion of the real issues. Speeches that make you feel instead of think are probably propaganda.

An ideal campaigner for public office is a consummate convincer. An ideal office holder is ethical and able. We usually elect the convincer and hope that he or she is ethical and able. When we buy the package without knowing the contents we are not making an informed decision. The common thread that runs through politics, journalism, and entertainment is that their most prominent people are the most believable. They are the best convincers and, given that they have the same abilities, it is not surprising that they can move effortlessly from one such occupation to another.

Some eyewitness accounts of Adolph Hitler's political rallies describe audiences as appearing mesmerized. Hitler began his speeches by speaking very softly. As he went on, his volume and demeanor would become more pronounced. By the time he finished speaking he was pounding on the podium. It is conceivable that, in addition to using propaganda techniques (his propaganda minister, Joseph Goebbels, reportedly kept a copy of Edward Bernays' book *Crystallizing Public Opinion* on his desk),

Hitler may have used a trance-inducing method to induce a receptive alpha brain state in his audiences. That would explain a great deal.

In addition to the news media, our information comes to us through the political process. However, the political process values gaining and holding power over everything, and, to this end, dispenses misinformation (what was once called lies) about the attributes of its candidates and the deficiencies of their opponents. It is a battle for our beliefs, and to the extent that false information is believed, informed decisions are an illusion.

Not long ago a very well educated Russian citizen in St. Petersburg, Russia, told me that she was angry with the Communist party. She was not especially upset with their unpleasant economic legacy. Given that St. Petersburg was a naval seaport, she expected it to experience economic hardship as the government cut back military spending. What aroused her anger was that she had been fed so much propaganda over her lifetime she did not know which of her beliefs were false. Since that conversation I have thought about which of my valued beliefs might be old propaganda. I was told that on the evening of the attack on Pearl Harbor, on hearing the news, an audience attending a concert in New York City rose and sang the Star Spangled Banner. According to a BBC program produced in the 1980s, President Roosevelt was aware of the coming attack from the time the Japanese fleet left harbor in Japan. The program suggested that his interest in entering the war in Europe would be served by such an attack. If their ostensibly well documented analysis is correct, the "date which will live in infamy" might do so for more reasons than one. Then again, could our allies and we have won the war if we had waited while Germany and Japan consolidated their positions?

The complex interactions of evolving science, technologies, economic strength, social trends, propaganda, and myriad other factors determine which forces will most influence our psychogenetic evolution. Further complicating the quality of our information is that journalism is a commercial enterprise run by people with beliefs, emotions, and economic necessities that alter their perceptions of reality. These biases are evident when the media turn a blind eye to the faults of people or organizations of which they approve, or when they refuse to allow publication of views that they oppose. In order to control market share, some journalists find a crisis where there is none, and sell it as news. In these cases information is distorted and public opinion suffers. It seems that the news and entertainment businesses focus on the sensational roughly within a context of contemporary views of propriety. As they do, their belief-altered perceptions of events are like circus mirrors that distort while they reflect their audiences. It is a self-reinforcing process that gives prominence to the sensational and reinforces resultant changes in social views by subsequently representing previous aberrations as normal. I recently heard a teenage girl asked what she wanted to be. She said a "porno" queen. Without the influence of the news and entertainment businesses, how could becoming a "porno" queen change from being viewed as less than admirable to a career goal in one generation? Entertaining news has its price. It remains to be seen what will change when we have the opportunity to select our news and entertainment from a wide array of decentralized sources over computer networks.

The control of modern media has fallen into the hands of a few major corporations. Owning television stations, radio stations, newspapers, magazines, book publishers, and the like has made it possible for such corporations to manipulate public opinion by denying access to essential information and by distorting what information is presented. With this power, the public can be led to believe that what is in the best interest of such corporations is in the best interest of the public. Given the three branches of government, the executive, legislative, and judicial, only the judiciary is relatively insulated from the power of such corporations to manipulate public opinion. In a recent attempt of the U.S. Senate to pass a law to resolve issues of damage to the public caused by the tobacco industry, a bill that came out of committee with an overwhelming vote (19 to 1), was defeated in a Senate vote after an enormously expensive propaganda campaign orchestrated by the tobacco industry. Senators were intimidated into voting against the legislation by threats to prevent their reelection through distorted advertising directed against them individually. They were induced as well to vote against the legislation through promises of favorable advertising. Failing a legislative resolution to the question of how tobacco companies should be held liable for the damage they have done by misrepresenting the deleterious effects of the products they sell, state attorneys general banded together in a settlement negotiation with the tobacco industry to resolve outstanding litigation. State attorneys general were less influenced by tobacco industry propaganda and were freer to exercise the power of government to control an industry capable of manipulating public opinion thorough propaganda. Subsequently, a jury in Florida returned a verdict against the tobacco industry and awarded damages large enough to threaten its future. The judiciary appears to be the only branch of government left that cannot be manipulated by propaganda.

Suppression of news about another piece of legislation, one which provided broadcasting high-definition television bandwidth to television companies without charge, was another coup of corporate media. Arguments against the giveaway were not reported by the major news organizations. If the public could be kept ignorant of the giveaway, lobbying by media corporations would be successful. It worked.

Through control of the media, either by concentrated ownership or pervasive propaganda, power elites manipulate what the public believes and thereby what the government does. If we permit this to continue by interpreting the constitutional protection of free speech to extend to corporations and the army of propagandists whose purpose is to thwart free speech, are we jeopardizing the right of future generations to balanced and open debate intended by the U.S. Constitution?

Whose Psychogenes Are Being Passed to Our Young?

Inadvertently, late 20th century humanity is engaged in an experiment unique in our history. In one aspect of the experiment, the normal intergenerational transmission of psychogenes from parent to child is being altered by communications technology. Exposure of our young for a substantial part of their formative years to public relations and information about other beliefs and values interrupts the traditional process of enculturation. To the extent that it exposes youth to a broader, non-parochial view of the world, communications technology might promote tolerance in an intolerant culture. Alternatively, it might destroy creativity, promote materialism, hedonism, nihilism, and insensitivity, and create in young minds a distorted view of humanity and history. This is not to say that parents are not capable of all these things without the assistance of commercial mass media. That notwithstanding, for the most part, parents are motivated to replicate their beliefs and values in their children from an intent to do what is right for their children. Commercially disseminated beliefs and values, on the other hand, have numerous motivations, few if any of which are concerned with the long-term welfare of their consumers.

The economy has also influenced our beliefs. After World War II, Americans experienced higher incomes, better educational opportunities, increased mobility, and other changes that favored nuclear families and disfavored more traditional extended families. Educated parents of nuclear families bought books such as *Dr. Spock's Baby and Child Care* to guide them through child rearing. They relied very little on the psychogenes of family members who were no longer present to advise or participate in child rearing. The books they bought were written by psychologists and were based on psychology theory. The new psychology placed the importance of self-esteem above that of self-discipline. What was not clear at the time was that "teaching" self-esteem is not a simple matter. It appears to be less a matter of teaching and more a matter of creating opportunities for learning. Attaining self-esteem is much like attaining happiness, it is the result of attaining something else. Our need for self-esteem derives from our fundamental need to perceive ourselves as valuable. To feel valuable, each of us needs purpose. Our self-esteem increases when we feel we are fulfilling the purpose that gives meaning to our lives. During our formative years, when self-esteem is being established, we are also learning behaviors and information necessary to prepare us for life. An essential part of that learning process involves being corrected or "criticized" when we are wrong. However, criticism is a double-edged sword. Although it is essential to correct our faults, if inappropriate or excessive, criticism can damage self-esteem. The damage caused by excessive or inappropriate criticism in teaching self-discipline appears to be what the new psychology intended to prevent. However, the other edge of the sword is that insufficient criticism can produce ignorant, undisciplined people with a false sense of self-worth, unprepared to deal with the problems of life. The relationship between criticism and self-esteem can be described by analogy. As a flame can be diminished by the wind, so too self-esteem can be diminished by criticism. However, as the absence of wind cannot create a flame, the absence of criticism cannot create self-esteem. It can create egocentricity and perhaps vindictiveness when faced with contradiction. Self-esteem derives from our own perception that we have achieved something and not merely from someone telling us that we have. No matter how well-intentioned we might be, too much or too little criticism can be destructive in their own ways. Later in his career, Dr. Spock said he never intended that children not be disciplined and that interpretations of his books to the contrary were wrong. Apparently some had concluded that any physical discipline was violent behavior, and its use, even in benign moderation, constituted teaching that any degree of violence was acceptable. Dr. Spock's comment suggests that substituting psychology theory for traditional child-rearing psychogenes has not been a resounding success in determining how much criticism is just right.

What we find is that the post-World-War-II generations, raised and educated according to new psychology theory, are fundamentally different from prior generations. Although signs appeared in the late 1950s, the difference had clearly become established with the Woodstock generation. The increasing reach of television and other means of communication, together with rising teenage affluence, also became significant influences. Given their affluence and the increasingly large number of hours children began to spend watching television, the youth market became attractive to large commercial interests. Targeted television advertising and entertainment introduced commercial values based on defying authority and other themes popular among the young. The advertising approach of pandering used for adults was now used in advertising to children. These economic and technological changes had two effects on the intergenerational transmission of traditional psychogenes. Once television programming was introduced into the home, parents no longer represented the principal source of beliefs and values. In addition, the beliefs and values introduced by television eroded traditional views of self-discipline and responsibility (they don't sell) and replaced them with beliefs and values based on consumerism, self-indulgence, and instant gratification, while mocking traditional values. Although hedonism and materialism have always been with us, beginning with the postwar generation, they became sanctioned. What appears to have happened in the second half of the 20th century is that technological and economic change created social change that caused psychology theory and consumerism to replace child-rearing traditions evolved over countless generations. Additional factors included opposition to the Vietnam War, the civil rights movement, the rise of cultural relativism, the current phase of the women's liberation movement, and increasingly sophisticated manipulation of public opinion by political and other groups. These and other forces apparently motivated the radical minorities of the sixties to replace, in great part, the World War II generation's conservatism with the political correctness and multiculturalism of current liberalism.

Although psychological research has taught us much about ourselves, such research can be difficult because of the complexity of the mind, difficulty in determining which factors cause which results, and the length of time required to establish the credibility of some theories. Good-sounding reasons can be given to explain behavior, but are they true? Are theories being implemented for their quality or for their compatibility with political and social movements? A generally accepted experiment regarding the effect of competition on creativity was done using two groups of pre-teenage children. They were asked to create a collage from provided materials. In one group, prizes were offered for the three collages judged by adult supervisors to be the best. In the other, the children were told that the prizes would be awarded randomly at the end of the session. Ostensibly, competition was the only variable. When the art works were judged for creativity, it was decided that the competitive group's work showed the least creativity. The conclusion drawn by the creators of this experiment was that competition was destructive to creativity. Was it? If the creators of this experiment believed that competition is destructive, they would not consider variables not germane to confirming that belief, unless they were scrupulously scientific. Was the only difference between the two groups the pressure of competing for a prize? Perhaps not. Perhaps what the students believed about the artistic tastes of the adult judges influenced their work. If this were considered, one might conclude that the competitive group created art they thought the judges would like, and the other group created art to their own liking. Would this be the first time students gave answers they thought teachers expected? Did the judges know which group they were judging when they formed their opinions? Would the result have been different if the students had been told that the judges would be other students? Do the conclusions suggest that pre-teenagers believe that adults are artistically conservative? Do the beliefs of the self-selected population of those in public education influence the agenda of this kind of research? Is this a case of belief creating its own reality?

I once heard a psychologist explain out-of-body experiences during surgery (when people seem to look down on themselves as if out of their bodies). The explanation was that the mind was trying to separate itself from the body because of some body-related situation the mind was trying to avoid. Where did that thought come from? How can it be tested? Interestingly, some aircraft pilots who have blacked-out in centrifuge tests (due to blood flowing from the head to the lower body) have had out-of-body experiences within minutes after leaving the centrifuge area. May we properly theorize that out-of-body experiences do not result from the mind trying to escape the body, but from something related to depriving the brain of oxygen, which occurs during centrifuge training and, at times, during surgery?

Compared with out-of-body experiences, theories of self-esteem, theories on the rehabilitation of criminals, theories about the influence on our young of beliefs conveyed through television and other media, and theories concerning countless other phenomena are extremely difficult to test. Evaluation is difficult in part because the observer's political, social, and other biases adversely influence the perceived results or lack thereof. But, verified or not, such theories are being used by educators and others to teach our young, and are shaping not only our society, but those influenced by the American model as well.

Test scores are the only largely objective means we have to verify the effectiveness of psychology-based teaching theory. Is it a coincidence that test scores have been under attack since the new education paradigm has been introduced? Is our present system of education attempting to avoid exposure of its failures under the artifice of claiming that testing (competition) is harmful to student self-esteem?

Recently, a particularly sad event took place involving autistic children. Parents were told that their children were more intelligent than was previously realized and that their intelligence could express itself through "facilitated communications." It required facilitators to function as interpreters for the children. Unfortunately, the facilitators' imaginations proved to be the source of the newly discovered intelligence. This is one example of what appears to be a junk science epidemic.

Gerd Gigerenzer, Director of the Center for Adaptive Behavior and Cognition at the Max Plank Institute for Psychological Research in Munich, Germany, has said recently:

> Much of psychology now consists of vague theories that don't spell out precise predictions ... Productive theories about the mind will have to risk being precise and opening themselves up to being disproved. Then we can begin to work out the ecology of rationality.[18]

If we tend to perceive what our beliefs predict we will observe, then belief in fiction or the secular mythology of propagandists is self-reinforcing. As long as a belief is satisfying, we are unlikely to cast it aside for a less satisfying but more intellectually defensible belief. To compound the problem, the more unrealistic the fiction the more likely rational argument will be perceived as not only wrong, but a threat to the believer. An essential part of the scientific method is to identify and discount personally satisfying, arbitrary beliefs that might distort our perceptions of the thing being studied. And, if the result of our study conflicts with our beliefs, our willingness to question, if not change, what we believe consistent with such result is a measure of our intellectual honesty and our capacity to do quality science.

All sorts of social, developmental, psychological, and other theories presented as fact have been influencing the evolution of our combined psychogenetic makeup by displacing beliefs evolved over generations. It is generally true in science that experiment is the means by which a theory is tested. However, psychological experiments on the scale we have been undertaking require generations to test and cannot be run under controlled conditions. Whether these theories will prove correct and will benefit us in the long run is not yet known. What we do know is that they are altering our psychogenes.

Before they are passed to the next generation, the inherited beliefs of each generation are changed. We might adapt them to new circumstances of living, or we might decide to do things differently from the way our parents or others have taught. In this way cultures evolve from what they were (what they believed) to what they are (what they believe now). The process is influenced by so many factors that it is largely uncontrollable. This realization has no doubt motivated the Amish and others to freeze their culture's evolution. However, everything is in the process of becoming something else; only the rates of becoming are different. Given that psychogenetic changes from generation to generation can weaken as well as strengthen a culture, our challenge is to predict whether our changes will be beneficial. Interfering with the teaching of established beliefs and values threatens religious, parental, and other traditional repositories of beliefs and values. Are the politically and commercially driven changes in our cultural psychogenes at the root of recent political, religious, and social movements back to more traditional values and beliefs? That some psychogenes of the new social paradigm are being rejected is not new. This is a cyclic social process of testing and reforming, driven by the population segments most offended by the way things are. Whether they come as unintended consequences of other changes or by the intentional distortions of belief managers, if new psychogenes are in fact based on untruth or unreality, they are probably damaging to social cohesion and strength, and are a potential threat to our future. If we act, not on what is true, but on what we believe to be true or what we wish were true, then, to the extent that the negligent or corrupt masters of the biology of belief influence what we believe to be true, we will likely act against our best interests and in favor of theirs.

Chapter 13

Reason, Myth, Psychogenetic Inertia, and the Future

In examining the biology of belief, we have considered how the structure of our brains influences what we believe, how our beliefs are transmitted, by what means they change, how they define our realities, determine our actions, alter our perceptions, perpetuate our cultures, and enable others to manipulate our beliefs and actions. We have yet to consider a scenario by which the biology of belief is likely to influence our collective future.

We See the Universe through Our Ancestors' Eyes

As we have seen, the present model of Homo sapiens comes with both amygdalae and prefrontal lobes. Unlike philosophical or mystical dualities, these brain structures comprise a true physical duality, which provides us with our fear and reason. They are the source of our Jekyll and Hyde nature. However, while fear, other reptilian passions, and reason provide our minds with essential life-sustaining processes, our humanness resides in what we have learned to believe. Our myths and ideals assuage our fears and control our aggressions. As the Greek historian Polybius (200?-118? BCE) wrote of the undisciplined of his day:

> [A]s every multitude is fickle, full of lawless desires, unreasoned passion, and violent anger, it must be held in by invisible terrors and religious pageantry.[1]

If our passions were not moderated by reason or by controlling myths, our behaviors would reflect our baser urges and not the human values of which we are capable. However, controlling myths deal with the effect and not the cause of our unreasoned behaviors. They control primal passions with emotion-stirring images, stories, and rituals.

Beginning with our ancient animist ancestors, it seems that our social evolution has directly influenced our mythologies. When we evolved pharaohs, we added the concepts of immortality and god-kings to our worship of animals, the sun, and other objects. When our ancestors in ancient India discovered how to control alpha trances, they incorporated them into their myths and philosophies as transcendental experiences and heightened states of spiritual awareness. Modern occult beliefs have replaced older concepts of supernatural forces with the more modern concept of energy. *Energy* is another word for "power" or "control." And whether in the form of God, energy, supernatural forces, or spirits, control serves the same purpose. Thinking that we have it or understand how it works gives us comfort in dealing with the otherwise uncontrollable, mysterious and dangerous things we encounter.

In its two-thousand-plus years of existence, Western philosophy has also reflected our cultural evolution. However, notwithstanding our greater understanding of our universe and ourselves, modern philosophy is about as ineffectual as that of the early Greeks in influencing the mythical and ethical beliefs of the general population. Modern philosophies, which have divested themselves of all vestiges of myth, find little support for their emotionally unfulfilling views. How fortifying is the belief that the universe is hostile and indifferent? How satisfying is the belief that our existence is unexplainable? And who is comforted in believing that we—alone—are responsible for the foolish things we do, with no way to absolve our guilt?

Perhaps, excepting the influence scientific discoveries have had on our worldview, we are not very different from our ancestors. They have lived in many places and spoken many languages, and, given our common emotional needs and our inheritance of their psychogenes, we have more in common with them than we realize. For better or worse, to the extent that we have inherited their psychogenes, we see the universe through their eyes. Unfortunately, although their myths were effective in dealing with their fears, when mythologies are dominant, those guided by reason are well advised to hide their true beliefs in a thicket of carefully phrased obscure language. As British philosopher and economist John Stuart Mill (1806-73) observed,

> The world would be astonished if it knew how great a proportion of its brightest ornaments, of those most distinguished even in popular estimation for wisdom and virtue, are complete skeptics in religion.

Averroes and others have suggested that mature philosophers should not openly criticize mythologies for their transgressions against reason, because myths are the source of morality and piety for a substantial part of society. The reciprocal view would be that mature theologians should not demonize philosophers for seeking the truth, even though it might conflict with myth. Unfortunately, it is more likely that less-mature philosophers will bemoan mythological hypocrisies and transgressions against reason to audiences rendered unreceptive by their fears and inherited beliefs. So too, less-mature theologians will continue to rationalize the inhuman results of their zealotry, refuse to acknowledge the "legitimacy" of other mythologies, and fail to realize that scientists, for the most part, are merely Nature's messengers. If so inclined, secular philosophers should be free to live by their own morality without having to twist it into a form acceptable to intolerant, powerful theologians. That is a price exacted from philosophers that would have been avoided if mature theologians had encouraged their zealous brethren not to demand from others what they demand from their flocks. Mature theologians have learned to adapt their mythologies to discoveries about Nature without denigrating the natural philosophers whose quest for wisdom continues to reveal Nature's secrets. Philosophers will continue to point their telescopes to the heavens looking for knowledge, while mythologists will continue to point their obelisks, minarets, and spires to the heavens looking for reassurance. How we deal with our inherent need for both will determine our future as it has our past.

Old Psychogenes in a New World

The following description of a population-driven embrittlement scenario is an example of how psychogenetic inertia might influence our future. Religious wars and self-perpetuating ethnic conflicts are other examples of psychogenetic inertia that seem destined to remain with us indefinitely.

Historically, cultures experience cycles of adversity and plenty, peace and confusion. In times of stress, fears beget myths that tend to focus our collective efforts, simplify our common worldview, and stimulate our passions, giving us strength and conviction to overcome adversity. During such times, reason is little respected, as Socrates and Bruno discovered. When times are good, religious passion fades as fear fades. Unneeded virility gives way to pleasures and soft comforts while diminished fears permit reason to question myth. In the past, changes brought by plenty would have invited attack by cultures experiencing times of adversity or transition. It is highly probable that that is behind us. Instead, barbarians at the borders are being replaced by something with which our fortifying myths, inspirational chants, and God-based morality have never prepared us to deal: success!

We owe our success as a species to our ability to understand and control the things around us. Our dilemma is that the unintended consequences of controlling the things around us might threaten our way of life. Our psychogenes, which were great for low-tech animists, might be devastating for high-tech mythologists. Given the virtually nonexistent technology of our animist ancestors, they dealt with their adversities by imagining a spirit world. They dealt with their lack of power over Nature by bargaining with prayers, sacrifices, chants, dances, and other rituals of respect for the spirits they believed could help them. These were fear-based belief systems that did not ignore Nature; they became one with it. Our population is expected to increase by sixty percent in less than forty years. But animist cultures in forests around the world are helpless before our technology as it destroys their life-sustaining balance with Nature to support our growing numbers. The cultural imperatives of primitive animistic societies acknowledge that their survival depends on Nature, while they are unaware of Nature's underlying laws. We, on the other hand, understand much about and utilize the laws of Nature, but have lost cultural imperatives that acknowledge our dependence on it. American psychogenes relevant to these matters were formed at a time when there was no limit to available land. The frontier had not yet reached the Pacific Ocean. The frontier mentality of our forefathers respected individual initiative, self-reliance, and strong religious convictions. Their religion taught them that they had dominion over all other living things and that to increase knowledge was to increase sorrow. They had little need and less respect for intellectual pursuits and resource conservation. Believing as they did helped them survive in their physically harsh and unforgiving world. And, directly or indirectly, we inherited their beliefs.

It would be a mistake to force the belief that our technology is the problem. Technology (applied science) is a tool, or more precisely, millions of tools. Intelligently applied, our technology can be compatible with Nature. However, toxicity is a matter of dosage, and otherwise ecologically compatible technologies can become toxic by increasing the volume of their usage. Increasing population and increasing usage drives increasing volume, as populations become more affluent. Methane is produced as a byproduct of digestion by the cattle we eat. It is believed by some that the world cattle population is now producing enough methane to influence global surface temperatures. A huge amount of methane is stored in ice crystals in the seafloor. They are called methane hydrates.[2] Were ocean currents to warm just enough to melt the ice, sufficient methane might be released to vastly accelerate global warming, as some believe it did at the end of the Paleocene era, about 55 million years ago.

Whether increasing Earth's surface temperature would be beneficial or otherwise in the long run is not the point. We might be unable to stop or reverse a possible rising-temperature trend because of psychogenetic inertia; e.g., our inability to control our procreation—because psychogenes relevant to reproduction are replicated without change in each new generation. Although recent population growth rates seem to be declining, our global population is still expected to double in about 50 years. Increases in the production rate of chemicals used to produce our food parallel increases in our population and in our affluence. Each year rain washes millions of tons of fertilizers,[3] herbicides, pesticides, and animal wastes into our waters, causing disease and death throughout the food chain. Recent tests have shown that drugs excreted by humans and animals are building up in our waterways and aquifers. And there has been a marked loss of bio-diversity and of arable land to housing construction and erosion.

Movements against nuclear power, deforestation, over-fishing, chemical pollution, *et cetera*, are attacking the symptoms. The need for power, lumber, and fish at ever-increasing levels is the result primarily of our growing population. We are not in balance with Nature. Changing laws to protect depleted fishing regions is relatively simple. Changing belief-driven behavior that increases the demand for fish is another matter. It is easier to force the belief that technology is the problem than to admit that our increasing population is the underlying cause. It seems apparent that our biological drive to reproduce, operating with the biology of belief, as manifested in cultural and myth-based psychogenes, encourages population growth and is at the root of our increasing numbers. In addition, high birth rates are very effective at swelling religious populations. Psychogenes that encouraged geometric population growth might have been affordable in the age that created them, when large families ensured our survival against disease or other disasters, and when we believed that the Earth was a limitless resource; since then, however, our life expectancies and affluence have increased, and we have become aware that we are depleting our resources at unsustainable rates. But once such psychogenes are embedded in a religious culture, how can they be changed?

It is possible that pollution-related infertility and premature death, reduced birth rates associated with increasing affluence, increasing numbers of educated women, drug-resistant lethal organisms, the migration of rural populations to urban centers, and other such factors might turn the tide of increasing population. If so, this would be the result of natural forces acting on the product of our collective inability to make rational choices about our own destiny. But superstition-based psychogenes, such as the belief that powdered rhinoceros horn is an aphrodisiac, drive demand for animals and animal parts, forcing prices higher and making illegal hunting of endangered species extremely difficult to stop. Our irrational psychogenes can have very real and completely irreversible consequences. Apparently, how our future evolves will be influenced less by our capacity to solve problems through rational thought than by our increasing affluence and the psychogenetic inertia inherent in the biology of belief.

Although our population has proliferated in the past two thousand years, some of our more important psychogenes have not changed significantly. They are potentially dangerous anachronisms. The potential danger inherent in failing to control our population rationally is not in some unrealistic projection of future population. History is filled with overpopulation scenarios, none of which have materialized to date. Unfortunately, the problem is more subtle. By pushing our life-sustaining systems to the limit, we embrittle ourselves. We lose the ability to accommodate Nature's surprises. California, a major producer of food, panicked at a five-year drought. Historically, a five-year drought for southern California is considered short. The droughts that ended the Anasazi culture in the southwest United States, the pre-Incan civilization of South America, and possibly the Sumerian culture lasted decades, if not centuries.

At the present time, Earth has about 1,500 active volcanoes. No one knows when we will experience an eruption sufficient to interrupt food production and exhaust global food reserves. What we do know is that the more we must consume everything we produce to keep up with our growing numbers, the smaller a volcanic eruption needs to be to create a catastrophe.

Dealing with rapidly rising ocean levels resulting from the dislodgment and subsequent melting of Antarctic ice is quite another matter. One theory that explains the movement of ice flows in Antarctica suggests that the Antarctic ice cap has a cycle of about 7,000 years. As snow accumulates on Antarctic land, the ice cap increases in size. This lowers ocean levels, as water is stored on land as packed snow and ice. As the cap thickens, it better insulates the region where the cap attaches to land. Heat rising from deep in the Earth, possibly due to volcanism, eventually causes melting of the ice that locks the cap to land. Water mixed with earth in a kind of slippery muck lubricates the ice sheets and their attachment to the land is lost. Sections begin to flow more rapidly to the ocean where they breakup and melt. If this were to happen on a large enough scale, melting ice could raise ocean levels. Some estimate that the present cycle will be completed within about 100 to 200 years. If this information is combined with the history that some believe led to the Sumerian culture in the Middle East, one might conclude that a pre-Sumerian flood did happen and that ocean levels are about to rise again, sans Noah. Global ocean levels might rise about ten meters or thirty feet. How would rising ocean levels contribute to embrittlement? If coastal areas were to flood, would food-producing land be needed for housing? Could the remaining land accommodate our present population?

Different beliefs and circumstances create different perceptions of which actions are appropriate and which are not. Those with a Genesis view of Nature see us as dominating all other life forms and have no problem with our causing the extinction of other species. They tend to see the Earth as an infinite reservoir for our procreation and mindless use of technology, and to believe that Nature will adjust the future to whatever we do. It will. How we will be a part of that future is another question. Others believe that allowing Nature to be itself is the answer to our problems. They say we should revert to a simpler time (before modern technology and the population explosion). This thinking assumes that Nature is benevolent or stable. The problem is that Nature is mindless, and we have come to rely on a state of Nature that is not permanent. Sea levels are not fixed. They vary at least 300 feet. The intelligent use of technology might be the only way to keep sea levels constant, whether it is used to compensate for the glaciation cycle or the possible warming effects of greenhouse gas emissions. What some of us seek is an idyllic status quo, not reliance on Natural forces. Those who will not or cannot address the underlying problem of population growth and the appropriate use of technology will find themselves stumbling into the future.

Were the Earth larger, or had we continued Greco-Roman and Arab inquiry into science and technology instead of losing almost a thousand years of myth-suppressed scientific inquiry during the Dark and Middle ages, it is likely that we would have arrived at our present level of scientific understanding when our global population was a fraction of what it is today. It is also possible that we would not have inherited the present high level of myth-driven psychogenes imploring us to procreate. Had our history been different we would have more time to deal with the problem of balancing our procreation psychogenes, our inherent, mindless drive to reproduce, and our need to live in balance with Nature. The longer we do nothing to correct the imbalance, the more our decisions will have to rely on objective reasoning and not on our anachronistic psychogenes.

Compounding our anachronistic beliefs is our lack of concern for all but immediate problems. Changing psychogenes on a global scale to prevent a disaster fifty years from now is, at best, a remote likelihood. If psychogenes evolve one funeral at a time, we might not be able to change quickly enough to influence our collective future. It will be a race between our rational understanding and our anachronistic psychogenes. Politicians and community leaders who must accommodate public beliefs to maintain their power, do not, in these matters, shape public opinion as much as reflect it. They power-surf on waves of today's beliefs and leave to our descendants the predictable future disasters that will be unleashed when reality can no longer accommodate our illusions. Leaders of faith-based organizations are less influenced by public opinion. Rather than being subject to public opinion, they influence it, because their beliefs are magnified by the number and influence of their followers. And, since faith-based belief systems are subjective, their administrators are seldom affected when their beliefs conflict with reality. Rational or not, the process is self-validating. Those who look to such belief systems to find their way will be using outdated maps. It is unfortunate that the belief-altered perceptions of mythologists do not permit them to learn from the experiences of extinct mythologies.

For mythologies that find their origins in the fear of death, among other things, it is not surprising that preserving and proliferating life would be core beliefs. If philosophers are denigrated or ignored, and if politicians and priests cannot provide rational guidance in matters as fundamental as avoiding outgrowing our life-sustaining resources, then Nature is the only force left that can cause us to discard our outdated psychogenes.

If we are better driven by crisis than by reason, then we can expect serious challenges to the present mythologies and psychogenes, as global food and energy become valuable and life becomes cheap. Computer models predict food and energy scarcities by the middle of the 21st century.[4] Thomas Homer-Dixon, director of the Peace and Conflict Studies Program at the University of Toronto said: the more resource scarcity and population stresses rise, "the smarter we have to be, both socially and technically, just to maintain our well-being." The more dire the problem "the more quickly we're going to have to respond."[5] It is ironic that revered myth-based psychogenes might create a future that will envy the past.

Can Our Mythologies Adapt?

If, as creatures of our biological inheritance, we must use myth to alter our perception of reality to survive it, perhaps the problems that come with dominance of our world will require that our next successful mythology defines all of humanity as its congregation. It might require that we create a supernatural parent interested in compassion over retribution, and see ourselves as a recent part of an ancient evolving universe. It might demand that we have respect for each other and our world, while rejecting the chauvinistic view of ourselves as God's chosen creatures, and that we act morally less out of fear of supernatural retribution and more as a collective decision to benefit ourselves and our descendants by leaving things better than we find them. And it might stress the importance of rational planning, and define transcendence as subordinating our inheritance as masters of predation to our inheritance of reason and the capacity for tolerance and enlightened self-interest. Instead of teaching fear to the young on the assumption that they all need fear to control their urges, a way might be found to stress the importance of rational thinking for those capable of controlling their urges without fear.

Joseph Campbell said that the old mythologies, which were useful in their time, are no longer relevant. We are faced with the prospect of embrittling the Earth's capacity to sustain us, and our world is fundamentally different from that of our ancestors. To blindly follow the dictates of their psychogenes is to invite a global version of the overpopulation disaster that befell the inhabitants of Easter Island. Our mythological beliefs must change before Nature bursts our psychogenetic bubble. The core psychogenes of influential Western mythologies developed almost two thousand years ago, when Western culture was dominated by a militaristic Roman state. The view that life on Earth at that time was a vale of tears was fertile ground for the formation of mythological beliefs that could find happiness only in a life to come. Although the military power of the Western Roman Empire has been gone for some fifteen hundred years, the mythology that it spawned has remained virtually unchanged. If such institutionalized anachronistic beliefs fail to recognize that we are not only capable of shaping our future on Earth, but have a responsibility to our descendants to shape it in a way that reflects our best objective judgment and not our unreasoned fears, then our time in history might be remembered less for our accomplishments in science and more for how unwilling the keepers of our mythologies were to adapt ancient beliefs to the present necessities of surviving on a small, fragile planet. If history teaches anything, it is that the uncontrolled excesses of pious zealots have caused at least as much damage and suffering as the similarly uncontrolled acts of political demagogues. Perhaps it is time that theologians saw themselves as shepherds, not only of their flocks, but of all flocks and the Earth as well. In the process, it would be well if they addressed honestly the pious zealotry of their policies, which motivate fundamentalist assassins and terrorists, and considered as well their resistance to changing attitudes about people not like themselves and the logical consequences of their teachings on overpopulating the Earth.

The traditional social dominance of emotion-based theologies appears to be undergoing a challenge. Whether it is for the better is not yet clear. Emotion-based social engineers in politics and various social movements are competing with established religions for control in determining social beliefs and values. In general, religions are motivated by the need for self-preservation and their historical desire to control the anxieties and baser urges of mankind through emotion-based myth. Some social engineers appear to be using pseudo-psychology to support an egalitarian or cultural relativist belief that equal outcome is more desirable than equal opportunity, and that self-esteem and not self-discipline will achieve the ultimate good. Unfortunately, the attempt to make every child feel good about her or his cultural heritage appears to have reduced educational standards. If cultural pride and self-esteem require not being disappointed by one's grades relative to those of others with different cultural heritages, and if grades can be manipulated by using psychology theory to establish that competition for grades is destructive, then cultural pride and self-esteem can be bolstered by marginalizing competition for grades and simplifying course content to ensure that the least capable will be able to succeed. In so doing, cultural relativists, more commonly seen as political multiculturalists who believe that cultures are equal but different, achieve their goals at the expense of educational excellence. Some social engineers appear to have faith in what might be a new secular mythology, based more on opinion than on science.

Do new social engineers represent a force capable of countering anachronistic mythological psychogenes, environmental embrittlement, opposition to fetal cell research, and other similar public policy issues? Social engineers and theologians both deal with the same malleable, emotion- and symbol-driven public, whose primary concerns are with their more immediate problems of making a living and raising their families. Theologians have used emotional mechanisms for millennia to control the behavior and anxieties of their flocks. In the process, they have attempted to conform public policy to their myth-based beliefs. Today, however, it appears that social engineers using modern belief-management techniques have reduced religion's influence over public policy. On the positive side, this could mean that anachronistic myth-based prejudices might lose influence over public policy. On the other hand, the collective beliefs of these social engineers would determine what is politically correct. As major corporations have acquired control of the means of distribution for news and information, via television, radio, books, magazines, *et cetera*, they too have become part of the new power elite. Given the covert nature of belief management, how would the new power elite be identified? Moreover, if they operate outside the structure of government, by what mechanism would this new power be kept in balance? If such a power elite is not elected and does not reveal their true beliefs regarding their public policy goals, we, the public, are subject to belief management on a grand scale and thereby lose influence over our future. Is this a significant threat to representative democracy? Was Edward Bernays correct in thinking that belief management would succeed in circumventing the democratic process and perpetuate elite power? In Stuart Ewen's analysis of the influence of belief management on the democratic process, he queried:

- Can there be democracy when public agendas are routinely predetermined by "unseen engineers?"
- Can there be democracy when public opinion is reduced to the published results of opinion surveys, statistical applause tracks?
- Can there be democracy in a society in which emotional appeals overwhelm reason, where the image is routinely employed to overwhelm thought?[7]

Foreign democracies that express concern about how the American model might be influencing their cultures should not be concerned with rock music and blue jeans. They should be wary of the culture-altering implications inherent in importing American public relations expertise and the concentration of ownership of the news and information systems. At the beginning of this century a number of researchers expressed concern about how democracy would bring with it a tyranny of the masses.[6] Visions of the French Revolution come to mind. This belief, perhaps self-serving, justified in the minds of many early public relations practitioners and theorists the notion that fraud, deceit, and the intentional thwarting of reasoned debate were necessary tactics if not an obligation of a power elite to preserve society from the barbaric tendencies of the masses. What has not been generally expressed is concern for what might happen if a power elite uses their position to force their will on the public. Worse yet, what if the power elite falls under the control of one person in a time of economic and social upheaval, as happened not long ago in Germany. Inasmuch as the jury system works fairly well, we might do better taking our chances with the so-called barbaric masses while avoiding a potentially lethal concentration of power. Perhaps reason could be put back into public debate to some degree, if the judiciary could find a way to distinguish free speech from blatant public relations fraud, and treat those who intentionally and blatantly deceive the public for personal or corporate gain the same way we treat fraud when committed between individuals.

What of conflicts between social engineers and religious groups? It is not inconceivable that social engineers might be trying to marginalize religious influence over public policy. This might account for recent apparent vying for control of social agendas. Examples include social engineers attempting to restructure education by replacing traditional religious values with psychology-based education theory, legal challenges to the use of social discrimination as a tool of religion to scorn behavior unacceptable to religious belief systems, and legislative attempts by religions to impose their beliefs through various anti-abortion, anti-evolution and pro-school prayer proposals.

It appears that the American experiment with independence has taken a new turn. What began as a refuge from religious persecution has succeeded in creating a culture influenced by religious values. At first, we sought to establish religious and political independence, and since have sought independence for those of us who were enslaved, for women, and for others who were denied their constitutional rights. Now, in attempting to declare independence from religious influence, it appears that some of us are willing to declare our independence from beneficial religious psychogenes, with little concern for how equivalent secular psychogenes will be created to replace them. As a society we cannot survive for long if laws alone are relied on to control our behavior. There would never be enough police. Ethical traditions from wherever derived are the primary source of restraint for civilized cultures. As Voltaire said through the character of Pope Benedict XIV in his Epilogue to *Elysium*,

> BENEDICT. And I often wished that I might speak with you. I must confess that I enjoyed your wit and your artistry. But it was your brilliance that led you astray. It

is difficult to be brilliant and conservative; there is little charm, for active minds, in standing for tradition and authority; it is tempting to be critical, for then you can feel the pleasure of individuality and novelty. But in philosophy it is almost impossible to be original without being wrong. And I should like to talk with you not as a priest or a theologian, but as one philosopher to another.

VOLTAIRE. Thank you. There has been considerable doubt as to my being a philosopher.

BENEDICT. You had the good sense not to fabricate a new system. But you made a fundamental and grievous mistake.

VOLTAIRE. What was that one?

BENEDICT. You thought it possible for one mind, in one lifetime, to acquire such scope of knowledge and depth of understanding as to be fit to sit in judgment upon the wisdom of the race—upon traditions and institutions that have taken form out of the experience of centuries. Tradition is to the group what memory is to the individual; and just as the snapping of memory may bring insanity, so a sudden break with tradition may plunge a whole nation into madness, like France in the Revolution.

History has shown that most of us need mythology to control our unreasoned passions and that reason is not an effective teacher of morality for the majority, driven by emotion. Perhaps our striving for independence has reached its limit when some of us, in an attempt to apply so-called psychology theory to real social systems, attempt to declare reason independent from emotion. It seems apparent that our internal conflict of reason and emotion is mirrored in our social conflicts. By ignoring the biological relationship between reason and emotion as we attempt to change traditions or perceived biases we do not like, we might be altering our collective character, and, in turn, our psychogenetic legacy, in ways we neither intend nor understand. That risk notwithstanding, it appears that we are in little danger of altering our religious psychogenes any time soon. The following is from a recent article regarding the Gallup polling organization:

> America's religious faith has proved constant too—much more so, at least, than is popularly supposed. Today's Christian right-wing trades on the idea that religious observance is in decline, and in dire need of rescue. The truth, according to Gallup's surveys, is close to the opposite. Religion seems to have undergone a surge of interest after the second world war, reflected in an increase in Bible reading, church giving and church building. These gains were undermined later on, when the social turmoil of the 1960s and 1970s took its toll on churches, as it did on most other institutions. But in the 1990s the decline seems to have stopped. The Princeton Religion Research Centre index, an ongoing measurement of eight key religious beliefs and practices, hit a ten-year high in 1995. The proportion of Americans telling Gallup that they have attended a church or synagogue service in the past week has increased from around 37% in the 1930s to around 42% in the 1990s, and those who went to college (70%) are now more likely to be a member of a church or synagogue than those who did not (67%).
>
> Whatever these ups and downs, the United States remains much more religious than any other rich industrial country. A Gallup Poll conducted in 1995 found that 61% of Americans say that democracy cannot survive without a widespread belief in a god of some kind. Surveying a variety of evidence that same year, the younger Gallup wrote that virtually all Americans say

they believe in God or a universal spirit [96%]; most believe God watches over and judges people; most believe he still performs miracles [78%]; many say they have felt his presence. More than one in three American adults says that God speaks to them directly. Virtually all Americans pray, and believe prayers are answered.

Religious passion, in turn, explains other singular features of the United States. One American in two gives two or three hours per week to a volunteer cause; and much of this effort is organized through churches. Religion may be at the root of America's optimism, too. A Gallup survey in 1989 found a correlation between religious faith and happiness, job fulfillment, excitement about the future and family ties.[8]
...

But for our constitutional requirement that church and state remain separate, one would think from Gallup's polls that the United States would be a virtual theocracy. What the Gallup article does not reveal is that many who comprise our governmental, educational, entertainment, news, and other elite groups appear to be self-selected participants who favor more the values of our social engineers than our theologians and who have influence disproportionate to their numbers. This social value dichotomy might be at the root of much of current competition for control of our social agenda. It might also explain what appears to be a defensive reaction by theologians, reflected in increased religious broadcasting and an increasingly overt involvement of religious leaders in politics. On the other hand, religious leaders might be merely updating their belief-management technology. Social engineers have managed to offend secular values as well. In the past, home education was practiced mostly for religious reasons. Today, however, increasing numbers of children are being educated at home for the secular goal of avoiding the influence of politically correct psychology theory and standards-reducing multicultural curricula taught in public schools. The various battles taking place elsewhere in the world between religious extremists and secular movements or between ultraconservative and progressive political movements do not appear to include a social engineering component such as ours. They seem to be more traditional battles that derive from a perceived threat to regional cultural, political, or religious psychogenes—resulting from the homogenizing effect of mass communications technology, economic globalization, rising ethnic and religious zealotry, and other factors. It appears that our future is caught up in a war of bubbles. Albert Einstein's view was that "Politics is a pendulum whose swings between anarchy and tyranny are fueled by perennially rejuvenated illusions." [9]

In the United States, if we assume that belief management by social engineering and other elite groups succeeds in dominating the public policy agenda, who will decide which beliefs should dominate? What would happen to the governmental balance of power if control of the public policy agenda resides in the hands of a non-elected, belief-managing elite whose actions are governed solely by their own secular mythology or commercial interests? Without constitutional control of such power, how can we describe our government as a representative democracy? Should such belief management be allowed protection of the first amendment guarantee of free speech?

Blurring the Line between Myth and Science

It appears that mythologists are attempting to marry science (rational analysis) with religion once again, this time using the Big Bang instead of Neoplatonism. If what is not yet known or not knowable to science is the only safe haven for myth, then the impossibility of knowing what, if anything, happened before the Big Bang represents an opportunity for mythologists to claim that the Big Bang is the mythological moment of Creation. Not only would such a claim be impossible to prove or disprove, it would support, in the minds of many, claims that myth has a way of knowing that science does not. If this line of reasoning were to become widely accepted, it follows that mythologists would use the Big Bang-Creation argument to impugn whatever established scientific knowledge they find most irritating. In all likelihood, Darwinism would be a prime target, and present efforts by anti-abortionists to control fetal tissue research[10] would acquire new vigor. Myth does not seek the truth about Nature. To the extent that truth contradicts myth, mythologists are irritated by the truth, to wit, the burning of Giordano Bruno for his contradiction of myth-endorsed geocentricity. If mythologists were to succeed in convincing the public that emotional myth is superior to rational science, then the problems mythologists created for the scientists studying the biochemistry that was used to produce a morning-after pill to avoid pregnancy, and for the scientists studying molecular biology, including cloning, will be considered small compared with the limits mythologists could impose on science with wide public support and eager legislatures.

For about a thousand years, from the fall of the Western Roman Empire to the Renaissance, Western science languished while mythologists dominated scientists and other philosophers. The contributions of Arab scientists to mathematics and medicine ceased with the burning of Averroes' books in the twelfth century and have not recovered to this day. It is one thing for scientists to invoke mythological references in personal conversations while discussing the Big Bang's apparent limit on the ability of science to pursue the truth. However, when prominent scientists invoke mythological references in otherwise scientific presentations to the public, it appears that science is worshipping at the altar of myth. As personally satisfying as such mythological references might be, those views are personal, unscientific, and as immune from scientific assessment as creation myths. We know that the only social environments in which science has flourished have been predominantly secular. For a scientist to endorse mythology with the imprimatur of a body of knowledge created in part by scientists who, in their quest to understand Nature, suffered or died at the hands of mythologists, is not good science nor is it good for science. How would such endorsements of myth by scientists be explained to Bruno, Galileo, and Descartes? Neither are such endorsements representative of the views of contemporary scientists, 60 percent of whom in the United States are not theists, with astronomers among the most skeptical.[11] Although prominence may justify hegemony in politics and theology, it does not in science.

There are others who put forth the idea that the natural world is the province of science and morality is the province of religion. But for Christian morality, would the Albigensians of southern France have been slaughtered in the 13th century? Would the Jewish victims of the Spanish Inquisition have been persecuted had the Roman Catholic Church not blamed all Jews for the death of Christ? And, at the beginning of this century, when both the Roman Catholic and Lutheran churches taught their flocks that Jews were responsible for the death of Christ, what effect did such beliefs have on a zealous Roman Catholic altar boy we know today as Adolph Hitler,[12] the architect of the Final Solution? In view of religion's abominable moral history, were Plato and Epicurus alive today they would no doubt laugh at the proposition that morality is the province of mythology. In an interview, the English writer Arthur C. Clarke said that

> One of the greatest tragedies of mankind is that morality has been hijacked by religion. So now people assume that religion and morality have a necessary connection. But the basis of morality is really very simple and doesn't require religion at all. It's this: 'Don't do unto anybody else what you wouldn't want to be done to you.' It seems to me that that's all there is to it.[13]

In addition, recent endorsements of mythology by a minority of prominent scientists come at a time when understanding science is the exception among otherwise educated people, and when mass media are blurring the lines between science and science fiction. Parapsychology, junk science, and cults are thriving. Some institutions of higher learning appear to have lost sight of their obligation to educate, not indoctrinate. They apparently lost focus beginning in the 1960s when social stresses generated by the Vietnam War caused some movements to apply pressure to university administrators. Consequently, many college-level diplomas today are equivalent to degrees in philosophy in Europe during the Middle Ages. Almost two generations after Woodstock, antiscience mythologists are being joined by new antiscience movements that define the real world with nihilistic or politically correct biases. These movements perceive the world through lenses distorted by forced beliefs, undisciplined reason, a victim mentality, or self-inflicted or institutionally inflicted ignorance. They reject science as mere politics, self-serving opinion, or a body of collected white European male prejudices, and they do not distinguish between theist and nontheist scientists. They are particularly disturbed by Darwin's view of biological evolution. Nature has no such bias and yields to those who best understand it. How many of our lives have benefited from the same scientific knowledge that is criticized by parsons, politicians, and pseudo-philosophers who confuse thoughts with things?

Since the Renaissance, the free pursuit of scientific inquiry has made possible most of what we associate with the advance of Western civilization. In contrast, we have seen from history that free scientific inquiry has been stifled when mythology has controlled political policy, as it did during the Dark and Middle Ages, and does today in parts of the world. For this reason, no matter how well intentioned they are, recent attempts to marry myth and reason pose a danger to science. Although mythology helps many of us deal with our fears and urges, the necessary reliance of myths on various imagined realities puts them at odds with science. At one point in the past, the conflict centered on heliocentricity. Contemporary examples would be challenges to Darwinism and fetal cell research. Some mythologies create emotionally satisfying images and stories embodying cultural values, superstitions, and incorporate perception-distorting anthropocentrism, dreams, the planning assumption, extra-experiential intuitions, our psychogenetic inheritance, and our need to ascribe meaning to everything. It follows that mythologies rooted in such things are as different from science as myth is different from objective reason.

For over 2,000 years, ecclesiastical courts have been condemning scientists and philosophers to death for making statements incompatible with their arbitrary, unreasoned, and emotion-based myths. During that same time, society has accepted and even embraced ecclesiasticism-justified slavery, monarchy, propaganda, war, patriarchy, plunder, and the murder of nonbelievers. Even today, the animosity that religion holds for science is alive and well. Ask any creationist, antiabortion activist, or religious fundamentalist. Better still, ask any victim of their zealotry. And the animosity is not limited to Western mythologists. Some believers in Indian mysticism not only attack Darwinism, but see European scientists themselves as denigrators of Eastern "mystical wisdom."[14] Although the Big Bang theory (conceived by a Roman Catholic theologian) is thought by some— through a strained analogy—to be compatible with the Creation in Genesis, it is not compatible with other creation myths. Consequently, the Big Bang theory, like Darwinism, is under attack by some believers in eastern myth.

To see religion solely as a benevolent force is to ignore its history. In its record of success at controlling the primal instincts of its followers, religion is formidable. However, science is seen as interfering with that formidability each time it threatens religion's authority by contradicting mythical "truths" on which religions rely for power over their followers. The only compatibility that seems likely between science and religion would be based on reason. But it would be extremely unrealistic to expect to reason with the religious masses, driven by emotion. To them, reason is a threat to the religious faith they need to help them survive reality. The most one might hope for is a reasoned accord between ecclesiastics and the secular minority. Excepting situations where those in control of religious movements are zealots, religious leaders understand full well the function of religion in society.

Given their familiarity with the shortcomings and contradictions of their myths, and the ease with which theocracies violate their own ethical codes, reason would suggest that leaders of religions should restrain their antiscience zealots. Although there are occasional hopeful signs that this might be happening, the unwillingness of religious leaders to condemn transgressions committed in the name of religion—and their readiness to criticize scientific inquiry in areas that conflict with their dogma—suggests that religious leaders are not interested in an accord. It appears that much of the impetus for accord is originating with a small minority of scientists and others who have strong religious beliefs. It follows that any accord between science and religion would be one-sided and might precipitate a future threat to science if such an accord were to upset the present balance between religion and secularism.

What does the future hold? If history repeats itself, and if science is not weakened by well-meaning people who might be seeking an accord to resolve their own myth–science paradox, then, in time, Darwinism will be rationalized and accepted by mythologists. In my view, any accord between religion and science would be an illusion. They are systems with different beliefs, purposes, and perceptions of reality. Moreover, their conflicting beliefs reflect the biology of the minds Nature has given us. Individually, most of us manage the internal conflict between our emotions and reason well enough to be productive and content. In the same way, our collective social mind should benefit, not when we try to force myth and science to agree, but when their different ways of dealing with the world are maintained in balance. Given the violence visited upon scientists and others when theologians have dominated, the future would probably be served best if mature theologians learned not to force the edicts of their mythologies on those with different beliefs, and if the line between science and myth were kept clear and unequivocal.

Philosophers and Shamans

In attempting to understand the human paradox, we have considered much about our universe and ourselves. We are at a point in our social evolution when we may be forced to reconsider our parochial beliefs, when our psychogenes and our institutions might prevent us from avoiding self-inflicted global disaster, when growing numbers of us lament our collective irrationality, and when the vast majority of us, while certain of our immortality, have no clue as to how our perceptions of the world came to be. It seems clear that the properties of energy-matter, and space-time have determined the evolution of our universe as well as life on Earth. In addition, it appears that our diverse perceptions of the universe result from the way in which our brains and our various psychogenetic inheritances have evolved.

We find ourselves looking back on some 12 or more billion years of evolution, attempting to comprehend it with the paradoxically conflicted minds Nature has given us. What seems clear is that our difficulties with perceiving the universe correctly have been understood better by philosophers than by shamans. Whether there was a first cause, and if so what it was, may never be resolved objectively. If there was a first cause, there is no reason to conclude that the planning-assumption-based anthropocentric God-hypothesis is correct. If black holes, quantum theory, and Einstein's general and special relativity are barely comprehensible to the average educated person today, why should we think that whatever created the Big Bang would be obvious to our primitive ancestors?

It seems clear that while philosophers are better able to suggest ways of coping with our future, their reasoned advice will go unheeded by populations more interested in assuaging their fears than in understanding them, unaware of the conflict Nature has built into their brains. The dominance of fear over reason in our minds will continue to be reflected in our reverence for shamans and our denigration of scientists and other philosophers whose inquiries we will continue to condemn as irreverent, and whose useful discoveries we will continue to embrace, oblivious to our hypocrisy.

In one quatrain of his *Rubáiyat*, the Persian astronomer, poet Omar Khayyám (1050?,1123 CE) lamented:

> Ah Love! Could you and I with Fate conspire
> To grasp this sorry Scheme of Things entire,
> Would not we shatter it to bits—and then
> Re-mold it nearer to the Heart's Desire! [15]

It is the misfortune of many philosophers, who understand the overall nature of things so clearly, that they become disillusioned and fail to experience the joys of life. In Schopenhauer's gloomy perspective,

> [G]enius [intellect unencumbered by emotion and desire] holds up to us the magic glass in which all that is essential and significant appears to us collected and placed in the clearest light, and what is accidental and foreign is left out.[16] ... If, now, we contemplate the turmoil of life, we behold all occupied with its want and misery, straining all their powers to satisfy its infinite needs and to ward off its multifarious sorrows, yet without daring to hope for anything else than simply the preservation of this tormented existence for a short span of time.[17]

It is clear that the Bible was correct in stating, "he that increaseth knowledge increaseth sorrow." Schopenhauer was correct, as well, in observing that those who see things in the clearest light of intellect are more likely to suffer than those who rely on comforting, but clarity-obscuring myth. However, it is also true that those capable of perceiving subtle pain are more likely to perceive subtle joy. And, given a choice, many would prefer the possible melancholy that accompanies wisdom to the bliss that often accompanies ignorance. In Anatole France's (1844-1924) view,

"[T]he joy of understanding is a sad joy, [yet] those who have once tasted it would not exchange it for all the frivolous gaieties and empty hopes of the ... [common] herd."[18] It might be said that Omar Khayyám's perception of the world would have been more optimistic if he had gone to sleep believing in a fortifying myth. Perhaps. It might also be said that Omar knew that the consequences of the unreasoned mythical and other inherited beliefs of his time would be waiting inevitably for him in the morning. Given that he had no apparent need of myth to assuage a fear of death, he might have benefited more from a non-mythical ethical community that created feelings of kinship and peace of mind through group ritual, music, art, singing, intellectual exchange, and the like while linking his purpose in life to a philosophy of self-improvement, benefiting his family and the common good, and leaving the Earth a better place for his having lived.

Given the nature of the biology of belief, it seems certain that myth will shape much of our future. The history of the Enlightenment shows that a non-mythological understanding of reality leads society to disillusionment and to subsequent reliance on comforting myths. Given this reality, and realizing that their power derives from this biological propensity of our species, perhaps the keepers of our mythologies will make future decisions reflective of a better understanding of the flaws inherent in the biology of belief. Perhaps they will be motivated to accommodate our avoidance of reality without abusing the power it bestows on them. Would we and our descendants not benefit if the keepers of our mythologies were less inclined to see nonbelievers as a threat, and, when interpreting their mythological writings, were less literal and more inclined to see themselves as stewards of humanity and the Earth?

Appendix A

DNA Sequence Trial & Error Computer Program

```
     'Randomly reproduce a simulated 1000 character
DNA code string.
     'Determine maximum and minimum number of
iterations required.

     CLS
     DELAY = 0: 'slow display to make random
selections visible
     DNA$ =
"ACTGGATCGGCATTACGGTCGAGTCCAGATCTACTGGTCATCCATCCGTT"
     DNA$ = DNA$ + DNA$ + DNA$ + DNA$ + DNA$
     DNA$ = DNA$ + DNA$ + DNA$ + DNA$

     RANDOM$ = "ACTG"

1    COUNT = 0
     DARWIN$ = " "

     FOR I = 1 TO LEN(DNA$)
20       COUNT = COUNT + 1
         K$ = INKEY$
         IF K$ = "-" THEN K = K + 1
         IF K$ = "+" THEN K = K - 1
         IF K <= 0 THEN K = 0
         FOR DELAY = 0 TO K * 100: NEXT DELAY

30       RANDOMIZE VAL(RIGHT$(TIME$, 1))
         T = INT((100 * RND) / 10)
         IF T < 1 GOTO 30
         D$ = INKEY$
         IF D$ = "-" THEN D = D + 1
         IF D$ = "+" THEN D = D - 1
         IF D$ = " " GOTO 100
         IF D < 0 THEN D = 0
         FOR J = 0 TO D * 100: NEXT J
         LOCATE 22, 1
         PRINT "DELAY = "; D
         IF T > LEN(RANDOM$) GOTO 30
         T$ = MID$(RANDOM$, T, 1)
         TEST$ = LEFT$(DARWIN$, I) + T$
         LOCATE 1, 1: PRINT TEST$
```

```
      LOCATE 16, 1
      PRINT "Guesses required to match `In God We
Trust' = "; COUNT; "       "

         FOR J = 1 TO DELAY: NEXT J
         IF LEFT$(DNA$, I) <> TEST$ GOTO 20
         DARWIN$ = TEST$
      NEXT I

      ITERATION = ITERATION + 1
      IF COUNT > MAX THEN LET MAX = COUNT
      IF ITERATION = 1 THEN LET MIN = COUNT
      IF COUNT < MIN THEN LET MIN = COUNT

      LOCATE 17, 1
      PRINT "Number of attempts = "; ITERATION
      LOCATE 18, 1
      PRINT "Maximum number of guesses = "; MAX; : IF
OLDMAX <> MAX THEN PRINT " on attempt "; ITERATION
      LOCATE 19, 1
      PRINT "Minimum number of guesses = "; MIN; : IF
OLDMIN <> MIN THEN PRINT " on attempt "; ITERATION
      OLDMAX = MAX
      OLDMIN = MIN
      LOCATE 21, 1
      PRINT "Pressing `+' speeds the process.
Pressing `-' delays the process."
      LOCATE 23, 20
      PRINT "Press the space bar to stop the
program."
      GOTO 1

100   END
```

Appendix B

"In God We Trust" Trial & Error Computer Program

```
'Randomly reproduce an "In God We Trust" DNA
code string.
'Determine maximum and minimum number of
iterations required.

    CLS
    DNA$ = "In God We Trust"
    RANDOM$ = "abcdefghijklmnopqrstuvwxyz
ABCDEFGHIJKLMNOPQRSTUVWXYZ"

1   COUNT = 0
    DARWIN$ = ""

    FOR I = 1 TO LEN(DNA$)
20      COUNT = COUNT + 1
30      RANDOMIZE VAL(RIGHT$(TIME$, 1))
        T = INT(100 * RND)
        IF T < 1 GOTO 30
        IF T > LEN(RANDOM$) GOTO 30
        T$ = MID$(RANDOM$, T, 1)
        TEST$ = LEFT$(DARWIN$, I) + T$
        LOCATE 2, 5: PRINT "               "
        LOCATE 2, 5: PRINT TEST$
        D$ = INKEY$
        IF D$ = "-" THEN D = D + 1
        IF D$ = "+" THEN D = D - 1
        IF D$ = " " GOTO 100
        IF D < 0 THEN D = 0
        FOR j = 0 TO D * 100: NEXT j
        LOCATE 10, 1
        PRINT "DELAY = "; D
    LOCATE 4, 5
    PRINT "Guesses required to match `In God We
Trust' = "; COUNT; "      "
        IF LEFT$(DNA$, I) <> TEST$ GOTO 20
        DARWIN$ = TEST$
    NEXT I

    ITERATION = ITERATION + 1
    IF COUNT > MAX THEN LET MAX = COUNT
    IF ITERATION = 1 THEN LET MIN = COUNT
```

```
     IF COUNT < MIN THEN LET MIN = COUNT

     LOCATE 5, 5
     PRINT "Number of attempts = "; ITERATION
     LOCATE 6, 5
     PRINT "Maximum number of guesses = "; MAX; : IF
OLDMAX <> MAX THEN PRINT " on attempt "; ITERATION
     LOCATE 7, 5
     PRINT "Minimum number of guesses = "; MIN; : IF
OLDMIN <> MIN THEN PRINT " on attempt "; ITERATION
     LOCATE 9, 1
     PRINT "Pressing `+' speeds the process.
Pressing `-' delays the process."
     LOCATE 10, 20
     PRINT "Press the space bar to stop the
program."
     OLDMAX = MAX
     OLDMIN = MIN

     GOTO 1
100  END
```

Appendix C

Brain Wave Types

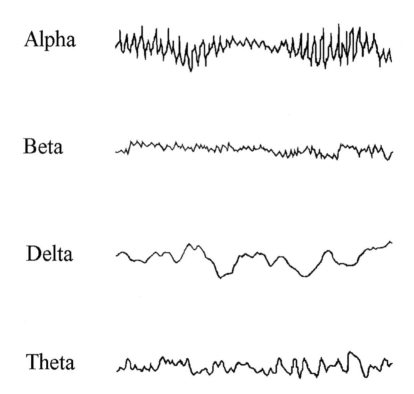

Alpha

Beta

Delta

Theta

Appendix D

Medial view of Right Brain Hemisphere

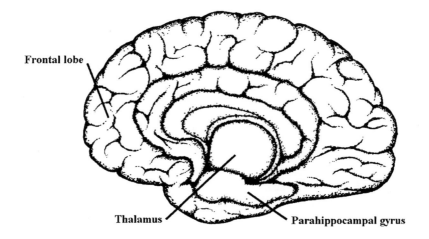

Frontal lobe

Thalamus

Parahippocampal gyrus

Appendix E

Specific Limbic Brain Components

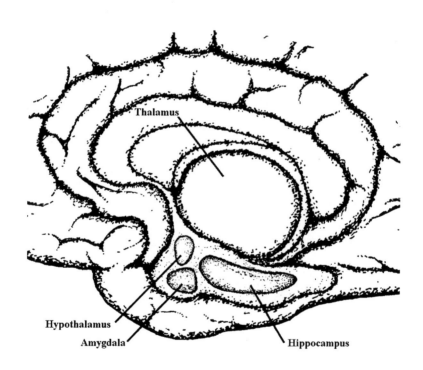

Appendix F

Inferred Black Sea Flood Migrations

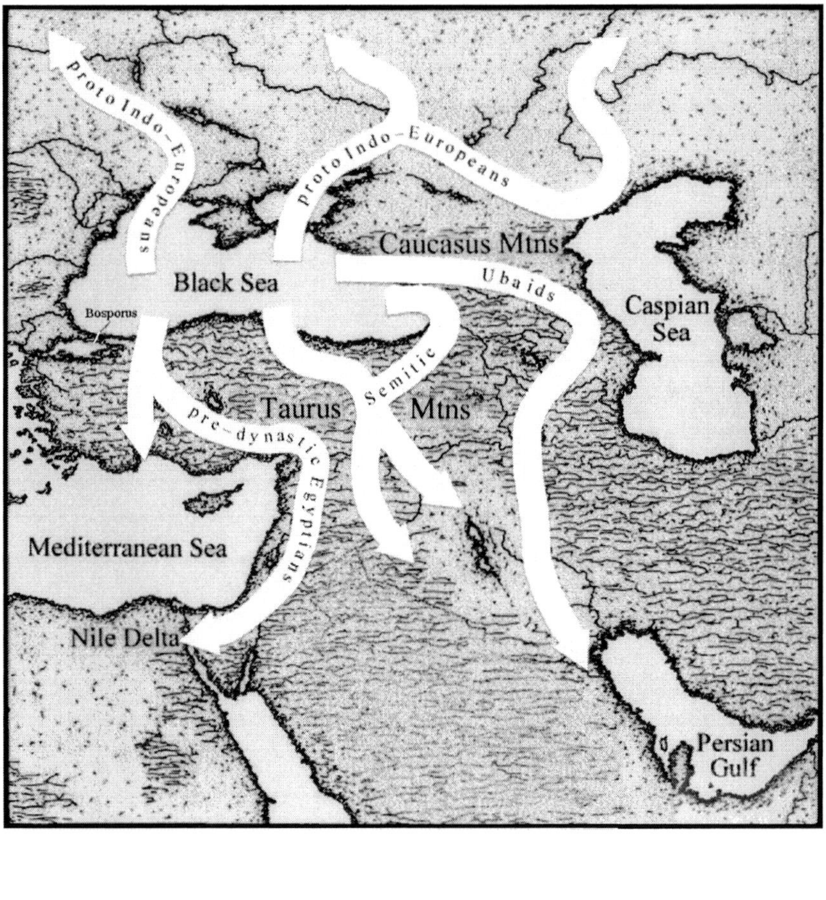
proto Indo-Europeans
proto Indo-Europeans
Caucasus Mtns
Black Sea
Ubaids
Caspian Sea
Bosporus
Semitic
Taurus
Mtns
pre-dynastic Egyptians
Mediterranean Sea
Nile Delta
Persian Gulf

Notes

PREFACE

1. Schopenhauer, Arthur, *The World as Will and Idea*, II, 254; "Books and Readings"; "Counsels and Maxims," p. 21, quoted in Durant, Will, *The Story of Philosophy*, 2nd Edition, Simon and Schuster, New York, 1926, p. 250, footnote 104.
2. Popper, Karl, *Through the Experience of Evolutionary Epistemology*, 1985, quoted in Cristianini, Nello, University of Trieste, Italy , "Evolution and Learning: an Epistemological Perspective," http://www.univ.trieste.it, March 21, 1995.
3. Wilson, Edward O., "Back from Chaos," in the <u>Atlantic Monthly</u>, March, 1998, pp. 41-62.

Chapter 1

THE MIND OF GOD AND THE MIND OF MAN

1. What we now call "science" is actually a branch of philosophy. It was considered by the early Greeks to be the study of natural philosophy. Today this is reflected in the highest academic degree awarded in science, the Ph.D. or Doctor of Philosophy.
2. Durant, Will and Ariel, *The Story of Civilization*, Simon and Schuster, New York, 1961, Vol. 7, Bk. 3, Ch. 22, Sec. 1, Par. 1.
3. Tipler, Frank J., *The Physics of Immortality,* Doubleday, New York, 1994.
4. Capra, Fritjof, *The Tao of Physics,* Shambhala Publications, Boston, 1991.

5. Dukas, Helen and Hoffman, Banesh, eds., *Albert Einstein: The Human Side,* Princeton University Press, Princeton, 1979, p. 43.

6. Dukas, Helen and Hoffman, Banesh, eds., *Albert Einstein: The Human Side*, 1979, p. 39.

7. Stenger, Victor J., "Quantum Spirituality," in Free Inquiry, Winter, 1997, pp. 57-9.

8. Descartes, Principia Philosopheiae, 1, 71, in Meditations and Principles of Philosophy, 168, referenced in Durant, Will and Ariel, *The Story of Civilization,* 1961, Vol. 7, Bk. 3, Ch. 23, Sec. 6, Par. 7.

9. Discours, Part 11, in Selections, 12, Discours de la methode, quoted in Durant, Will, *The Story of Civilization,* 1939, Vol. 2, Bk. 4, Ch. 21, Sec. 3, Part 4, Par. 1.

10. Gorgias, 495; Rep., 619; Philebus, 66, Plato, Rep., quoted in Durant, Will, *The Story of Civilization,* 1939, Vol. 2, Bk. 4, Ch. 21, Sec. 3, Part 4, Par. 1.

11. Ockham, Super IV Lib. Sentent., IV, 12, K, in Tornay, I, iii, 2, in Owen, II, 378, quoted in Durant, Will, *The Story of Civilization,* 1957, Vol. 6, Bk. 1, Ch. 12, Sec. 5, Par. 7.

12. Durant, Will, *The Story of Civilization*, 1935, Vol. 1, Bk. 2, Ch. 19, Sec. 2, Part 6, Par. 7.

13. Locke, John C., "An Essay Concerning Human Understanding," 1690. Bk. 1, Ch. 1, Sec. 5.

Chapter 2

PROBLEMS OUR MINDS HAVE WITH PERCEPTION

1. Hume, *Enquiry concerning Human Understanding*, quoted in Durant, Will and Ariel, *The Story of Civiliazation, 1965,* Vol. 9, Bk. 1, Ch. 4, Sec. 6, Part 3, Par. 8.

2. "Rational Mind Designs," in Science News, July 13, 1996, Vol 150, p. 24.

3. Meslier, Jean, *Superstition in All Ages* or *Last Will and Testament*, XXXII, referenced in Durant, Will and Ariel, *The Story of Civilization,* 1965, Vol. 9, Bk. 5, Ch. 18, Sec. 3, Par.15.

4. "Dioxin's fowl deed; Misshapen brains," in Science News, August 30, 1997, Vol. 153, p. 133.

5. Bower, Bruce, "Tots show signs of intentional minds," in Science News, February 24, 1996, Vol. 149, No. 8, p. 118; Bower, Bruce, "Kids take mental aim at others' goals," in Science News, September 18, 1995, Vol. 148, No. 12, p. 181.

6. "Dolphin perception," in The Economist, December 21, 1996, p. 118.

7. Shaw, George Bernard, *Back to Methuselah: A Metabiological Pentateuch*, Brentano's, New York, 1929, p. XIVI, quoted in Sagan, Carl, and Druyan, Ann, *Shadows of Forgotten Ancestors*, Random House, New York, 1992, p. 64.

8. Connor, Steve, "God Spot is found in brain," in The Sunday Times (Britain), November, 2, 1997.

9. Raloff, J., "Patients savor this brain disorder," in Science News, June 7, 1997, Vol. 151, No. 23, p. 348.

10. West, Thomas G., *In the Mind's Eye*, Prometheus Books, Buffalo, 1991, p. 143.

11. West, *In the Mind's Eye*, 1991, pp. 101-29.

12. UNIVERSAL PRAYER: *CONFESSION OF SINS AND ASKING FOR FORGIVENESS,* Part II, *CONFESSION OF SINS COMMITTED IN THE SERVICE OF TRUTH,* http://www.vatican.va...20000312_prayer-day-pardon-en.html, March 17, 2000.

13. Apostolic Letter *Tertio millennio adveniente,* 35, *MEMORY AND RECONCILIATION: THE CHURCH AND THE FAULTS OF THE PAST,* December, 1999, http://www.vatican.va/roma_curia/...20000307_memory-reconc-Itc_en.html, March 7, 2000.

14. John Paul II, *General Audience Discourse* of September 1, 1999, in *L'Osservatore Romano*, Eng. Ed., September 8, 1999, 7, *MEMORY AND RECONCILIATION: THE CHURCH AND THE FAULTS OF THE PAST,* December, 1999, http://www.vatican.va/roma_curia/...20000307_memory-reconc-Itc_en.html, March 7, 2000.
15. Apostolic Letter *Tertio millennio adveniente,* 35. The citation from the Second Vatican Council is from *Dignitatis humanae,* 1, *MEMORY AND RECONCILIATION: THE CHURCH AND THE FAULTS OF THE PAST,* December, 1999, http://www.vatican.va/roma_curia/...20000307_memory-reconc-Itc_en.html, March 7, 2000.

Chapter 3

THE BIOLOGY OF BELIEF MANIPULATION

1. McCabe, Joseph, *The Columbia Encyclopedia's Crimes Against the Truth,* Haldeman-Julius Publications, Girard, Kansas, 1950, Foreword.
2. Doyno, Victor, ed., *Bible Teaching and Religious Practice,* Mark Twain, reprinted in *Selected Writings of an American Skeptic,* Prometheus Books, 1995, pp. 421-2.
3. "Neural development," in <u>The Economist</u>, July 15, 1995, pp. 62-3.
4. "Memory building," in <u>The Economist</u>, August 29, 1998, electronic version .
5. Rosen, Laura Epstein, Ph.D., and Amador, Xavier Francisco, Ph.D., *When Someone You Love is Depressed*, The Free Press, New York, 1996, p. 129.
6. "Wake up, sleepy brain," in <u>Science News</u>, September 21, 1996, Vol. 150, No. 12, p. 184.

7. Chandogya Upanishad vi. 7, quoted in Durant, Will, *The Story of Civilization,* 1935, Vol. 1 Bk. 2, Ch. 14, Sec. 7, Par. 19.
8. Smith, Vincent A., *Akbar,* Oxford, 1919, p. 412, quoted in Durant, Will, *The Story of Civilization,* 1935, Vol. 1, Bk. 2, Ch. 14, Sec. 7, Par. 19.
9. Bower, Bruce, "Bridging the Brain Gap," in <u>Science News</u>, November 2, 1996, Vol. 150, No. 18, p. 280.
10. *Encyclopedia of Psychology*, 2nd Edition, John Wiley & Sons, New York, 1994, Vol 2. pp. 197-9.
11. *Encyclopedia of Psychology*, 1994, Vol. 1, pp. 183-4.
12. "Neural ties that bind perception," in <u>Science News</u>, February 20, 1999, Vol. 155, p. 122. More in Bower, Bruce, "Brain cells work together to pay attention," in <u>Science News</u>, March 11, 2000, Vol 157, p. 167.
13. Gazzaniga, Michael S., "The Split Brain Revisited," in <u>Scientific American</u>, July, 1998, pp. 51-5.
14. Evangelista, Anita, *Dictionary of Hypnotism,* Greenwood Press, New York, 1991, p. 121.
15. *Dictionary of Hypnotism,* 1991, p. 205.
16. *Encyclopedia of Psychology*, 1994, Vol. 2, p. 197.

Chapter 4

THE GENESIS OF MIND, SELF-ORGANIZING KNOWLEDGE, AND PSYCHOGENES

1. Popper, Karl, *Thought and Experience and Evolutionary Epistemology,* 1985, quoted in Cristianini, Nello, <u>Evolution and Learning: An Epistemological Perspective,</u> March 21, 1995, University of Trieste, Italy.
2. "ATCG Puzzle Pieces," in <u>Scientific American</u>, December, 1997, p. 22.
3. Levy, Steven, *Artificial Life*, Pantheon Books, New York, 1992, pp. 155-87.

4. Levy, Steven, *Artificial Life*, 1992, pp. 216-30.
5. Levy, Steven, *Artificial Life*, 1992, pp. 191-211.
6. David, Kosa, Bennett, Forrest H., Keane, Martin A., and Andre, John R., eds., *Genetic Programming III: Darwinian Invention and Problem Solving*, Morgan Kaufmann Publishers, San Francisco, 1999.
7. Simmons, Robert, "How the Giraffe Got Its Neck," in Discovery Magazine, March, 1997, p. 14.
8. James, Peter and Thorpe, Nick, *Ancient Inventions*, Ballantine Books, New York, 1994, pp. 476-7.

Chapter 5

OUR ANCESTORS' BELIEFS AND THE ORIGIN OF CREATION MYTHS

1. Smith, Dr. Henry, "Scraps from a Diary - Chief Seattle - A Gentleman by Instinct - His Native Eloquence," in the Seattle Sunday Star, October 29, 1887.
2. Freud, Sygmund, *The Interpretation of Dreams,* translated by James Strachery, Standard Edition, V, pp. 350-1, quoted in Campbell, *The Hero with a Thousand Faces*, Princeton University Press, Princeton, 1968, p. 19.
3. Campbell, Joseph, *The Hero with a Thousand Faces,* 1968, p. 19.
4. Bacon, Francis, Essay "Of Atheism," quoted in Durant, Will and Ariel, *The Story of Civilization,* 1961, Vol. 7, Bk. 1, Ch. 7, Sec. 5, Par. 4.
5. Meslier, Jean XII, quoted in Durant, Will and Ariel, *The Story of Civilization,* 1965, Vol. 9, Bk. 5, Ch. 18, Sec. 3, Par. 23.
6. Katha Lipanishad, ii, 23 1; Radhakrishnan, i, 158, quoted in Durant, Will, *The Story of Civilization,* 1935, Vol. 1, Bk. 2, Ch. 14, Sec. 7, Par. 17.

7. Durant, Will, *The Story of Civilization*, 1935, Vol. 1, Bk. 1, Ch. 14, Sec. 17, Par. 16.

8. Meslier, Jean, *Superstition in All Ages,* or *Last Will and Testament*, XII, quoted in Durant, Will and Ariel, *The Story of Civilization,* 1965, Vol. 9, Bk. 5, Ch. 18, Sec. 3, Par. 21.

9. Hall, Manly P., *The Secret Teachings of All Ages*, 19th Edition, The Philosophical Research Society, Inc., Los Angeles, 1973, p. XLIX.

10. Hall, Manly P., *The Secret Teachings of All Ages*, 1973, p. L.

11. Hall, Manly P., *The Secret Teachings of All Ages*, 1973, p. LI.

12. Campbell, Joseph, *The Hero with a Thousand Faces*, 1968, p. 248.

13. "Wisdom of the Ages," MCR Agency, Inc., 6116 Merced Avenue, Oakland, Calif., 94611, (electronic resource).

14. Tornay, Steven C., *Ockham: Studies and Sketches,* Open Court Publishing, LaSalle, Illinois, 1938, quoted in Durant, Will, *The Story of Civilization,* 1957, Vol. 6, Bk. 1, Ch. 12, Sec. 5, Par. 6.

15. *Encyclopedia of Psychology,* 1994, Vol. 2, Ch. 6, p. 505.

Chapter 6

CREATION ACCORDING TO SCIENCE— HOW THE EARTH FORMED

1. Peebles, P. James E., Schramm, David N., Turner, Edwin J., and Kron, Richard G., "The Evolution of the Universe," in <u>Scientific American</u>, October, 1994, p. 53.

2. Cowen, Ron, "Opening the Door to the Early Cosmos," in <u>Science News</u>, August 3, 1996, Vol. 150, No. 5, p. 68.

3. "Satellites hint sun is growing stronger," in <u>Science News</u>, September 27, 1997, Vol. 152, p. 197.

4. Cowen, Ron, "The Once and Future Sun," in <u>Science News</u>, March 26, 1994, Vol. 145, pp. 204-5.

5.   Kirshner, Robert P., "The Earth's elements," in <u>Scientific American</u>, October, 1994, p. 44.
6.   Weinberg, Steven, "Life in the Universe," in <u>Scientific American</u>, October, 1994, p. 59.
7.   Cowen, Ron, "Chemical Pathway Links Stars, Meteorites," in <u>Science News</u>, November 6, 1993, Vol. 144, p. 292.
8.   Kirshner, Robert P., "The Earth's Elements," 1994, pp. 59-65.
9.   Cowen, Ron, "Bright Comet Poses Puzzles (Hyakutake's Tails of Mystery)," in <u>Science News</u>, June 1, 1996, Vol. 149, pp. 346-7.
10. Kirshner, Robert P., "The Earth's Elements," 1994, pp. 59-65.
11. "A moon for Dionysus," in <u>Science News</u>, September 27, 1997, Vol. 152, No. 13, p. 200.
12. Cowen, Ron, "The real meaning of 50 billion galaxies," in <u>Science News</u>, February 3, 1996, Vol. 149, No. 5, p. 77.
13. Winters, Jeffrey, "The Answer in the Voids," in <u>Discover Magazine</u>, March, 1996, p. 27.
14. Frank, Adam, "In the Nursery of the Stars," in <u>Discover Magazine</u>, February, 1996, p. 30.
15. Gehrels, Tom, "Collisions with Comets and Asteroids," in <u>Scientific American</u>, March, 1996, pp. 54-59.
16. Gehrels, Tom, "Collisions with Comets and Asteroids," 1996, pp. 54-59.
17. Cowen, Ron, "New link between Earth and asteroids," in <u>Science News</u>, November 6, 1993, Vol. 144, p. 300.
18. Gehrels, Tom, "Collisions with Comets and Asteroids," 1996, pp. 54-59.
19. Gehrels, Tom, "Collisions with Comets and Asteroids," 1996, pp. 54-59.
20. "Old equipment finds big asteroid nearby," in <u>Science News</u>, June 8, 1996, Vol. 149, No. 23, p. 365.
21. "The Doomsday Asteroid," WGBH Educational Foundation, Nova program #2212, Air Date 10-31-95, Journal Graphics, Inc., Transcript, p.5.

22. Monastersky, Richard, "The Moon's Tug Stretches Out the Day," in <u>Science News</u>, July 6, 1996, Vol. 150, No. 1, p. 4.
23. Allegre, Claude J., and Schneider, Stephen H., "The Evolution of the Earth," in <u>Scientific American</u>, October, 1994, pp. 66-75.

Chapter 7

BRAIN EVOLUTION AT THE DNA LEVEL

1. Lucretius, Vol. 3, IV, page 834, quoted in Durant, Will, *The Story of Civilization,* 1944, Vol. 3, Bk. 2, Ch. 8, Sec. 2, Par. 15
2. Lucretius, Vol. 3, V, page 419, quoted in Durant, Will, *The Story of Civilization,* 1944, Vol. 3, Bk. 2, Ch. 8, Sec. 2, Par. 15.
3. Lucretius, Vol. 3, V, Page 837, quoted in Durant, Will, *The Story of Civilization,* 1944, Vol. 3, Bk. 2, Ch. 8, Sec. 2, Par. 15.
4. Bakewell, C., *Sourcebook in Ancient Philosophy*, 1909, New York, p. 6 , referenced in Durant, Will, *The Story of Civilization,* 1939, Vol. 2, Bk. 2, Ch. 6, Sec. 14, Part 1, Par. 14.
5. Zimmer, Carl, "Life Takes Backbone," in <u>Discovery Magazine</u>, December, 1995, p. 38-9.
6. "Origin of Life on the Earth," in <u>Scientific American</u>, October, 1994, pp. 77-83.
7. de Duve, Christian, " The Birth of Complex Cells," in <u>Scientific American</u>, April, 1996, pp. 50-57.
8. Travis, John, "How many genes does a bacterium need?" in <u>Science News</u>, September 28, 1996, Vol. 150, No. 13, p. 198.
9. Lipkin, R., "Early life: In the soup or on the rocks?" in <u>Science News</u>, May 4, 1996, Vol. 149, No. 18, p. 278.

10. Fackelmann, Kathleen, "The Cortisol Connection," in <u>Science News</u>, November 29, 1997, Vol. 152, No. 22, p. 350.

11. "The Slime Alternative," in <u>Discover Magazine</u>, September, 1998, pp. 86-93.

12. "The Origin of Species," in <u>The Economist</u>, November 25, 1995, pp. 85-87.

13. Nusslein-Volhard, Christianne, "Gradients That Organize Embryo Development," in <u>Scientific American</u>, August, 1996, pp. 54-55, 58-60.

14. Travis, John, "The Ghost of Geoffroy Saint-Hilaire," in <u>Science News</u>, September 30, 1995, Vol. 148, No. 14, pp. 216-8.

15. Monastersky, Richard, "Jump-Start for the Vertebrates," in <u>Science News</u>, February 3, 1996, Vol. 149, No. 5, pp. 74-7.

16. Zimmer, Carl, "Breathe Before You Bite," in <u>Discover Magazine</u>, March, 1996, p. 34.

17. Travis, John, "Yeast genetic blueprint publicly unveiled," in <u>Science News</u>, May 4, 1996, Vol. 149, No. 18, pp. 278-8.

18. Pennisi, E., "Mice, Flies Share Memory Molecule," in <u>Science News</u>, October 15, 1994, Vol. 146, p. 244.

19. "Repeating DNA surprises once again," in <u>Science News</u>, March 16, 1996, Vol. 149, No. 11, p. 171.

20. Travis, John, "Let's repeat: Mutation gums up brain cells," in <u>Science News</u>, December 20/27, 1997, Vol. 152, No. 25/26, p. 390.

21. Travis, John, "Repeating DNA linked to schizophrenia," in <u>Science News</u>, December 8, 1997, Vol. 152, No. 19, p. 294.

22. "How brain cells make up their minds," in <u>Science News</u>, October 28, 1995, Vol. 148, No. 18, p. 284.

23. "Mind Forming," in <u>The Economist</u>, July 15, 1995, p. 63.

24. "Anatomy of the Human Nervous System," *The Encyclopedia Britannica,* Multimedia Disc, 1994-1998, Encyclopedia Britannica Inc.

25. Begley, Sharon, "Your Child's Brain," in <u>Newsweek Magazine</u>, February 19, 1996, pp. 55-62.

26. Goleman, Daniel, *Emotional Intelligence,* Bantam Books, New York, 1994, p. 5.
27. Bower, Bruce, "Brain structure sounds off to fear, anger," in Science News, January 18, 1997, Vol. 151, No. 3, p. 38.
28. "Anatomy of apprehension," in Science News, November 9, 1996, Vol. 150, No. 19, p. 301.
29. Bower, Bruce, "The social brain: New clues from old skull," in Science News, May 21, 1994, Vol. 145, pp. 326-7.
30. Goleman, Daniel, *Emotional Intelligence*, 1994, pp 8-9.

Chapter 8

THE OVERT PROCESS OF BRAIN EVOLUTION

1. Bakewell, 6, referenced in Durant, Will, *The Story of Civilization,* Simon and Schuster, 1939, Vol. 2, Bk. 2, Ch. 6, Sec. 14, Part 1, Par. 14.
2. Diog. L., i.c., referenced in Durant, Will, *The Story of Civilization,* 1939, Vol. 2, Bk. 3, Ch. 15, Sec. 2, Par. 3.
3. Aristotle*, De Partibus Animalium*, i. 10, iv, 10, referenced in Durant, Will, *The Story of Civilization,* 1939, Vol. 2, Bk. 3, Ch. 15, Sec. 2, Par. 3.
4. Tarn, W.W., "J.R.: Studies of the Greek Poets" *Hellenistic Civilization,* London, 1927, p. 238, referenced in Durant, Will, *The Story of Civilization,* 1939, Vol. 2, Bk. 4, Ch. 21, Sec. 4, Part 2, Par. 15.
5. Travis, John, "Third Branch of Life Bares Its Genes," in Science News, August 24, 1996, Vol. 150, No. 8, p. 116.
6. "Hot Stuff," in The Economist, August 24, 1996, p. 63.
7. "Earliest Earthlings," in Scientific American, January, 1997, p. 29.
8. "When glaciers covered the entire Earth," in Science News, March 29, 1997, Vol. 151, No. 13, p. 196.
9. "When glaciers covered the entire Earth," 1997, p. 196.
10. Monastersky, Richard, "Popsicle Planet," in Science News, August 29, 1998, Vol. 154, No. 9, pp. 137-41.

11. Monastersky, Richard, "Jump-Start for the Vertebrates," in <u>Science News</u>, February 3, 1996, Vol. 149, No. 5, pp. 74-7.

12. Zimmer, Carl, "Breathe Before You Bite," in <u>Discover Magazine</u>, March 1996, p. 34.

13. Monastersky, Richard, "The first shark: To bite or not to bite?," in <u>Science News</u>, February 17, 1996, Vol. 149, No. 7, p. 101.

14. Monastersky, Richard, "Walking away from a fish-eat-fish world," in <u>Science News</u>, July 30, 1994, Vol. 146, p. 70.

15. Erwin, Douglas H., "The Mother of Mass Extinctions," <u>Scientific American</u>, July, 1996, pp. 70-78.

16. Padian, Kevin, and Chiappe, Luis M., "The Origin of Birds and Their Flight," in <u>Scientific American</u>, February 1998, pp. 38-47.

17. Monastersky, Richard, "The Lost Tribe of the Mammals," in <u>Science News</u>, December 14, 1996, Vol. 150, No. 24, pp. 378-9.

18. Monastersky, Richard, "The pushy side of mammalian brains," in <u>Science News</u>, November 18, 1995, Vol. 148, No.21, p. 330.

19. Monastersky, Richard, "Impact Wars," in <u>Science News</u>, March 5, 1994, Vol. 145, pp. 156-7.

20. Cowen, Ron, "51 Pegasi: A star without a planet?" in <u>Science News</u>, March 1, 1997, Vol. 151, No. 9, p. 133.

21. "The Doomsday Asteroid," WGBH Educational Foundation, Nova program #2212, Air Date 10-31-95, Journal Graphics, Inc., Transcript, p.4.

22. Ryan, William and Pitman, Walter, *Noah's Flood*, Simon & Schuster, New York, 1998.

23. CAH, i, 456, referenced in Durant, Will, *The Story of Civilization*, 1935, Vol. 1, Bk. 1, Ch. 7, Sec. 2, Part 1, Par. 6.

24. Durant, Will, *The Story of Civilization*, 1935, Vol. 1, Bk. 1, Ch. 7, Sec. 2, Part 5, Par. 15.

Chapter 9

WHERE DARWINIAN EVOLUTION ENDS AND PSYCHOGENETIC EVOLUTION BEGINS

1. Wilson, Edward O., *Consilience*, Vintage Books, a division of Random House, Inc., New York, 1998, pp. 188-9.
2. Dawkins, Richard, *The Selfish Gene*, 2nd Edition, Oxford University Press, New York, 1989, pp. 189-92.
3. Cavalli-Sforza, L.L. and Feldman, M.W., *Cultural Transmission and Evolution*, Princeton University Press, Princeton, 1981, p. 73.
4. Cavalli-Sforza, L.L. and Feldman, M.W., *Cultural Transmission and Evolution*, 1981, p. 70.
5. "Biology isn't Destiny," in <u>The Economist</u>, February 14, 1998, pp. 83-4.
6. Diodorus, iii, 66; Siculus: *Library of History*, Loeb Classical Library, Vol 7, New York, 1933, quoted in Durant, Will, *The Story of Civilization,* 1939, Vol. 2, Bk. 2, Ch. 8, Sec. 5, Par. 1.
7. Coulanges, 213; Rohde, pp. 295-6, quoted in Durant, Will, *The Story of Civilization,* 1939, Vol. 2, Bk. 2, Ch. 8, Sec. 5, Par. 2.
8. Nilsson, p. 83, quoted in Durant, Will, *The Story of Civilization,* 1939, Vol. 2, Bk. 2, Ch. 8, Sec. 5, Par. 2.
9. Nilsson, p. 85, quoted in Durant, Will, *The Story of Civilization,* 1939, Vol. 2, Bk. 2, Ch. 8, Sec. 5, Par. 2.
10. Theophrastus, *Characters,* Loeb Library, XVI, quoted in Durant, Will, *The Story of Civilization,* 1939, Vol. 2, Bk. 2, Ch. 8, Sec. 5, Par. 6.
11. Plutarch, "Solon," quoted in Durant, Will, *The Story of Civilization,* 1939, Vol. 2, Bk. 2, Ch. 8, Sec. 5, Par. 6.
12. Sophocles, *Trachinian Women,* 584; Lacroix, Paul, *The History of Prostitution,* 2V. New York, 1931, I , 117; Becker, W.A., *Charicles,* Tr., Metcalfe, London, 1886, p.

381, quoted in Durant, Will, *The Story of Civilization,* 1939, Vol. 2, Bk. 2, Ch. 8, Sec. 5, Par. 6.

13. Plato, *Laws,* 933; Harrison, J.E.: *Prolegomena to the Capital* (Study of Greek Religion) Cambridge, England, 1922, p. 139, quoted in Durant, Will, *The Story of Civilization,* 1939, Vol. 2, Bk. 2, Ch. 8, Sec. 5, Par. 6.

14. "Letter to Bishop Mellitus Written by Pope Gregory" (601 C.E.), http://www/Source.com/history/docs/mellitus.html, 10/5/99.

15. *Encyclopedia Britannica,* 1960, Vol. 5, p. 643.

16. Spinoza, Baruch, *Tractatus Theologico-Politicus,* Ch. 5, quoted in Durant, Will, *The Story of Philosophy*, 2nd Edition, Simon and Schuster, New York, 1926, p.125, footnote 21.

17. Spinoza, Baruch, *Tractatus Theologico-Politicus,* Ch. 6, quoted in Durant, Will, *The Story of Philosophy*, 1926, p.125, footnote 22.

18. Spinoza, Baruch, *Tractatus Theologico-Politicus,* Ch. 6, quoted in Durant, Will, *The Story of Philosophy*, 1926, p.125, footnote 23.

19. Armstrong, Karen, *A History of God,* Alfred Knopf, New York, 1994, pp. 395-6.

20. Seppa, N., "Nailing Down Pheromones in Humans," in Science News, March 14, 1998, Vol. 153, No. 11, p. 164.

21. Raloff, Janet, "When Science and Beliefs Collide," Science News, June 8, 1996, Vol. 149, No. 23, p. 360-4.

22. "Culture wars," in The Economist, September 12, 1998, pp. 97-9.

Chapter 10

Psychogenes and Cultural Evolution

1. Bower, Bruce, "My Culture, My Self," in Science News, October 14, 1997, Vol. 152, p. 248.

2. Bower, Bruce, "My Culture, My Self," 1997, Vol. 152, p. 248.
3. "The Western Tradition," video series transcribed by Thomas Michael Kowalick, PBS Adult Learning Service, Alexandria, Va., 1989, p. 26.
4. Silberman, Neil Asher, "The World of Paul," in <u>Archeology Magazine</u>, Vol. 49, Nov./Dec., 1996, p. 30.
5. Cicero, *De re Publica*, ii, 19. quoted in Durant, Will, *The Story of Civilization,* Simon and Schuster, 1944, Vol. 3, Bk. 1, Ch. 5, Sec. 4, Par. 1.
6. Polybius, vi, 56. *Histories.* 6v, Loeb Library quoted in Durant, Will, *The Story of Civilization,* 1944, Vol. 3, Bk. 1, Ch. 5, Sec. 3, Par. 2.
7. "The Western Tradition," video series transcribed by Thomas Michael Kowalick, PBS Adult Learning Service, Alexandria, Va., 1989, p. 29.
8. "Constantine The Great," Infopedia, Softkey Multimedia, Inc., Funk and Wagnalls' *New Encyclopedia* (CD ROM), 1996.
9. Tacitus, *Histories; Annals,* i.ll. TR Murphy, London, 1930, quoted in Durant, Will, *The Story of Civilization,* 1944, Vol. 3, Bk. 3, Ch. 13, Sec. 1, Par. 4.
10. C.F. Burckhardt, 252 F, quoted in Durant, Will, *The Story of Civilization,* 1944, Vol. 3, Bk. 5, Ch. 30, Sec. 3, Par. 1.
11. Hist. Aug., "Elagabalus, " xxiv, 4, quoted in Durant, Will, *The Story of Civilization,* 1944, Vol. 3, Bk. 5, Ch. 30, Sec. 3, Par. 1.
12. Lot, 29, referenced in Durant, Will, *The Story of Civilization,* 1944, Vol. 3, Bk. 5, Ch. 30, Sec. 3, Par. 1.
13. Cf. Augustine, Ep. 232, quoted in Durant, Will, *The Story of Civilization,* 1950, Vol. 4, Bk. 1, Ch. 2, Sec. 3, Par. 5.
14. Salvian, iv, 15; vii, passim; and excerpts in Heitland, W.E., Agricola, 423, Boissier, II, 410, 420, and Bury, Later Roman Empire, 307, quoted in Durant, Will, *The Story of Civilization,* 1950, Vol. 4, Bk. 1, Ch. 2, Sec. 3, Par. 4.

15. Durant, Will, *The Story of Civilization,* 1950, Vol. 4, Bk. 1, Ch. 3, Sec. 5, Par. 4.
16. Machiavelli, "Discourses, iii, #1, quoted in Durant, Will, *The Story of Civilization,* 1957, Vol. 6, Bk. 1, Ch. 1, Sec. 4, Par. 10.
17. McCabe, Joseph, *The Columbia Encyclopedia's Crimes Against The Truth,* Haldeman-Julius Publications, Girard, Kansas,1950.

Chapter 11

The Noble Experiments and Aristotle's Resurrection

1. *Encyclopedia of Psychology,* 2nd Edition, John Wiley & Sons, New York, 1994, Vol. 1, pp. 68-9.
2. *Encyclopedia of Psychology,* 1994, Vol. 1, p. 69.
3. Zeller, E., *Socrates and the Socratic Schools*, London, 1877, p.327, quoted in Durant, Will, *The Story of Civilization,* 1939, Vol. 2, Bk. 5, Ch. 29, Sec. 4, Par. 3.
4. Durant, Will, *The Story of Civilization*, Simon and Schuster, New York, 1939, Vol. 2, Bk. 5, Ch. 29, Sec. 4, Par. 2.
5. Tarn, 238; Symonds, 21, quoted in Durant, Will, *The Story of Civilization,* 1939, Vol. 2, Bk. 4, Ch. 21, Sec. 4, Part 2, Par. 16.
6. Phaedrus, 245, referenced in Durant, Will, *The Story of Civilization,* 1939, Vol. 2, Bk. 4, Ch. 21, Sec. 3, Part 3, Par. 3.
7. Mahaffy, 455; id., Greek Life, 382, quoted in Durant, Will, *The Story of Civilization,* 1939, Vol. 2, Bk. 4, Ch. 21, Sec. 4, Part 3, Par. 3.
8. Gilson, *Philosophie au Moyen Age*, LL 104; Tornay, 58, 191-2, quoted in Durant, Will, *The Story of Civilization,* 1957, Vol. 6, Bk. 1, Ch. 12, Sec. 5, Par. 8.

9. Tornay, 186; Owen, II, 377, quoted in Durant, Will, *The Story of Civilization,* 1957, Vol. 6, Bk. 1, Ch. 12, Sec. 5, Par. 8.

10. Philebus, 57-8, quoted in Durant, Will, *The Story of Civilization,* 1939, Vol. 2, Bk. 4, Ch. 21, Sec. 4, Par. 2.

11. Crito, 49, quoted in Durant, Will, *The Story of Civilization,* 1939, Vol. 2, Bk. 4, Ch. 21, Sec. 4, Par. 2.

12. Crito, 49; Laws, 951; Phaedo, 82, quoted in Durant, Will, *The Story of Civilization,* 1939, Vol. 2, Bk. 4, Ch. 21, Sec. 4, Par. 2.

13. Laws, 885, 908-9, quoted in Durant, Will, *The Story of Civilization,* 1939, Vol. 2, Bk. 4, Ch. 21, Sec. 3, Part 6, Par. 3.

14. James, Peter and Thorpe, Nick, *Ancient Inventions*, Ballantine Books division of Random House, Inc., New York, 1994, pp. 483-4.

15. Sarton, II (i), 305, quoted in Durant, Will, *The Story of Civilization,* 1950, Vol. 4, Bk. 2, Ch. 14, Sec. 8, Par. 7.

16. Averroes, *Exposition of Methods of Argument Concerning the Doctrimes of the Faith*, 230, quoted in Durant, Will, *The Story of Civilization,* 1950, Vol. 4, Bk. 2, Ch. 14, Sec. 8, Par. 9.

17. Id., *A Decisive Discourse on the Relation Between Religion and Philosophy,* 52, quoted in Durant, Will, *The Story of Civilization,* 1950, Vol. 4, Bk. 2, Ch. 14, Sec. 8, Par. 9.

18. Id., *Exposition,* 190; *Discourse,* 50-1; Gilson, E., *Reason and Revelation in the Middle Ages,* 40f, quoted in Durant, Will, *The Story of Civilization,* 1950, Vol. 4, Bk. 2, Ch. 14, Sec. 8, Par. 9.

19. Averroes, *Exposition*, 193, quoted in Durant, Will, *The Story of Civilization,* 1950, Vol. 4, Bk. 2, Ch. 14, Sec. 8, Par. 9.

20. Averroes, *Discourse,* 14, quoted in Durant, *The Story of Civilization,* 1950, Vol. 4, Bk. 2, Ch. 14, Sec. 8, Par. 8.

21. Plato, Phaedo, 74-5, Theaetetus, 185-7, quoted in Durant, *The Story of Civilization,* 1939, Vol. 2, Bk. 4, Ch. 21, Sec. 3, Part 3, Par. 2.

22. Durant, Will, *The Story of Civilization*, 1939, Vol. 2, Bk. 4, Ch. 21, Sec. 3, Part 3, Par. 4.
23. Philebus, 64-6, quoted in Durant, *The Story of Civilization,* 1939, Vol. 2, Bk. 4, Ch. 21, Sec. 3, Part 4, Par. 2.
24. Durant, Will, *The Story of Civilization*, 1939, Vol. 2, Bk. 4, Ch. 21, Sec. 3, Par. 1.
25. Laws, 885, 908-9, referenced in Durant, *The Story of Civilization,* year 1939, Vol. 2, Bk. 4, Ch. 21, Sec. 3, Part 6, Par. 3.
26. Phaedo, 66, referenced in Durant, *The Story of Civilization,* 1939, Vol. 2, Bk. 4, Ch. 21, Sec. 3, Part 6, Par. 5.
27. Owen, II, 410, quoted in Durant, *The Story of Civilization,* 1957, Vol. 6, Bk. 1, Ch. 12, Sec. 5, Par. 15.
28. Kessler, John J., *Giordano Bruno: The Forgotten Philosopher,* http://www.infidels.org/library/historical/john_kessler/giordano_bruno.html, undated.
29. Durant, Will, *The Story of Philosophy*, 2nd Edition, Simon and Schuster, New York, 1926, p. 116.

Chapter 12

The Battle for our Psychogenes

1. Kurtz, Howard, *Spin Cycle*, Touchstone Books, New York, 1998, p.xiii.
2. Kurtz, Howard, *Spin Cycle*, 1998, p.xiii.
3. Ewen, Stuart, *PR! A Social History of Spin,* Basic Books, New York, 1996, p. 15.
4. Ewen, Stuart, *PR! A Social History of Spin*, 1996, p. 13.
5. Ewen, Stuart, *PR! A Social History of Spin*, 1996, p. 154.
6. Lippmann, Walter, *Public Opinion*, p. 234, quoted in Ewen, Stuart, *PR! A Social History of Spin*, 1996, p. 157, note 24.

7. Lippmann, Walter, *Public Opinion*, pp. 37-38, quoted in Ewen, Stuart, *PR! A Social History of Spin*, 1996, pp. 157-8, note note 25.

8. Lippmann, Walter, *Public Opinion*, pp. 206-7, quoted in Ewen, Stuart, *PR! A Social History of Spin*, 1996, p. 158, note 26.

9. Bernays, Edward, *Propaganda*, pp. 27-34, quoted in Ewen, Stuart, *PR! A Social History of Spin*, 1996, p. 166, note 39.

10. Bernays, Edward, *Crystallizing Public Opinion*, p. 51,quoted in Ewen, Stuart, *PR! A Social History of Spin*, 1996, p. 167, note 41.

11. Bernays, Edward, *Propaganda*, p. 25, quoted in Ewen, Stuart, *PR! A Social History of Spin*, 1996, p. 167, note 43.

12. Engelberg, Stephen, "A New Breed of Hired Hands Cultivates Grass-Roots Anger," *New York Times*, May 17, 1993, pp. A1, A17, quoted in Ewen, Stuart, *PR! A Social History of Spin*, 1996, p. 29, note 5.

13. Ewen, Stuart, *PR! A Social History of Spin*, 1996, p. 29.

14. Schackne, Steward, "Some Considerations Underlying Jersey's Public Relations Activities," Standard Oil Company (New Jersey) and Affiliated Companies, 1948 Public Relations Conference, *Proceedings* (New York, October 21-22, 1948), p. 82, quoted in Ewen, Stuart, *PR! A Social History of Spin*, 1996, pp. 384-5, note 15.

15. Ewen, Stuart, *PR! A Social History of Spin*, 1996, p. 28-9.

16. John R. MacArthur, *The Second Front: Censorship and Propaganda in the Gulf War.* (New York: Hill and Wang, 1992, pp. 58-59), quoted in Ewen, Stuart, *PR! A Social History of Spin*, 1996, p. 29, note 4.

17. Ewen, Stuart, *PR! A Social History of Spin*, 1996, p. 40.

18. Bower, Bruce, "Rational Mind Designs," in <u>Science News</u>, July 13, 1996, Vol. 150, No. 2, p. 24-8.

Chapter 13

Reason, Myth, Psychogenetic Inertia and the Future

1. Polybius, vi. 56, quoted in Durant, Will, *The Story of Civilization,* Simon and Schuster, New York, 1944, Vol. 3, Bk. 1, Ch. 5, Sec. 3, Par. 2.
2. Erwin Suess, Gerhard Bohrmann, Jens Greinert and Erwin Lausch, "Flammable Ice," in Scientific American, November, 1999, pp. 77-83.
3. Beardsley, Tim, "When Nutrients Turn Noxious," in Scientific American, June, 1997, p. 24-6.
4. "The End of Cheap Oil," in Scientific American, March, 1998, pp. 78-95.
5. Raloff, Janet, "The Human Numbers Crunch," in Science News, June 22, 1996, Vol. 149, No. 25, pp. 396-7.
6. Ewen, Stuart, *PR! A Social History of Spin*, Basic Books, New York, 1996, pp. 409-10.
7. Ewen, Stuart, *PR! A Social History of Spin*, 1996, pp. 140-6.
8. "Dr. Gallop's Finger on America's Pulse," in The Economist, September 27, 1997, pp. 95-7.
9. Dukas, Helen and Hoffman, Banesh, eds., *Albert Einstein: The Human Side,* Princeton University Press, Princeton, 1979, p. 38.
10. Regalado, Antonio, "The Troubled Hunt for the Ultimate Cell," in Technology Review, July-August, 1998, pp. 34-41.
11. "Faith Steady Among Scientists – Or Is It?," in Free Inquiry, Summer, 1997, pp. 7-8.
12. Murphy, John Patrick Michael, "Hitler was Not an Atheist," in Free Inquiry, Spring, 1999, p. 9.
13. "God, Science and Delusion—a Chat with Arthur C. Clarke," in Free Inquiry, Spring, 1999, pp. 36-7.
14. Johnsen, Linda, "Evolution and Yoga," in Yoga International, October/November, 1998, pp. 35-9.
15. Khayyám, Omar, *Rubáiyat,* rendered into English by Edward Fitzgerald, first published in 1909 by Hodder and Stoughton,

England, this reference edition published by Weathervane Books, New York, 1985, CVIII.

16. Schopenhauer, Arthur, *The World as Will and Idea*, I, 321, quoted in Durant, Will, *The Story of Philosophy,* 1926, p. 252, footnote 114.

17. Schopenhauer, Arthur, *The World as Will and Idea*, II, 374; I, 423, quoted in Durant, Will, *The Story of Philosophy,* 1926, p. 257, footnote 144.

18. France, Anatole, *The Human Tragedy*, quoted in Durant, Will, *The Story of Philosophy,* 1926, p. 261, footnote 162.

Bibliography

Allegre, Claude J., and Schneider, Stephen H. "The Evolution of the Earth." *Scientific American* (October, 1994): 66-75.

"Anatomy of apprehension." *Science News* (November 9, 1996): 301.

"Anatomy of the Human Nervous System." *The Encyclopedia Britannica,* Multimedia Disc. 1994-1998, Encyclopedia Britannica Inc.

Armstrong, Karen. *A History of God.* New York: Alfred Knopf, 1994.

"ATCG Puzzle Pieces." *Scientific American* (December, 1997): 22.

Beardsley, Tim. "When Nutrients Turn Noxious." *Scientific American* (June, 1997): 24-6.

Begley, Sharon. "Your Child's Brain." *Newsweek Magazine* (February 19, 1996): 55-62.

Bernays, Edward L. *Crystallizing Public Opinion.* 1923.

----------. *Propaganda.* 1928.

"Biology isn't Destiny." *The Economist* (February 14, 1998): 83-4.

Bower, Bruce. "Brain cells work together to pay attention." *Science News* (March 11, 2000): 167.

----------. "Bridging the Brain Gap." *Science News* (November 2, 1996): 280.

----------. "Kids take mental aim at others' goals." *Science News* (September 18, 1995): 181.

----------. "My Culture, My Self" *Science News* (October 14, 1997): 248.

----------. "Rational Mind Designs." Science News (July 13, 1996): 24-8.

----------. "The social brain: New clues from old skull." *Science News* (May 21, 1994): 326-7.

----------. "Tots show signs of intentional minds." *Science News* (February 24, 1996): 118.

----------. "Brain structure sounds off to fear, anger." *Science News* (January 18, 1997): 38.

Campbell, Joseph. *The Hero with a Thousand Faces*. Princeton: Princeton University Press, 1973.

Capra, Fritjof. *The Tao of Physics*. Boston: Shambhala Publications, 1991.

Cavalli-Sforza, L.L., and Feldman, M.W. *Cultural Transmission and Evolution*. Princeton: Princeton University Press, 1981.

Connor, Steve. "God Spot is found in brain." *The Sunday Times (Britain)*, November, 2, 1997.

Corsini, Raymond J., Ed. *Encyclopedia of Psychology*, 2nd. New York: Wiley, 1994.

Cowen, Ron. "51 Pegasi: A star without a planet." *Science News* (March 1, 1997): 133.

----------. "Bright Comet Poses Puzzles (Hyakutake's Tails of Mystery)." *Science News* (June 1, 1996): 346-7.

----------. "Chemical Pathway Links Stars, Meteorites." *Science News* (November 6, 1993): 292.

----------. "New link between Earth and asteroids." *Science News* (November 6, 1993): 300.

----------. "Opening the Door to the Early Cosmos." *Science News* (August 3, 1996): 68.

----------. "The Once and Future Sun." *Science News* (March 26, 1994): 204-5.

----------. "The real meaning of 50 billion galaxies." *Science News* (February 3, 1996): 77.

"Culture wars." *The Economist* (September 12, 1998): 97-9.

David, Kosa, Bennett, Forrest H., Keane, Martin A., and Andre, John R., Eds. *Genetic Programming III: Darwinian Invention and Problem Solving*. San Francisco: Morgan Kaufmann, Publishers, 1999.

Dawkins, Richard. *The Selfish Gene*, 2nd Edition. New York: Oxford University Press, 1989.

de Duve, Christian. "The Birth of Complex Cells." *Scientific American* (April, 1996): 50-57.

"Dioxin's fowl deed; Misshapen brains." *Science News* (August 30, 1997): 133.

"Dolphin perception." *The Economist* (December 21, 1996): 118.

Doyno, Victor. *Bible Teaching and Religious Practice, Mark Twain.* Reprinted in *Selected Writings of an American Skeptic.* Buffalo, New York: Prometheus Books, 1995.

"Dr. Gallop's Finger on America's Pulse." *The Economist* (September 27, 1997): 95-7.

Dukas, Helen, and Hoffman, Banesh, eds. *Albert Einstein—The Human Side.* Princeton: Princeton University Press, 1979.

Durant, Will and Ariel. *The Story of Civilization.* New York: Simon and Schuster, 1935-1965.

"Earliest Earthlings." *Scientific American* (January, 1997): 29.

"The End of Cheap Oil." *Scientific American* (March, 1998): 78-95.

Engelberg, Stephen. "A New Breed of Hired Hands Cultivates Grass-Roots Anger." *New York Times*, May 17, 1993, A1, A17.

Erwin, Douglas H. "The Mother of Mass Extinctions." *Scientific American* (July 1996): 70-78.

Evangelista, Anita. *Dictionary of Hypnotism.* New York: Greenwood Press, 1991.

Ewen, Stuart. *PR! A Social History of Spin.* New York: Basic Books, 1996.

Fackelmann, Kathleen. "The Cortisol Connection." *Science News* (November 29, 1997): 350.

"Faith Steady Among Scientists—Or Is It?" *Free Inquiry* (Summer, 1997): 7-8.

Fitzgerald, Edward. *Rubáiyat of Omar Khayyám.* New York: Weathervane Books, 1985.

Frank, Adam. "In the Nursery of the Stars." *Discover Magazine* (February, 1996): 30.

Gazzaniga, Michael S. "The Split Brain Revisited" *Scientific American* (July, 1998): 51-5.

Bibliography

Gazzaniga, Michael S., Ivry, Richard B., and Mangun, George R. *Cognitive Neuroscience*. New York: Norton, 1998.

Gehrels, Tom. "Collisions with Comets and Asteroids." *Scientific American* (March, 1996): 54-59.

"God, Science, and Delusion—a Chat with Arthur C. Clarke." *Free Inquiry* (Spring, 1999): 36-7.

Goleman, Daniel. *Emotional Intelligence*. New York: Bantam Books, 1994.

Hall, Manly P. *The Secret Teachings of All Ages*, 19th Edition. Los Angeles: The Philosophical Research Society, Inc., 1973.

"Hot Stuff." *The Economist* (August 24, 1996): 63.

"How brain cells make up their minds." *Science News* (October 28, 1995): 284.

Hume, David. *Enquiry concerning Human Understanding*. LaSalle, IL: Open Court Publishing, 1956.

James, Peter, and Thorpe, Nick. *Ancient Inventions*. New York: Ballantine Books, 1994.

Johnsen, Linda. "Evolution and Yoga." *Yoga International* (October/November, 1998): 35-9.

Kirshner, Robert P. "The Earth's Elements." *Scientific American* (October, 1994): 44, 59-65.

Kurtz, Howard. *Spin Cycle*. New York: Touchstone Books, 1998.

Levy, Steven. *Artificial Life*. New York: Pantheon Books, 1992.

Lipkin, R. "Early life: In the soup or on the rocks?" *Science News* (May 4, 1996): 278.

Lippmann, Walter. *Public Opinion*. New York: Macmillan, 1961.

Locke, John C. *An Essay Concerning Human Understanding*, Dutton.

MacArthur, John R. *The Second Front: Censorship and Propaganda in the Gulf War*. New York: Hill and Wang, 1992.

McCabe, Joseph. *The Columbia Encyclopedia's Crimes Against The Truth*. Girard, Kansas: Haldeman-Julius Publications, 1950.

"Memory building." *The Economist* (August 29, 1998): Electronic version .

Meslier, Jean. *Superstition in All Ages* or *Last Will and Testament.* New York: Truth Seeker Co., 1950.

"Mind Forming." *The Economist* (July 15, 1995): 63.

Monastersky, Richard. "The Moon's Tug Stretches Out the Day." *Science News* (July 6, 1996): 4.

----------. "Impact Wars." *Science News* (March 5, 1994): 156-7.

----------. "Jump-Start for the Vertebrates." *Science News* (February 3, 1996): 74-7.

----------. "Popsicle Planet." *Science News* (August 29, 1998): 137-41.

----------. "The first shark: To bite or not to bite?" *Science News* (February 17, 1996): 101.

----------. "The Lost Tribe of the Mammals." *Science News* (December 14, 1996): 378-9.

----------. "The pushy side of mammalian brains." *Science News* (November 18, 1995): 330.

----------. "Walking away from a fish-eat-fish world." *Science News* (July 30, 1994): 70.

"A moon for Dionysus." *Science News* (September 27, 1997): 200.

Murphy, John Patrick Michael. "Hitler was Not an Atheist." *Free Inquiry* (Spring, 1999): 9.

"Neural development." *The Economist* (July 15, 1995): 62-3.

"Neural ties that bind perception." *Science News* (February 20, 1999): 122.

Nusslein-Volhard, Christianne. "Gradients That Organize Embryo Development." *Scientific American* (August, 1996): 54-55, 58-60.

"Old equipment finds big asteroid nearby." *Science News* (June 8, 1996): 365.

"Origin of Life on the Earth." *Scientific American* (October, 1994): 77-83.

"The Origin of Species." *The Economist* (November 25, 1995): 85-87.

Padian, Kevin, and Chiappe, Luis M. "The Origin of Birds and
　　　Their Flight." *Scientific American* (February, 1998): 38-
　　　47.
Peebles, P. James E., Schramm, David N., Turner, Edwin J., and
　　　Kron, Richard G. "The Evolution of the Universe."
　　　Scientific American (October, 1994): 53.
Pennisi, E. "Mice, Flies Share Memory Molecule." *Science News*
　　　(October 15, 1994): 244.
Popper, Karl. "Through the Experience of Evolutionary
　　　Epistemology." In Atti del convegno *Che cos'e il
　　　pensiero?* Accademia Nazionale dei Lincei, 1985.
Raloff, Janet. "Patients savor this brain disorder." *Science News*
　　　(June 7, 1997): 348.
----------. "The Human Numbers Crunch." *Science News* (June 22,
　　　1996): 396-7.
----------. "When Science and Beliefs Collide." *Science News*
　　　(June 8, 1996): 360-4.
"Rational Mind Designs." *Science News* (July 13, 1996): 24.
Regalado, Antonio. "The Troubled Hunt for the Ultimate Cell."
　　　Technology Review (July-August, 1998): 34-41.
"Repeating DNA surprises once again." *Science News* (March 16,
　　　1996): 171.
Rosen, Laura Epstein, and Amador, Xavier Rosen Francisco.
　　　When Someone You Love is Depressed. New York: The
　　　Free Press, 1996.
Ryan, William, and Pitman, Walter. *Noah's Flood.* New York:
　　　Simon & Schuster, 1998.
"Satellites hint sun is growing stronger." *Science News*
　　　(September 27, 1997): 197.
Schopenhauer, Arthur. *The World as Will and Idea,* 9th ed. New
　　　York: Scribner's, 1948.
Seppa, N. "Nailing Down Pheromones in Humans." *Science
　　　News* (March 14, 1998): 164.
Shaw, George Bernard. *Back to Methuselah: A Metabiological
　　　Pentateuch.* New York: Brentano's, 1929.

Silberman, Neil Asher. "The World of Paul." *Archeology Magazine* (Nov/Dec, 1996): 30.

Simmons, Robert. "How the Giraffe Got Its Neck." *Discovery Magazine* (March, 1997): 14.

"The Slime Alternative." *Discover Magazine* (September, 1998): 86-93.

Smith, Henry. "Scraps from a Diary—Chief Seattle—A Gentleman by Instinct—His Native Eloquence." *Seattle Sunday Star*, October 29, 1887.

Stenger, Victor J. "Quantum Spirituality." *Free Inquiry* (Winter, 1997): 57-9.

Suess, Erwin, Bohrmann, Gerhard, Greinert, Jens, and Lausch, Erwin. "Flammable Ice." *Scientific American* (November, 1999): 77-83.

Tipler, Frank J. *The Physics of Immortality.* New York: Doubleday, 1994.

Tornay, Steven C. *Ockham: Studies and Sketches.* La Salle, IL: Open Court Publishing, 1938.

Travis, John. "How many genes does a bacterium need?" *Science News* (September 28, 1996): 198.

---------. "Let's repeat: Mutation gums up brain cells." *Science News* (December 20/27, 1997): 390.

---------. "Repeating DNA linked to schizophrenia." *Science News* (December 8, 1997): 294.

---------. "The Ghost of Geoffroy Saint-Hilaire." *Science News* (September 30, 1995): 216-8.

---------. "Third Branch of Life Bares Its Genes." *Science News* (August 24, 1996): 116.

---------. "Yeast genetic blueprint publicly unveiled." in *Science News* (May 4, 1996): 278-8.

"Wake up, sleepy brain." *Science News* (September 21, 1996): 184.

Weinberg, Steven. "Life in the Universe." *Scientific American* (October, 1994): 59.

West, Thomas G. *In the Mind's Eye.* Buffalo: Prometheus Books, 1991.

"When glaciers covered the entire Earth." *Science News* (March 29, 1997): 196.

Wilson, Edward O. "Back from Chaos." *Atlantic Monthly* (March, 1998): 41-62.

----------. *Consilience.* New York: Random House, 1999.

Winters, Jeffrey. "The Answer in the Voids." *Discover Magazine* (March, 1996): 27.

Zimmer, Carl. "Breathe Before You Bite." *Discover Magazine* (March, 1996): 34.

Acknowledgments

I would like to express my gratitude to David Boccagna, Colin Foote, Myra Jerome, John Ryland Mickowski, and my wife Shirley for their constructive comments and for finding time in their busy lives to critique my manuscript. In addition, I would like to thank my editor, Dan Wilson of The Editor's DeskTop, my indexer, Cynthia Landeen of In.dex.trous, and my illustrator, Thomas Giovannoli, for their fine work.

Permissions Acknowledgments

Grateful acknowledgment is made to the following for permission to reprint previously published material:

Simon & Schuster: Excerpts from *The Story of Civilization* by Will Durant. Copyright © 1935 by Will Durant. Copyright renewed 1963 by Will Durant. Reprinted by permission of Simon & Schuster.

Basic Books: Excerpts from *PR!* by Stewart Ewen. Copyright © 1996 by Basic Books, Inc. Reprinted by permission of Basic Books, a member of Perseus Books, L.L.C.

John Wiley & Sons: Excerpts from *Encyclopedia of Psychology*, 2/e by Corsini. Copyright © 1994 by John Wiley & Sons. Reprinted by permission of John Wiley & Sons, Inc.

Williamson Music Co.: Lyric lines of "You've Got To Be Carefully Taught" by Richard Rodgers and Oscar Hammerstein II appear on pages 16–17. Copyright © 1949 by Richard Rodgers and Oscar Hammerstein II. Copyright Renewed. WILLIAMSON MUSIC owner of publication and allied rights throughout the world. International Copyright Secured. Reprinted by Permission. All Rights Reserved.

The Philosophical Research Society, Inc.: Excerpts from *An Encyclopedic Outline of Masonic, Hermetic, Qabbalistic and Rosicrucian Symbolical Philosophy* by Manly P. Hall. Copyright © 1962 by The Philosophical Research Society, Inc. The Philosophical Research Society, Inc. could no be located to acquire permission.

Haldeman-Julius Publications: Excerpts from *The Columbia Encyclopedia's Crimes Against The Truth* by Joseph McCabe. Haldeman-Julius Publications could not be located to acquire permission.

In addition to the above, grateful acknowledgment is made to authors whose copyrights have expired and to those whose excerpts fall within the category of fair comment.

Index

2001: A Space Odyssey (Clarke), 43

A

abortion rights and psychogenetic inheritance, 170
Abu Yaqub Yusuf, Emir, 216
The Academy, 221
adaptation. *See* evolution
adenine sequences. *See* DNA
advertising. *See* belief manipulation
Africa, formation of, 144, 147
African-Americans, 19–20, 178. *See also* slaves
alertness reduction in brainwashing, xxiv, 51
Alexander (the Great), 210, 222–223
Alexandrian Library, 196, 215
al-Farabi, Arab philosopher, 216
Alpha Centauri (star), 106
Alvarez, Luis, 146
Alvarez, Walter, 146
Amish attempts to limit cultural change, 176, 251
amphibian evolution, marine, 123, 139
amygdalae
    emotions and, xxxvi, 126–129, 132
    fear and, 86
    in human brain, xxx, xxxvi, 126–128, 148, 253
    in reptile brain, 140
    role in memory, 43
    role in survival, 128
Anaxagoras, 133–134, 212
Anaximander, 133–134, 212

Ancestor (computer program), 66–67
angiosperms role in evolution, 143
animism
    in ancestral beliefs, xxix, 79–81, 206
    evolution of, 27
    and modern religion, 81–82
    the planning assumption in, 22, 35, 111
    and voodoo, xxiv, 56
Antarctic ice melt, 260
anthropocentric, 277
anthropomorphism, xxiii, 3, 27, 94–95
Aquinas, Thomas, 8, 218, 225, 227
Arabs, and Greek philosophical tradition, 193, 196, 216–217
archaea branch, tree of life, 115, 135
Aristocles. *See* Plato
Aristotle
    about, 222–223
    and Averroes, 216–217
    contradicted by Bruno, 227–228
    on dreams, 208
    on evolution theory, 134
    on Final Cause, 212
    on God, 212–213
    on natural selection, 212
    on reincarnation, 211
    secular reasoning method applied by others, 218–219
Armstrong, Karen, 167–168
Asia, formation of, 148
Ass (constellation), 92
assassin, derivation of, 53
asteroids, 105, 108

astrology, 81, 88–89, 174
astronomy, 88–89
Astro Turf organizing in public
    relations, 237–238
Atlantic Ocean, formation of, 144
ATP (adenosinetriphosphate), 117
Augustine, a philosopher, 202, 215,
    220, 224–229
Australopithecus afarensis (Lucy),
    148
autism and intelligence, 249–250
autogenesis, 104, 113–114
Averroes, Moorish philosopher (Ibn
  Rushd)
    about, 202, 224–226
    and Aristotelian logic, 218–220
    library of burned, 272
    on myth as source of morality,
      257
    on religion and philosophy, 216–
      217
    view of God, 217
Avicenna, Arab philosopher (Ibn
  Sina), 216, 225

B

Bacon, Francis, 17, 85
Bacon, Roger, 196
bacteria, evolution of, 115–117, 135–
    136
bacterial flagellum, 70
Bavaria, Louis of, 226
Bayes' theorem, 13
behavior/behavioral attributes
    DNA-derived, 156–159
    genetic adaptation and, xxx, 71–
      73
    psychogenetic influences, 153–
      159

belief alters perception, xxii, xxv, 5–
    6, 11–18, 231. *See also*
    propaganda
belief manipulation. *See also*
  propaganda; public relations
    and brainwashing, 47–52
    covert nature of, 265
    in democracy, 236–240, 266
    dominant beliefs in, 231, 271
    happy face photo example, 240–
      241
    the media and, 232, 243–249
    persuasion techniques, 55–57
    through propaganda, 231–244
    and trance, 48–57
beliefs. *See also* faith; psychogenes
    absence of, effect on perception,
      18
    adaptation, 162–164
    ancestral, xxvi–xxvii, 6, 41, 79–
      81, 111
    ancient Greek, 160–162
    astrology and inherited, 81, 88
    competition among, damage
      resulting, xxvii, 82
    core, cultural, 5–6, 74, 178, 182,
      262–263
    criminal behavior and systems of,
      51, 55, 171
    delusions, 29, 44
    early Christian, 88–92, 186–189
    emotional needs in creation of,
      xxxiii, 85–88, 96, 210, 229,
      254
    evolution of, 88–92, 164
    faith-based, 85–86, 262
    forced, xxii, 27–28, 30, 35, 274
    group, psychotic (examples),
      177–179

and information value, 53
inheritable, xxv, xxvi, 73–78, 159
inheritance value of, xvi–xvii,
    73–74, 155, 158
knowledge v., 7–8
linked, xxii, 28, 34–35
management of in psychogenetic
    perpetuation, 193–203
perceived value, xxxi,151, 155
psychoanalysis role in changing,
    29
and reality, xxiv, 29, 166–179,
    248, 262, 276
self-limiting, 20, 55
self-perpetuating, 19–20, 34
skill evolution as refinement, 156
and social behavior, 132, 156
survival value of, xxv, xxxi, 14,
    24, 28, 73–74
television as source of, 247–249
transitory, xxiii, 27–29, 35
transmission through children,
    xxxii, 166, 245, 247
and written language, xxvi, 76–77
believing is seeing, 5–6, 11–18, 34.
    See also propaganda
Benedict XIV, Pope, 267–268
Bergson, Henry-Louis, 88
Bering Strait, formation of, 148
Bernays, Edward
    on belief management in
        democracy, 236–237, 266
    public relations, xxxiv, 233–234
    work used in Nazi Germany, 243
bias. *See* belief manipulation
Bible (Christian)
    Augustine's faith in, 224
    Ecclesiastes (1:18), xxviii, 1, 88
    Matthew 1:20, 207

role of dreams in, 207
Big Bang-Creation argument, xviii,
    xxi, xxxviii, 271–275
Big Bang Theory, xviii, xxi, 3–4, 34,
    100. *See also* universe
black holes, 102–105, 277
Black Sea migrations, 149–150, 291
body temperature regulation in
    evolution, 140–143
Bohr, Niels, 2
Bosporus Strait, 149–150
brain, human
    amygdalae, role of, xxx, xxxvi,
        43, 126–129, 253
    axon growth, 125
    brainstem, 126–127
    cerebral cortex, 43, 118
    chemistry and reality, 42–47, 51
    in dyslexics, 25–26
    emotions in, 38–39, 130
    evolution of, xviii, xxx–xxxi, 24–
        26, 34, 124–127
    glia (cells), 124–127
    God module, xxiii, 24–26, 86,
        229
    hemisphere domination in, xxii,
        xxiv, xxxiv, 11–15
    hippocampus, 41–42, 86, 126–
        128, 148
    limbic system, xxiv, 43–44, 127,
        130, 287–289
    the mind and, xviii, xxi–xxvii, 5–
        8, 14–15, 37
    neural network maturation, xxii,
        11, 25–26
    neurons (cells), 124–125
    olfactory lobe, 126–127
    prefrontal cortex, 41–42
    pre-frontal lobes (neocortex),

xxx, xxxiv, xxxvi, 42–45, 51,
  83–84, 128–132, 205, 229,
  253
reptilian component, xxx, 38–39,
  118, 127, 140, 144, 149
structural development, 124–131
temporal lobes, 24–25, 41
thalamus, 45, 83–84, 126–128
trance and, xxiv, 45–50, 52, 56–
  57, 80, 242, 254
wave charts, 285
brainstem, role in evolution of human
  brain, 126–127
brainwashing, xxiv, 37, 47–52, 55–
  58. *See also* belief
  manipulation; persuasion
  techniques
Brandeis, Louis D., 53
breast cancer research example, 13–
  14
A Brief History of Time (Hawking),
  xxi, 1, 3, 5
Bruno, Giordano, 31, 219, 227–229,
  272
Bryan, William Jennings, 26–27
bubble reality, xxxii,176–179
Buffon, George de, 134
Burgess shale deposits, 137

C

Caesar, Augustus, 240
Caesar, Julius, xxxiii, 182, 185, 215,
  240
calcium storage, role in evolution,
  122–123, 137–138
Campbell, Joseph, xxvii, 84–85, 93,
  263
Canada, attempt to limit

psychogenetic migration, 176
Cancer (astrological sign), 92
cargo cults, 174
Carus, Titus Lucretius, 113–114
Catholic Church, 17, 30–33, 166,
  238–239, 273
cause and effect linkages, 12–14, 29,
  50
cause and effect relationships, 20, 78,
  156
On Cause, Principle, and Unity
  (Bruno), 227–228
Cavalli-Sforza, L.L., 154
censorship. *See* belief manipulation
cerebral cortex,
  blood flow, 118
  role in memory, 43
  in behavior, 157
Chicxulub (Mexico) meteor, 145–
  146
childhood. *See* infancy and childhood
chondriosome (mitochondria), 116–
  117
Christianity
  astrology, role in belief, 88–93
  astronomy, role in belief, 88–93
  Christmas celebration as
    psychogene, 165
  customs, evolution of, 88–93
  faith supported by reason
  disproved, 218–220
  Greco-Roman psychogenes and,
    190–193, 215–216
  monastic movement, 190–191
  myth and promise of eternal life,
    87, 187–188
  Neoplatonism embedded in, 214,
    222, 224

philosophy linked to mythology, 214

Plato's influence on, 214–215, 218, 222

psychogenetic evolution, 186–202

reason and faith in, 214–217, 227–230

Christmas celebration as psychogene, 91–92, 165–166

Christ the Redeemer. *See* Jesus

chromosomes. *See* DNA

Cicero, 183, 208

cilicin and hallucination, 45, 84

Clarke, Arthur C., 43, 273

Climbing Mount Improbable (Dawkins), 70

Clinton, Bill, 55, 232–233

clouds, interstellar, 103

coffin of Lazarus (constellation), 92

The Columbia Encyclopedia's Crimes Against The Truth (McCabe), 192–201

comets, 106, 108, 110, 115

communications technology and psychogene transmission, 245–247

computer simulation

and Chicxulub impact, 145

of DNA, 63, 281–282

"In God We Trust", 283–284

and formation of the moon, 108–109

and self-organizing knowledge, 64–65

sexual reproduction in, 67–68

Confession of Sins and Asking for Forgiveness, 31–33

confusion (programmed), role in brainwashing, 51

Congo (Zaire), Africa, 18

conifers role in evolution, 140, 142–145

consensus building, 231

consilience, xvii, xxix, 1, 153

Consilience (Wilson), 153

Constantine, Emperor of Rome, 188–191, 198–199

constellations. *See* stars

continental drift, 59, 109, 142, 148. *See also* tectonics

conversion. *See* brainwashing

convince, derivation of, 231

Cook, Captain James, 16

cosmos. *See* universe

Crab nebula, 103

creation according to science, xxviii, 99–112

creationism, 34, 166

creationist, 166, 275

creation myths

ancestral, xxvi–xxviii, 79, 97

Big Bang Theory, xviii, 3

contradiction of extant beliefs, 30

intuitions, 15, 80, 82, 88, 99, 209, 229

and life on earth, 114

science and, 166, 274

and our uniqueness, 171

creation of life, 115

creativity/competition experiment, 248

Cretaceous period, 107, 145–146

crimes of passion, reptilian brain and, 39

criminal behavior and belief systems, 171

critical mass concept, 175

Critique of Pure Reason (Kant), 7

Crito (Plato), 207
Crystallizing Public Opinion
(Bernays), 241
cults. *See* brainwashing
cultural dilution, attempts to limit,
176, 267
Cultural Transmission and Evolution
(Cavalli-Sforza and Feldman), 154
culture, human
attempts to limit change, 176
belief and behaviors in, 156
cycles of, 256
defined, 174
ethical systems establishment,
xxxiv, 205
evolution of, xxxi, 154–160, 181–
182, 203, 254–256
monoculture, 54, 75
polyculture, 54, 75
psychogenes as determinants, 75,
163, 174–177
and self-organizing knowledge,
151
success and, 256–257
unit of transmission, 156–157
cyanobacteria, evolution of, 135–136
cyber-bubble reality, 177
cytosine sequences. *See* DNA

D

The Daily Progress, 169
Darrow, Clarence, 26
Darwin, Charles
biological evolution, 33
final resting place, 30
on genetic knowledge, 72–73
on natural selection, 134–135
*On the Origin of Species by Way
of Natural Selection*, xxi–xxiii,

8, 22–23, 26, 72–73, 134–135
variations in attribute
mechanisms, 71
Darwin, Erasmus, 134
Da Vinci, Leonardo, 26, 86,
Dawkins, Richard, xvii, xxxi, 22, 70,
154–155
day-care services and political
correctness, 169
December 25th, evolution of
significance, 91–92, 165–166
Defender of the Peace (Marsilius of
Padua), 218
deities. *See also* gods
Goddess Pele, 85
Greek, associated with the sun,
90
Norwegian, associated with the
sun, 90
Ra (Sun god), 85
symbolic of the vernal equinox,
92
delusion, 29, 44
depression, gender specific response
to, 44–45
Descartes, René, 5–6, 228–229
Dicty (Dictyostelium amoeba), 118–
119, 136
diet, role in brainwashing, 51
differentiation, cellular, 117, 119–
122
digital DNA, xxv, 63
dinosaurs, 142–146
dioxin exposure and intelligence, 19
disinformation. *See* belief
manipulation
diversity (punctuated equilibrium),
xxv, 67–68
DNA (deoxyribonucleic acid)

about, 61–62, 112
behavior and, 156–157
brain evolution and, 124–127
chromosomal doublings, 122–
123, 137–138
chromosomes, defined, 119
computer simulation, xxv, 63,
281–284
differentiation in, 117
early, 116–118
gene inversion, 137
genes, defined, 119
genetic programming and, 68
knowledge and, xvi, xxv, 62
mathematical analog of, 65
messenger molecules in, 117–120
mutation caused changes, 63–64,
121–124
protein manufacture in, 114–115,
117, 120
refinement process, 62–63
self-replication of, 60–61, 115
sequences/components, 62–63
sexual reproduction and, 63–64,
67
dopamine, a neurotransmitter, 43–44
Down's syndrome, 122
Dr. Spock's Baby and Child Care
(Spock), 245
dreams
ancestral, xxvi–xxvii, xxix, 79, 83
annunciation (birth of Christ),
207
in Bible (Christian), 207–208
in brain evolution, 127
false, 207
forgetting of, 45
Greek philosophers on, 207–208
hallucinations and, xxiv, xxvi–

xxvii, xxix, 46
interpretation of, 84, 206–207
memory and, 42, 83
myth and, xxvii, 83–85
as prophesy, 208–209
symbolism and, 84
true, 207
Durant, Ariel, xvix, 2
Durant, Will, 2, 210–211
dyslexia as evolutionary advantage,
25–26

E

Earth (planet), xxviii, 102, 105–111,
115. *See also* planets;
tectonics
Easter Island, 263
Ecclesiastes (1:18), xviii, 1, 88
ecosystem, artificial, 65–68
Ecuador, Incan invasion of, 175
education of children
beliefs and curricula, xxxii
day-care services and political
correctness, 169
home-schooling, 270
as indoctrination, 6, 169
psychogenetic formation of
children, 169
Edwards, Jonathan, 57
Einstein, Albert, 2–3, 26, 271, 277
elements (chemical), formation of,
103
Elysium (Voltaire), 267–268
embrittlement, environmental,
xxxvii, 256–265
emotional intelligence, 130–131
Emotional Intelligence (Goleman),
130–131
emotional learning, 128

emotions
    amygdalae, role of, 126–129
    dreams and, xxvii
    gender-specific responses, 44–45
    as genetic knowledge, 71–73
    hippocampus, role of, 126–127
    human brain and, 38–39
    limbic system and, 43, 127, 130
    manipulation of by public
        relations, 234, 238–242
    in mythology, 86
    reason and, 234, 269
    survival value in evolution, 39
    symbols used to manipulate, 235
Empedocles, 133–134, 212, 223
The Encyclopedia of Psychology,
    xxviii
endorphins, 43–44, 47
Enlightenment, 18th century, xxxviii,
    168, 178, 218, 234, 279
entelechy, 134, 212
environment
    Antarctic ice melt, 260
    drought in California, 259
    ecosystem, artificial, 65–68
    embrittlement, xxxvii, 256–265
    global warming, 258–259
    greenhouse gases, 110, 147, 261
    greenwashing technique, 239
    impact winter, 146
    infertility and, 259
    ocean levels, global rising, 142,
        260
    population increases, xxxvii,
        256–259, 261–263
    resource scarcity, 262
    volcanic eruptions role in, 260
Epicurus, 209, 210
epigenetic rules, 153

epilepsy, 24–25, 41
equilibrium, punctuated, 67–68
An Essay Concerning Human
    Understanding (Locke), 7–8
eukarote organisms, 118–119, 135
Eurasia, formation of, 144, 147
European secular era, beginnings,
    219
evangelization. *See* brainwashing
evolution
    amphibian, marine, 123, 139
    and belief in intelligence of
        creation, 8
    and beliefs, survival value of, 14,
        30
    of body patterns, 121–122, 137
    body temperature regulation and,
        140–141
    calcium storage in, 122–123,
        137–138
    closed-loop behaviors in, 158–
        159
    cognitive tools of, 14
    creation story (biblical) xxii, 8,
        30, 111
    cultural, xxx, 153–160, 181–182,
        203, 254–256
    dinosaurs, 30, 142–147
    early life forms, 136–138
    extinction disaster series, 141–
        142
    fresh-water adaptation in, 137–
        138
    global warming, 257–258
    Greek version of, 113, 133
    human, 148–149
    of human brain, xviii, xxx–xxxi,
        19
    influences on (primary), 59

innovations derived from, 22
insects role in, 140, 143
intelligence and, xxv, 14
the jaw, role in, 122, 137–138, 141, 144
knowledge and, xvi–xvii, xxxi–xxxii, 61
land adaptation of animals, 133, 138–144
lung development in, 138–139, 141
of mammals, 144–149
multicellularity, 117–121, 136–138
plant, 137, 142–143
psychogenetic, xxv–xxvi, xxxi, xxxiii, 73–78, 133, 160, 175, 182, 192, 203, 242
religious faith and, 24–26
reptile, 122, 139–142
reptiles, mammal-like, 140–141, 143
rib cage, importance of, 139
salt excretion, role in, 138
Scopes trial, 26
self-organizing knowledge as, 62, 158
social
    acceleration of, xxv–xxvi, 76
    economic change as cause, 247
    large-scale, 149–151
    mythology, influence on, 254–256
    postmodernist approach, 173–174
    propaganda in, 160
    psychogenes role in, 73–78, 159, 177–178
reform movements as, 160, 172–173
and self-preservation, 219–220
technological change as cause, 247
successful adaptation and, 256–262
survival of the fittest, prenatal example, 135
vertebrate, 121–124
Ewen, Stuart, 233, 238
extinction and devastation, role of in evolution, 141–142, 145–146
extra-experiential intuitions. *See* intuition, extra-experiential

F

faith. *See also* beliefs
    belief and disbelief, 85–86
    in early Christianity, 214–216
    emotional basis of, 95
    heresy and use of force, 30–33
    role of mystery in, 87
    in supernatural as therapeutic, 15
    survival value of, 24–26
faith healings, causes of, 57
Falsafah, a philosophy, 225
false memory, 50, 83
fanatics (zealots), 52–58, 264
Faraday, Michael, 25
fatigue, role in brainwashing, 51
FDA (Food and Drug Administration) and food imports, 232–233
fear
    amygdalae, role of, 86
    fight or flight response, 117
    hippocampus, role of, 86

myth and, xxv, 86–87
origin of, 86
and reason, xxv, 86
survival value of, 86
Feldman, M.W., 154
feminism
and God, 95, 168
role in liberalism, 247
Ferdinand V, 216
Final Cause philosophy, 212
First Cause philosophy, 212–213, 277
first factor and rule of thumb, 13–14
On the First Principal (Scotus), 218
Fisher, R.A., 65
the flood
Black Sea migrations, 149–151, 291
Gilgamesh (Sumerian), 151
of Noah, 151
flying fish, example of evolved adaptation, 69
fractals, 121
France, Anatole, 278–279
France, attempt to limit psychogenetic migration, 176
fresh-water adaptation in evolution, 122, 137–138
Freud, Sigmund, 84, 233

G

Gage, Phineas, 129–130
galaxies. *See* universe
Galerius, Emperor of Rome, 189
Galileo (Galilei), 30, 219, 227, 229
Garnett, R. Jefferson, 169
genes. *See* DNA
The Genetic Theory of Natural Selection (Fisher), 65

genome, human, 63
Gibraltar Strait, 147–148, 150
Gigerenzer, Gerd, 13–14, 250
Gilgamesh, epic of, 206
giraffe, example of evolved adaptation, 69–70
glaciation cycles, 147–148, 261
glia (cells), role in brain evolution, 124–125
global warming, 257–258
God
Aristotle on, 212–213
Averroes view of, 217, 224–225
evolution of, 94
existence of, 8, 213
Faylasuf view of, 225
feminism and, 95, 168
in Genesis (Bible), 94
history of (commentary), 167–168
as metaphor for creative force, 5
the mind of, xxi, xxx, 1, 5, 132, 214
of the mystics, 168
neoplatonists view of, 214
of perfect ideas, 213–214
as "Prime Mover Unmoved"/"First Cause"/Soul of the World, 212
proof of existence of, 225
Seattle, Chief (native American) on, 81–82
sun as symbolic of, 89
God module, xxiii, 24–26, 86, 229
gods. *See also* deities
evolution from inherited belief, 81
evolution of from mythological spirits, xxvii, 79–81, 91

Greek version of, 94
the Kabbala on, 94
vengeful nature of, 93–94
Goebbels, Joseph, 241
Goleman, Daniel, 130–131
Greece, psychogenes assimilation in ancient, 183–186
Greek philosophical tradition, 207–214
greenhouse gases, 110, 147, 261
greenwashing technique in public relations, 239
Gregory I, Pope, 165
guanine sequences. *See* DNA
Guicciardini, historian, 219
Gurdjieff, Georgii, 22
gymnosperms role in evolution, 140

H

Hal (the thinking computer), 43
Hall, Manly P., 88–92
Halley, Edmond, 33
hallucinations
achieved by, 83–84
dreams and, xxvii, xxix, 45–46, 83
role of in brainwashing, 52
sensory deprivation and, 45–47
Hammerstein, Oscar, 16
Hasidic Jews attempts to limit cultural change, 176
Hawaiians and Captain Cook, 16
Hawking, Stephen, xxi, xxx, 1–5, 34, 132
Henry III, 227
heresy
of Bruno, 228
burning of heretics, 200–201
faith and use of force, 30–33

of Galileo, 30, 219, 229
of William of Ockham, 226
The Hero with a Thousand Faces (Campbell), xxvii
Hesiod, 206
heuristics (rule of thumb), 13–14
Hill and Knowlton, public relations firm, 239
Hillis, William Daniel, 68
Himalayan Mountains, formation of, 147
hippocampus, role of
in fear, 86
in human brain, 126–127, 148
in memory, 41–42
in reptile brain, 142
The Historia Augusta, 190
A History of God (Armstrong), 167–168
Hitler, Adolph, 241–242, 273
Hoffer, Eric, 52
Holland, John Henry, 65
Holland, Peter, 122
Holmes, Oliver Wendell, 54
Holy Roman Empire, creation of, 190–191
Homer, 206–207
Homer-Dixon, Thomas, 262
Homo erectus (the standing human), 149
Homo habilis (handy man), 148–149
Homo sapiens archaic, 149
Homo sapiens sapiens (the thinking human), 149
homosexuality and psychogenetic inheritance, 170
hormones, gender-specific role of, 44–45
Hubble, Edwin, 34

human evolution, 148–149. *See also*
    evolution
human genome, 63
human paradox, xxx, 1–5, 24, 127–
    132, 277
Hume, David, 12–13
hunches. *See* intuition
Huntington's disease, 124
Huxley, Thomas, 26
Hymel, Gary, 239
hypnosis and hypnotic trance, 47–48,
    50, 57

I

Ibn Bajja, Arab philosopher, 216
Ibn Rushd (Averroes). *See* Averroes
Ibn Sina (Avicenna). *See* Avicenna
Iliad (Homer), 206–207
impact winter, 146
improbability and belief systems, 12
Incan invasion of Ecuador, 17
infancy and childhood
    belief formation in, xxxii, xxxv–
        xxxvi, 5–6, 16–17, 245–249
    brain growth in, 19
    child rearing, 246–247
    day-care services and political
        correctness, 169
    education's role in psychogenetic
        formation, 169
    intention discernment in, 21
    language fluency ability, 125
    learning windows in, 125
    psychogenetic inheritance, 164,
        175
infertility, 259
information
    accumulation of and evolution,
        76
    organized reproduction, 60

information age, first, 76
Inquisition (of Medieval Christianity)
    Bruno, Giordano and, 219, 228
    Jewish victims of, 273
    McCabe, Joseph on, 198, 200–
        201
    zealot fundamentalist killings, 54
insects role in evolution, 141, 143
insight. *See* intuition
intellect, defined, 27
intelligence
    autism and, 249–250
    emotional, 130–131
    evolution and, 14, 59–60, 75
    malnutrition and, 19
    and mythology, 87–88
    and planning, 20–21
    success, attitude and, 20
    toxic substances and, 19
Internet and cyber-bubble reality,
    177
interstellar clouds, 103
intuition
    ancestral, 80
    animism and, 82
    emotional intelligence and, 131
    extra-experiential, xxii, xxvi,
        xxviii, 79, 99, 209, 275
    memes and psychogenes, 155
    and perception, 11–16
    poet and perception, 229
    role of, xxii, 11–16, 79–80, 82,
        87–88, 155, 206
    shamans use in dreams, xxii, 206
    Stekel, Wilhelm and, 84
    Upanishads and, xxviii, 46, 87–
        88
iridium (element), 146
irreducible complexity argument, 70–

71
Isabella I, 216
Islam
    attempt to limit psychogenetic
        migration, 176
    mysticism as core of, 225
Italian culture
    beliefs, early, 182–183
    Christian (early) psychogene
        assimilation, 187–190
    empire phase of, 185–186
    fusion of religion and patriotism
        in, 187
    Germanic psychogenetic
        influence on, 186–187
    Greco-Roman psychogenes and,
        184–186, 191–192, 202–203
    Greek psychogene assimilation,
        183–186
    metamorphosis of religious
        psychogenes in, 186–190
    Oriental/Middle Eastern
        psychogenetic influence on,
        186–187
    Renaissance, 202–203

J

James, William, 240
the jaw, role in evolution, 123, 137–
        138, 141, 144
Jefferson, Thomas, xxii, 19, 20
Jekyll and Hyde nature of man,
        xxxiv, 253
Jekyll and Hyde story, 39
Jesus
    astrological evolution of
        birthdate, 92
    promise of eternal life, 187–188
    the Redeemer, allegorical

adaptation, 91–92
Joan of Arc, 88
John Paul II, Pope, 166
John XXII, Pope, 226
judgment and the brain, 12
judgment shortcut
    (representativeness), 13
Jupiter (planet), 105–107

K

the Kabbala, 94
Kant, Immanuel, xxiv, 7, 34
Kepler, Johannes, xxi, xxx, 2, 105,
        132
Khayy'am, Omar, poet, 278, 279
Kitayama, Shinobu, 182–182
knowledge
    belief v., 7–8
    Bible (Christian) as detractor, 88
    DNA (deoxyribonucleic acid)
        and, xvi, xxv, 61, 62
    evolution and, xxxi, 135, 151
    evolution of adaptive, 61
    genetic, 71–73
    genetic algorithm (computer
        simulation), xxvi, 65–68
    innate, possibility of, 7–8
    and mythology, 87–88
    as organized ignorance, 178–179
    psychogenetic, xxv–xxxii, 73–78
    role of brain hemispheres, 11–12
    self-organizing, 62–68, 78, 151,
        158
    self-organizing knowledge
        molecular, 60–62, 113, 151,
        158
    self-replicating, 21, 60–61
Kurtz, Howard, 232

L

Lamarck, Jean-Baptiste de, 134
language
    benefits of, 76
    development of complex, xxv–
        xxvi, 40–41
    evolutionary origin of, 83, 175
    fluency ability in childhood, 125
    history of, 76–77
    in psychogenetic evolution, 75–
        77, 175
    written, xxvi, 75–77
lead exposure and intelligence, 19
Leibniz, Gottfried, 228
Lemâitre, Georges Henri, 3, 34
Lies and Fallacies of the
    Encyclopedia Britannica
    (McCabe), 193
Life magazine, 233
limbic system
    in brain evolution, 127
    dopamine, role of, 44
    emotional intelligence in, 130–
        131
    emotion and, 38, 43
    representation, 287–290
Linde, Alex, 34
linked beliefs, xxiii, 28, 34–35
Linne, Karl von, 134
Lippmann, Walter, xxxv, 234–236
lobotomy, prefrontal, 130
Locke, John, 7–8
Lucretius. *See* Carus, Titus Lucretius
Lucy (Australopithecus afarensis),
    148
Luddites opposition to technological
    change, 176
lung development in evolution, 138–
    141

Luther, Martin, 192, 226
the Lyceum, 223

M

Machiavelli, Niccolo, 192, 202, 218
Magi, the three (constellation), 92
magical thought, origins of, 96
Magnus, Albertus, 92
malnutrition and intelligence, 19
mammals, evolution of, 144–149
man, evolution of, 148–149. *See also*
    evolution
Mandelbrot set, 121
Mankind-Their Origin and Destiny,
    92
mantle currents, 109
Marsilius of Padua, philosopher, 202,
    218
Martha and Mary (constellation), 92
matter, self-replicating, 60–62, 113–
    115
Matthew 1:20, 207
Maxentius, Emperor of Rome, 189
Maxwell, James, 25
McCabe, Joseph, 192–193
McNauqhton, Bruce, 42
media, modern communications,
    243–247
meditation and reality in trance state,
    50
Mediterranean Ocean, formation of,
    146–150
Melanesia, cargo cults in, 174
memes (self-reproducing ideas), xvi–
    xvii, xxxi, 154–155
memory
    amygdalae, role of, 43
    cerebral cortex, role of, 43

dreams and, 42, 83, 127

emotional, 129

false, 50, 83

hippocampus, role of, 41

limbic system and, 127

long-term potentiation, 42

neocortex role in, 144

permanent, 41–42, 83, 127

prefrontal cortex, role of, 41

and reason, 41

short-term, 41–42

and sleep, 42

Memory and Reconciliation: The Church and the Faults of the Past, 30–33

Meslier, Jean, 17, 87–88, 193

messenger molecules, 43, 118–120

metaphysical psychogenetic bubble reality, 177

Meteor Crater (Arizona), 107

meteors and meteorites, 103, 145–146

Michelangelo, 81

Milky Way, 104

Mill, John Stuart, British philosopher, 255

the mind, 37, 131. *See also* brain, human

mind-genes. *See* psychogenes

miracles

brain hemisphere dominance and, 12

cultural view of, 174

religious context, 57, 87, 270

superstitious belief, 161

misperceptions, self-perpetuating, 19–20, 34

molecules. *See also* matter

formation of, 103

self-organizing, xviii, 60–62, 115, 158

self-organizing, appearance of, 111

self-replication requirements, 115

Moncenigo, Giovanni, 228

moon(s), 104, 108–109

Moors, 202, 216–217

morality, xxxvii, 54, 209–219, 222–226, 255, 268, 273

Moslems, North African, 216–217

mountain chains, formation of, 109, 137, 147

multicellularity evolution, 117–119, 121

Multilateral Agreement on Investment, 176

Mulvian Bridge, battle of, 189

Murchison meteorite, 103

mutation, role in evolution, 66–68, 121–124

mystery, role of in mythology, 87–88

mysticism and scientific method

ancestral beliefs, 95–96

Averroes on, 217

Einstein, Albert on, 2–3

in Islam, 225

religious context, 275

mystics, 168. *See also* shamans

myth and mythology

adaptation, 263–271

belief and the self, 54

Christianity's promise of eternal life, 187–189

creation

ancestral, xxii, xxvi–xxix, 81, 99

Big Bang Theory, xviii, xxi, 4

contradiction of extant beliefs,

30
 intuitions, 15
 and life on earth, 114
 science and, 272
 and uniqueness beleifs, 171–
 172
dreams and, xxvii, 83–85
emotional needs in creation of,
 xxvii, 85–86
fear and, xxvii, 86–87
Francis Bacon on, 85
the future and, 279
Greek attempt to replace with
 reason, 206–214
and intellect, 87–88
key factors of, 82
and logic, 206–207
morality and, xxxvii, 255
mystery, role of, xxvii, 87–88
philosophy's link to, 214
planning assumption and, 30, 35
reality and, 93
science and, xxviii, 30, 33, 271–
 276
secular, creation of, xxxvii, 233,
 240, 250, 265, 271
secular, rise of, 233–244
and social evolution, 254–256
and theology, 255–256
Western, evolution of, 211

N

Natural History (Buffon), 134
natural selection. *See* evolution
near-death experiences, biology of,
 46–47
nebula formation, 104
neocortex
 in human brain, xv, xxx, xxxiv,
 37–45, 84, 126–132, 144–149,
 253
 in reptilian brain, 144
Neoplatonism, 214–215, 222–224
Neptune (planet), 105–106
neural network pattern recognition,
 xxii, 11
neurolinguistic programming (NLP),
 xxv, 48, 55–57
neurons (cells), role in brain
 evolution, 124–125
neurotransmitters, 41–44
neutron star, formation of, 102
New Guinea, cargo cults in, 174
Newton, Isaac, xxi, 2, 132, 177
Nietzsche, xxxii, 163–164, 166
NLP (neurolinguistic programming).
 See neurolinguistic programming
 (NLP)
no boundary proposal, 4, 34
North America, formation of, 144,
 146, 148

O

Ockham's Razor, 218, 226
Ockham, William of
 about, 225–226
 on belief and perception, 6–7
 on ego and will, 94
 faith supported by reason
 disputed, 202, 218
 on First Cause philosophy, 213
Odyssey (Homer), 206–207
olfactory lobe, role in evolution of
 human brain, 126–127
Origen, a philosopher, 215
*On the Origin of Species by Way of
 Natural Selection* (Darwin), xxi,
 xxiii, 8, 22–23, 26, 72–73, 134–

135
Origin of the Universe (Hawking), 4–
    5
Orion (constellation), 92
out-of-body experiences, 249
oxygen deprivation and
    hallucination, 46–47

P

Padua, Marsilius of, 202, 218, 226
Panama, formation of, 146, 148
Pangea, 140, 142–144
paradox, the human, xxi, xxx, 1–5,
    24, 127–132, 277
parasites role in adaptation and
    diversity, 66–68
Parkinson's disease, 44
Patton, George, 26, 187
Paul of Tarsus, 211
Pavlov, Ivan, 48
PCB (polychlorinated biphenyls) and
    intelligence, 19
Peale, Norman Vincent, 20
Pearl Harbor attack, 242
Pele, Goddess, 85
Penzias, Arno, 34
perception
    and belief, xvii, xxi–xxiii, xxxiii–
        xxxv, 5–6, 11–18, 166, 231,
        241, 248, 251
    and intuition, 14
persuasion techniques, 55–57. *See
    also* belief manipulation;
    propaganda
The Phantom Public (Lippman), 234
pheromones, 44, 171
philosophers
    derivation of term, 205
    dream interpretation by, 207–208

role of, xxxii, 229
    and shamans, 277–279
    theologians and, Chapter 13
philosophy
    ancient Greek, 207–214
    modern, 228, 254–256
    mythology's link to, 214
*The Philosophy of the Inductive
    Sciences* (Whewell), xvii
pipe dreams (phrase), 46
Pius XII, Pope, 166
planets
    Earth, 102, 105–111, 115
    formation of, 103
    Jupiter, 105–107
    Mars, 106–108
    Mercury, 107
    moons relationship to, 104
    Neptune, 105–106
    planetesimals, 108
    Pluto, 106
    Saturn, 105
    Uranus, 105
    Venus, 107
planning assumption, 275
    about, 20–27
    ancestral, 79–80
    key factors of, 82
    in philosophy, Greek, 209
    underpinnings, 35
    watchmaker argument, xxii–xxiii,
        21, 35
Plato, 6–7, 207–215, 221–223
Plotinus, founder of Neoplatonism,
    214, 215
political correctness
    day-care services and, 169
    reversing psychogenetic
        inheritance, 170, 247

and social reform, xxxii, 172–173 , 265

Polybius, Greek historian, 184, 253

Pomponazzi, Florentine statesman, 218

Popper, Karl, xvi, xxv, 61

population, global increase of, xxxvii, 256–263

postmodernism, xviii, 173–174

postwar (WWII) generation, 247

poverty and intelligence, 19

PR! (Ewen), 233–234, 238–239

Prarsepe Jovis (constellation), 92

prefrontal cortex, role in memory, 41

prefrontal lobes (neocortex), role of in human brain, xxx, xxxiv, xxxvi, 41–46, 51, 83–84, 128–132, 229, 253

problem solving, and cause and effect beliefs, 13

propaganda, xxxv. *See also* belief manipulation; public relations
for belief manipulation, 230–231
education as indoctrination, 169
emotions role in, 241
Hitler, Adolph's techniques of, 241–242
misinformation as, 242
and psychogenetic beliefs, 240
public opinion, forming of, xxxv, 56, 222, 234–236
and public opinion polls, 232
social evolution and, 160
and the subconscious, 234, 236

Propaganda (Bernays), 236

On Prophesying by Dreams (Aristotle), 208

Protagoras, Greek philosopher, 27

Prozac (pharmaceutical), 43, 171

psychoanalysis, role in belief, 29

psychogenes (heritable and transmittable beliefs). *See also* beliefs
ancestral, 169–170, 254–256
in ancient Greece, 183–186
biblical, allegorical nature of, xxxii, 167, 170
Christian, in Dark and Middle Ages, 191–192
commercially disseminated, 245–247
core, 74, 178
as cultural determinants, 163, 170, 174–177
cultural transmission of, xxxii, 154–156, 165–166, 245–247
defined, xvi, 73, 155
early Roman, 182–183
evolution of, 155
foreign, 175–176
genetic boundary of, 154–159
Greco-Roman, 191–192, 202–203
Greek, social and mythological, 209
inheritance value perceived, xvi–xvii, 73–74, 155, 158
memes and, xvi–xvii, xxxi, 154–155
migration of, 175–176
Nietzsche's allegory of change, 163–164, 166
perpetuation of, 193–202
political correctness movement and, 170
in population increase, xxxvii, 256–259, 261
population increase influenced by, 256–259

psychotic, 176–177
religious, 269–271
and social evolution, 159
technology and, 256–258
transmission of, 159, 162–163,
    245–249
Western v. Eastern, 181–182
psychogenetic evolution, xxv–xxvi,
    xxxi, xxxiii, 73–78, 182, 192,
    203, 242
psychogenetic inertia, 256–262
psychogenetic inheritance, 231, 234,
    247
psychogenetic knowledge, xxv–xxvi,
    xxix, xxxii, 73–78, 178
public opinion, forming of, xxxv,
    222, 231–237, 242–243
Public Opinion (Lippman), 234, 236
public relations. *See also* belief
    manipulation; propaganda
  Astro Turf organizing in, 237–
    238
  Bernays, Edward as father of,
    233–234
  clandestine nature of, 235
  emotional manipulation by, 235,
    238
  greenwashing technique, 239
  hospital atrocity story, 239
  junk science in, 238
  public opinion, forming of, xxxv,
    231–237, 242–243
  Standard Oil of New Jersey
    anecdote, 238–239
  tactics used to control the masses,
    266
  and tobacco industry, 238–239,
    243–244
Pythagoras, 211, 214

R

rationalism as religion, 225
Ray, Thomas, 65–67
reality
  beliefs and, 29, 162, 172, 176–
    177, 179, 248, 276
  brain chemistry and creation of,
    43–47
  bubble, 176–177, 179
  consensus and mass beliefs, 176–
    177
  individual perception of, 235
  meditation and, 50
  myth and, 93
  postmodern view, 173–174
  psychogenetic inheritance in, 166
  and scientific method, 33
  William James on, 240
reality model, 6–8, 172
reason
  ability to, 40–41, 132, 234
  Bible (Christian) approach to,
    xxviii, 8
  denigration of, 86, 88, 97, 202
  emotions and, 269
  and faith in early Christianity,
    214–216, 218–220
  and fear, xxvii, 86
  Greek attempt to replace myth
    with, 206–214
  memory and, 41
  and morality, 214
  neocortex role in ability, 144
red giant. *See* sun
Reformation, 218
reform movements and social
    evolution, 160, 172–173
reincarnation, 7, 211
religion

ancestral, xxvii
evolution from animism, 81
motivations of, 264, 267
neurobiological mechanism
  underlying, xxviii
psychogenes of, 269–271
science v., xxxviii, 271–276
and social engineering, 267
Renaissance, Italian, 202–203, 218,
  226, 229
representativeness, 13
reptile evolution, 139–140, 142
reptiles, mammal-like, 141
reptilian brain, 38–39, 140, 144, 149
The Republic (Plato), 207
revival meetings, religious, 56–57
rib cage, importance in evolution,
  139
ritual ceremonies
  hallucination in, 46
  psychogenetic redirection of, 165
  revival meetings, 56–57
  voodoo (vodoun), 48
River out of Eden (Dawkins), 70
RNA (ribonucleic acid)
  about, 114
  mathematical analog of, 65
  messenger, 62
  protein manufacture in, 114–115
  self-replication of, 60, 115
Rogers, Richard, 16
Roosevelt, Franklin Delano, 242
Rorschach test, 17–18
rule of thumb (heuristics), 13–14
runner's high, 44, 47

S

Salem witch-trial bubble, 177
Sallust, Roman historian, 184–185

salt excretion, role in evolution, 138
Salvian, a priest, 190–191
Saturn (planet), 105
schizophrenia, 124
Schopenhauer, Arthur, xv, 278
science
  and myth, 271–276
  religion v., xxxviii, 261, 271–276
  worshipping at altar of myth, 272
scientific method
  and belief evolution, 250
  invented by Aristotle, 223
  mysticism as counter to, 95
  and perceptual bias, 29
  reality and, 33
Scopes, John, 26
Scotus, Duns, Scottish theologian,
  218, 225–226
Seattle, Chief (native American), on
  God, 81–82
secular mythology, 265
seeing is believing, xxii–xxiv, 5–6,
  11–18
self-esteem, 245–247
The Selfish Gene (Dawkins), xvii
self-organizing knowledge
  and DNA simulation, 62–68
  evolutionary threshold, 151
  knowledge v., 78
  molecular, 158
self-organizing molecular
  knowledge, xvii, 60–62, 115, 158
self-perpetuating misperceptions, 19–
  20, 34
self-preservation instinct, 219
self-replicating knowledge, 60–61
self-replicating matter, 60–62
senses, denigration of, 88, 211,
  214–215, 218, 221

sensory deprivation in hallucination, 45–46

serotonin, a neurotransmitter, 43, 45

sexual relations between spirits and humans, 56

sexual reproduction
in computer simulation, 67–68
in DNA, 63–64

Shackne, Stuart, 238–239

Shakespeare, William, 86

shamans, xxxii, 205–207, 277–279

Shaw, George Bernard, 23–24, 169

Shoemaker-Levy 9 comet, 107

sin, origin of in Stoicism, 210

Singer, Wolf, 49

singularity theory, 4

skepticism, 225–226

skill evolution as belief refinement, 156

slaves and slavery, 20, 178

sleep, 42, 45, 83

social engineering, 264–265

social evolution
acceleration of, xxv–xxvi, 76
economic change as cause, 247
large-scale, 149–151
mythology, influence on, 254–256
postmodernist approach, 173–174
propaganda in, 160
psychogenes role in, 73–78, 159, 177–178
reform movements as, 160, 172–173
and self-preservation, 219–220
by social engineering, 267
technological change as cause, 247

Socrates, 221

solar systems, formation of, 103, 105. *See also* universe

solar wind, 105–106

Solomon (the Supreme Light), 90–91

solstice celebration as psychogene, 165

Somalia, Africa, 18

soul, the
derivation of, 81
in reincarnation, 211

South America, formation of, 144, 146

South Pacific (play), 16

South Sea Company bubble, 176–177

spin. *See* belief manipulation; public relations

Spin Cycle (Kurtz), 232

Spinoza, Baruch, xxxii, 88, 166–167, 228

spirit world
animism and, 27
of Homo sapiens sapiens (the thinking human), 149
intuition and, xxvi, 15
sexual relations with humans, 56
voodoo (vodoun), 48, 56

Spock, Benjamin, 245–246

spontaneous generation, 113–114

Stable (constellation), 92

Stamford Scales of Hypnotic Susceptibility, 48

stars. *See also* sun; universe
Ass (constellation), 92
of the Bear (constellation), 92
coffin of Lazarus (constellation), 92
Crab nebula, 103
exploding, 102, 104

formation of, 101
interstellar clouds, 103
lifetime of, 101–103
Magi, the three (constellation), 92
Martha and Mary (constellation), 92
nebula formation, 104
neutron, 102
Orion (constellation), 92
Prarsepe Jovis (constellation), 92
shooting, 106–107
Stable (constellation), 92
stellar radiation, 103
supernova, type II, 102–103
white dwarf, 102
stars of the Bear (constellation), 92
Stekel, Wilhelm, 84
Stoicism, evolution from philosophy to theology, 210–211
The Story of Civilization (Durant), xix, 2
stroke, cerebral, 130
success, role in culture, 20, 256–257
Sumerian culture, xxix, 150–151
Summa totius logicae (William of Ockham), 226
sun, 89–92, 101, 104. *See also* stars; universe
supernova, type II, 102–103
survival of the fittest. *See* evolution
suspicion. *See* intuition
Systema Naturae (Linne), 134

T

technology
derivation of, 156
and psychogenes, 256–258
role in evolutionary success, 260–261

tectonics (plate), 137, 148. *See also* continental drift
tektites, 110
television in belief manipulation, 244–247
temporal lobes, role of in memory, 41
Terence, 17
Tesla, Nikola, 25
testosterone, 44
thalamus, role of in human brain, 45, 84, 127–128
thalamus, role of in survival, 128
Thales, Greek philosopher, 206
Theogony (Hesiod), 206
theology
anthropomorphic, 94
mythology and, 255–256
social dominance of emotion based, 264–271
thinking, a benefit of language, 76
thought stopping in brainwashing, 52
The Three Metamorphoses (Nietzsche), xxxii, 163–164
Thus Spake Zarathustra (Nietzsche), 163
thymine sequences. *See* DNA
Tierra (computer simulation component), 65–68
tobacco industry and public relations, 238–239, 243–244
toxic substances and intelligence, 19
Tractatus Theologico-Politicus (Spinoza), 166–167
traits, cultural, 154–155
trance
alpha-state, 49–51, 57, 242
Hitler's use of, 242
hypnotic, 47–48

Triassic period, 142

Triceratops, 145

the trinity, origins, 87, 89–90, 190–191

tulip bubble, 176–177

Tullius, Marcus, 183

Tunguska Valley (Siberia), 107

Twain, Mark, 40, 77

twins and psychogenetic evolution, xxxii, 157–158

U

universe

    Big Bang Theory, xvii, xxix, 3–4, 34

    creation of, 34, 100–105

    galaxies relationship to, 4, 101, 103–104

    nature of and creation myths, xxviii, 99

    nebula formation, 104

    Neoplatonists view of creation, 5

    order in, 64

    planet formation, 103

    solar system formation within galaxies, 103

    star formation, 103

Upanishads, xxviii, 46, 87, 206–207

V

Vilenkin, Andre, 34

Virgil, 87

virgin birth story, 56

the Virgin mother, 92

Virgo (astrological sign), 92

volcanoes, formation of, 109

Voltaire, 267–268

vomero nasal organs (VNO), 44, 172

voodoo (vodoun), 48, 56

W

watchmaker argument, xxiii, 21, 35

The Wave Function of the Universe, 34

Weber, Eugene, 182–183

Whewell, William, xvii

white dwarf (star), 102

Wilberforce, William, 26

Wilson, Edward O., xvii, 153

Wilson, Matthew, 42

Wilson, Robert, 34

wisdom, denigration of, 87, 95, 164, 177, 255, 275

wisdom, evolution of, xxxi, 151

witchcraft, belief in, xxx, 2, 40, 132

Woodstock generation, 247

Woolf, Leonard, 39–40

written language, xxvi, 75–77

X

Xenophanes, Greek philosopher, 94

Y

You've Got to be Carefully Taught (song), 16–17

Z

Zaire, Africa, 18

zealots, xxiv, 37, 52–58, 264, 276

Zeno of Citium, 210

Zeno of Tarsus, 211

zircons (Australia), 110